BEYOND
PRODUCTIVITY

BEYOND PRODUCTIVITY

How Leading Companies Achieve Superior Performance by Leveraging Their Human Capital

GREGORY G. DESS AND JOSEPH C. PICKEN

AMACOM

American Management Association

New York • Atlanta • Boston • Chicago • Kansas City • San Francisco • Washington, D.C.
Brussels • Mexico City • Tokyo • Toronto

This publication is designed to provide accurate and authoritative
information in regard to the subject matter covered. It is sold with the
understanding that the publisher is not engaged in rendering legal,
accounting, or other professional service. If legal advice or other expert
assistance is required, the services of a competent professional person
should be sought.

Library of Congress Cataloging-in-Publication Data

Dess, Gregory G.
    Beyond productivity : how leading companies achieve superior
performance by leveraging their human capital / Gregory G. Dess and
Joseph C. Picken.
        p.   cm.
    Includes bibliographical references and index.
    ISBN 0-8144-0435-9 (hc.)
    1. Organizational effectiveness.   2. Organizational learning.
3. Leadership.   4. Labor productivity.   5. Human capital.
6. Organizational effectiveness—Case studies.   I. Picken, Joseph C.
II. Title.
    HD58.9 .D47   1999
    658.3—dc21   98-49319
                                                            CIP

Printing number

10   9   8   7   6   5   4   3   2   1

CONTENTS

PREFACE

For most of the twentieth century, the primary tools for the creation of wealth were physical: land, natural resources, human labor, and machines. The worth of a company was determined in large measure by the sum of its tangible resources. In recent years, however, companies like Microsoft, PeopleSoft, America Online, and Amazon.com have turned this model inside out. These companies, dealing in software and services and built on a foundation of intellectual capital with little or no tangible investment, have created extraordinary value for their investors, far in excess of the worth of their physical and financial assets. Traditional industries based on tangible assets, such as oil, autos, steel, and financial services, have lagged far behind, reinforcing the argument that value is determined not by the sum of an organization's resources but by how efficiently those resources are used and redeployed into new opportunities over time.

In his influential book, *Intelligent Enterprise*, James Brian Quinn declares "a new paradigm" and argues that "with little fanfare, over the last several decades the development and management of services, service technologies and human intellect have emerged as the primary determinants of business and national economic success."[1] More recently, he has argued that "intellect and innovation are the sources of virtually all economic value, growth and strategic edge today." In the future, successful strategies will focus on "investing in the special skills and intellect that only highly motivated, knowledgeable people can provide, and then . . . leveraging this intellect through a few 'best in world' internal systems and the integrated management of many outsourced activities." Throughout, Quinn argues that in an economy increasingly driven by knowledge and information, the returns to the effective management of human and intellectual capital will be greater than those available from the more efficient management of physical and financial assets.[2]

Although these notions have considerable appeal, no one has yet written the definitive book on how to transform the traditional organization into an intelligent enterprise. Much of the academic research to date has focused on defining and measuring intellectual capital. Collectively, we don't yet know very much about how managers can or should use these ideas to improve performance and create competitive advantage. Although most organizations haven't even begun to address these challenges, leading companies in almost every industry are beginning to experiment with new approaches. In the process, they are learning a great deal by trial and error. At this point in the early development of a new management paradigm, we believe that there is much to be gained from understanding these initiatives, learning what works and what doesn't from the experiences of others. And that is the purpose of this book: to provide managers at all levels with insights on how leading-edge organizations are leveraging their human capital and knowledge resources—going *beyond productivity*—to create winning strategies.

This book is written for managers, and our focus is decidedly practical. One of us is a leading academic researcher in the fields of leadership and strategy; the other is a management consultant and a former CEO with nearly thirty years of practical management experience. Our approach seeks to combine the best of both worlds: thorough investigation, analysis and documentation, and a no-nonsense, practical get-to-the-bottom-line orientation.

Our research was conducted over three years. We looked at the leading organizations in a broad cross section of industries and asked their leaders how they acquired, developed, and retained the best and brightest human capital resources. We looked at their structures, systems, processes, and procedures as we sought to understand how they used technology, structure, and management techniques to maximize the performance and productivity of their human capital resources. Our approach was qualitative and largely inductive.

The initial research base consisted of a sample of approximately one hundred leading-edge firms (the top two in each industry) selected on the basis of having been included in *Fortune*'s annual "most admired" lists for 1994 and 1997. To this sample we added approximately one hundred additional up-and-comers—smaller companies whose superior performance or innovative approaches made them worthy of investigation. Our research included a screening of the materials provided by these organizations in response to our initial queries, supplemented as required by e-mail surveys, follow-up queries, personal interviews with key executives, and a broad-based review of secondary sources from the business press and academic and trade journals.

This kind of research turns up hundreds of fascinating stories. But stories, no matter how interesting, don't lead to the kinds of insights managers can take action on. Although almost everyone is familiar with Microsoft Corporation, no one has yet been able to duplicate its success. The issues are complex, and there are many reasons for Microsoft's spectacular performance. It's not just the industry; software has its share of winners and losers, just like any other. Luck and timing? Bill Gates was clearly in the right place at the right time; the organization began with an almost exclusive franchise in an explosive-growth industry. But Microsoft has gone well beyond its roots in operating systems and has consistently built strong, often dominant, positions in one market segment after another. Clearly it has built a superior brand position and leveraged its power in the marketplace (perhaps too effectively, say some). But there's more to the story than marketing prowess. In an industry where product life cycles are brutally short and continuing innovation is key to survival, Microsoft has done an exceptional job of managing and leveraging its intellectual capital resources to deliver a steady stream of innovative new products. Although not every organization is blessed with the opportunities or the resources Microsoft has enjoyed, we are convinced that regardless of the industry, the companies that learn how to manage and leverage their intellectual capital resources more effectively will be the big winners over the next decade.

Our research has led to a number of key insights and an integrating framework that we have used to organize and interpret the qualitative data gathered in the course of the study. This conceptual framework extends current perspectives on intellectual capital and bridges the gap between theory and practice by focusing explicitly on how organizations can leverage their human and knowledge capital resources to create new sources of competitive advantage.

To fully exploit the potential of an organization's human capital and knowledge resources, management must venture beyond the traditional notions of productivity—more output from the same input—that usually focus on only a single resource at a time. Leveraging human capital and knowledge resources—going *beyond productivity*—requires much more.

Management faces two key challenges. The first is to address the quality and capabilities of the human capital resource itself: to recruit, develop, and retain the best talent available. The second is to design and configure the organization's structural capital*—the key processes and structures that link its human, knowledge and information, and tangible resources to each other and to its core value-creating processes—so as to maximize the potential and performance of the entire entity.

Our focus throughout this book is on how leading companies are meeting these challenges in a changing competitive environment. Chapter 1 lays the foundation, providing both a historical perspective and the conceptual framework. Chapter 2 focuses on the quality of an organization's human capital: how leading organizations recruit, select, develop, and retain a workforce composed of employees with the optimal mix of skills, attitudes, and capabilities to meet the needs of the organization. Chapter 3 looks at organizational systems, processes, and task designs. In it we address opportunities to leverage individual capabilities and improve collective performance through the application of technology. Macrolevel issues of organizational structure and design are addressed in Chapter 4. Chapter 5 deals with the roles of culture, incentives, and management control systems and illustrates with key examples how each can either complement or confound leverage initiatives in other areas. Chapter 6 focuses on organizational learning and the role of leadership in creating a learning organization. Finally, in Chapter 7, we recap our central themes and outline a practical, step-by-step approach to implementation.

Each of Chapters 2 through 6 concludes with a strategic inventory: a checklist of key issues and a series of questions focusing on the concepts and lessons from that chapter. These inventories are designed to help the reader identify opportunities, develop strategies and action plans, and evaluate progress toward the goal of realizing the full potential of human capital in his or her own organization.

Notes

1. James Brian Quinn, *Intelligent Enterprise: A Knowledge and Service Based Paradigm for Industry* (New York: Free Press, 1992).

2. James Brian Quinn, Jordan J. Baruch, and Karen Anne Zien, *Innovation Explosion: Using Intellect and Software to Revolutionize Growth Strategies* (New York: Free Press, 1997).

---

*The term "structural capital" includes the organization's core business processes, its organizational structures, information and communications infrastructures, internal support functions and processes, incentives, controls and performance measurement systems, culture, values and leadership. Chapter 1 more fully addresses the roles of and key interactions between human and structural capital resources.

ACKNOWLEDGMENTS

The preparation of a book is not a solo effort. Early on, AMACOM's publisher, Hank Kennedy, shared our vision. Without his backing, and the support and persistent prodding of our editor, Adrienne Hickey, and her capable colleagues at AMACOM, our vision would not have become a reality.

A book like this would not have been possible without the interest, support, and cooperation of key individuals in each of the companies we studied. Although it is impossible to recognize every contributor individually, we are deeply indebted to the individuals in dozens of organizations who provided access, answered our endless queries, and offered their wisdom and fascinating insights on the issues we address here. Thanks to each and every one of you.

Greg would like to thank many people who have provided support and encouragement over the years. These include Professors Nelson Rogers and Cecil Johnson at Georgia Tech and Don Beard, Monty Kast, and the late Charles Summer at the University of Washington. All have played important roles in stimulating his interests in learning and a career in academia. He has also benefited, both personally and professionally, from his associations with Clark Holloway, Jay Janney, Tom Lumpkin, Doug Lyon, Mike Martinko, Mike Hitt, Duane Ireland, Jeff Covin, Alex Miller, Abdul Rasheed, and Jackie Thompson. He also thanks C. M. Gatton, who endowed his chair at the University of Kentucky, and Dean Richard Furst, for their support. He owes a special debt of gratitude to his wife, Margie, daughter Taylor, and the two people who got it all started, Mary and Bill Dess.

Joseph thanks a number of individuals who have encouraged and inspired him throughout his business and academic careers. Professor James Brian Quinn, at the Amos Tuck School of Business Administration at Dartmouth, stimulated a desire to understand the inner workings of organizations. Dr. Robert C. Dean, Jr., and his associates at

Creare, Inc. planted a seed that grew into a lifelong fascination with technology and entrepreneurship. And Dr. Robert J. Potter, Jr., guided him through the early years of his management career at Xerox and has been a friend and counselor for more than two decades. Professors Greg Dess, Abdul Rasheed, Richard Priem, David Harrison, and Lawrence Schkade provided support, inspiration, and encouragement in his mid-life pursuit of a Ph.D. John Lundin and Tom Lumpkin also played an important role as companions on the academic journey, there to celebrate or commiserate as the occasion required. More recently, the clients of his consulting practice and his colleagues at Southern Methodist University, especially Gordon Walker, Robin Pinkley, Tammy Madsen, John Slocum, and Dean Al Niemi, have provided insight and inspiration. Finally, to his family—Mary, his wife; David, Matthew, Anna, and Christopher; and his parents, Dorothy and Joe Picken: Thanks for your patience, understanding, and support over the years (I'll be home as soon as I finish this chapter).

CHANGING THE RULES OF THE GAME

At the end of the 1800s, American football was a game of sheer muscle: sixty minutes of mass-attack running plays, after which the team with the most poundage and power was victorious. Yet, despite its predictability, football was fast becoming the most popular college sport of its day.

Then, in 1895, during a game between North Carolina and Georgia State, something unexpected occurred. A North Carolina fullback, in punt formation, was rushed. But instead of kicking, he *threw the ball*. Passing it forward to a teammate, who ran 70 yards for a touchdown. The Georgia State coach protested that the pass was illegal. But knowing of no rules against it, the referee allowed the play to stand.

In the years to follow, few teams attempted forward pass maneuvers. Football was played as usual, and reports of game-related injuries grew more common and more alarming. Finally, in 1905, President Roosevelt issued an ultimatum: The game's excessive roughness must end or the game itself would. A Georgia Tech football coach named John Heisman, recalling the controversial North Carolina play he had witnessed years before, decided the forward pass was just what football needed. He submitted his idea to the Rules Committee and, in 1906 the play was legalized.

Still, football didn't change overnight. It wasn't until 1913 that the tremendous possibilities of the forward pass were widely recognized. When Knute Rockne and Gus Dorias, players from a little-known college called Notre Dame, used the play to defeat nationally ranked Army. Their new passing offense transformed football into a strategic test of skill and intelligence, as well as power.[1]

Change doesn't just happen. It takes time for new ideas and new approaches to diffuse through an industry or a society and reach a critical mass, but once the advantages become apparent to a sufficient number of participants, the old order topples and is swiftly replaced by the new. The forward pass, first used in 1895 and formally written into the rulebook in 1906, didn't have much of an impact on the game until its potential for creating competitive advantage was demonstrated, in convincing fashion by Rockne and Dorias. And in a remarkably short time, the forward pass became the dominant offensive weapon in the game.

New ideas and new approaches are also changing the world of business. It hasn't happened everywhere, but the critical mass is building. In industry after industry, it's no longer just a game of market power and financial muscle, economies of scale and breadth of scope. Over the past century, the locus of wealth creation has shifted from capital-intensive industries like steel and automobiles to information-intensive industries like information services, financial services, and logistics. As we stand on the threshold of the knowledge age, the most powerful sources of growth, employment, and wealth creation are found in innovation-driven industries—computer software, biotechnology, and the like—industries where the keys to competitive advantage rely on the effective management of human resources.

A Changing Environment: The New Economy

In this new information-based economy, global financial markets have essentially become one; knowledge-based work is outsourced around the world; and specialist companies dealing in customized products are finding new ways to compete against mass production and mass marketing. The Internet has created a global market for ideas. Anyone can become a publisher on the World Wide Web. This unimpeded flow of information from anywhere to almost anywhere else on the globe facilitates free markets and makes it virtually impossible to repress ideas or maintain a closed society. *Business Week* calls it "a transcendent technology—like railroads in the nineteenth century and automobiles in the 20th."[2]

It's more than technology that has changed; it's the way it is being used. In a recent *Harvard Business Review* article, Philip Evans and Thomas Wurster proclaimed that "a new behavior is reaching critical mass. Millions of people at home and at work are communicating electronically using universal, open standards. This explosion in connectivity is the latest—and for business strategists, the most important—wave in the information revolution."[3]

Driven by the globalization of markets and enabled by the rapid diffusion of information and communications technologies, the developed economies of the world are coming to depend increasingly on the creation, distribution, and use of information and knowledge. Citing a recent study by the Organization for Economic Cooperation and Development, *The Economist* points out that "more than half of the total GDP in the rich economies is now knowledge-based, including industries such as telecommunications, computers, software, pharmaceuticals, education and television. High tech industries have nearly doubled their share of manufacturing output over the past two decades, to around 25%, and knowledge-intensive services are growing even faster. By one reckoning, 'knowledge workers'—from brain surgeons to journalists—account for eight out of ten new jobs." These changes are transforming the U.S. domestic economy. Today "intellectual capital drives the value of products—from 1990 to 1996, the number of people making goods fell 1%, while the number employed in providing services grew 15%." Echoing a similar theme in a 1996 speech, Federal Reserve chairman Alan Greenspan pointed out that "America's output, measured in tons, is barely any heavier now than it was twenty years ago, even though real GDP has increased twentyfold."[4]

Peter Drucker, whose keen insights have stimulated management thinking for more than sixty years, notes declining birthrates in the developed countries and concludes that future economic growth can no longer be based on expanding the workforce or increasing consumer demand. Rather, he argues, "It can come only from a very sharp and continuing increase in the productivity of the one resource in which the developed countries still have a competitive edge: knowledge work and knowledge workers."[5]

Gary Hamel and C. K. Prahalad, authors of *Competing for the Future*, also see profound changes in the ways organizations are structured and managed. In traditional organizations, authority was vested from the top down, and power was derived from control over resources, access to proprietary information, and the ability to impose sanctions. In the new economy, the resources that matter, knowledge and know-how, are embodied in people, personal computers, networks, and organization-wide e-mail systems. This focus on intellectual resources will redefine the boundaries of organizations, change the implicit contract between managers and workers, and erode the traditional power base of senior executives. Traditional managerial controls will give way to cooperative alliances as more and more of the resources critical to success will lie beyond organizational boundaries. The idea of loyalty to a workplace in exchange for a "job for life" no longer resonates; today, employees look out for themselves, and contract employment, flexible career paths, and frequent job changes are increasingly the norm. Top management jobs will change as well:

> Traditionally, the accumulated knowledge and industry experience of top managers has served as the implicit justification for their positions at the top of the hierarchy. But experience is of value only to the extent that the future is more or less like that past. In industry after industry, the terrain is changing so fast as to make much of their experience irrelevant, or—to the extent that experience blinds them to new opportunities—even dangerous.[6]

As the economies of the world become more closely intertwined and the effects of technology (for better or for worse) become felt in every corner of the globe, the rules of the game will be forever changed. How will organizations compete in a knowledge-based economy? Will the sources of competitive advantage be totally new, or just extensions of what we have been doing for years?

Beyond Productivity: Competitive Advantage in the Knowledge Age

For nearly a century, more efficient management and utilization of labor and physical and financial resources—increased productivity— has been a primary source of competitive advantage. But as the skills, approaches, and techniques for managing tangible resources have become widely known and practiced, the more efficient management of things no longer consistently leads to sustainable advantage. Most sophisticated companies know how to manage the intangibles as well— brands, image, reputation, and public opinion. If the significant allocation of resources (Washington lawyers and lobbyists) is any indication, the art of influencing public policy is also well known to many organizations. But times have changed. Hamel and Prahalad recently described it this way:

> The machine age was a physical world. It consisted of things. Companies made and distributed things (physical products). Management allocated things (capital budgets); management measured things (the balance sheet); management invested

in things (plant and equipment). In the machine age, people were ancillary, things were central. In the information age, things are ancillary, knowledge is central. A company's value derives not from things, but from knowledge, know-how, intellectual assets, competencies—all of it embodied in people.[7]

Although the practices of human resources management—focused primarily on the technical skills and labor inputs of employees—are well developed, most organizations have not yet developed the same degree of competence and sophistication in the management of the knowledge, know-how, and learning capabilities embodied in their employees. Drucker observes that "the productivity of knowledge and knowledge workers . . . is still neglected and abysmally low."[8] This rather pessimistic assessment is supported by the conclusion of a recent study which found that between 1986 and 1996, the top companies in the Fortune 500 had, on average, improved their gross profit margins by more than two percentage points. This improvement generally reflected better management of these organizations' tangible resources: inventories, capital equipment, and direct labor inputs. Over the same period, sales doubled, but selling and general and administrative expenses increased from 11 percent to 12 percent of revenue, continuing a trend that has seen overheads consume a steadily rising percentage of sales, from 8 percent in the 1920s to nearly 32 percent today. *Fortune*'s conclusion is that "on the operations side—the side that processes physical stuff—companies have improved productivity, leveraged growth and become more efficient. But on the staff side of the house—which processes information—they've gotten worse, unable even to achieve economies of scale, let alone truly take out costs."[9]

In a knowledge-driven economy, returns to the effective management of human capital are likely to exceed those available from the more efficient management of financial and physical assets. In order to realize these returns, however, companies must go *beyond productivity*—by developing and implementing new approaches and management techniques to tap the knowledge, intellect and creativity of each of their employees. And more effective management of the human capital resource should also improve the utilization of financial and physical assets, boosting overall firm performance.

Knowledge as a Manageable Resource

The management of the knowledge and know-how embodied in an organization's human capital resources presents a whole new set of challenges for managers. Traditional approaches simply don't apply. First of all, as an economic asset, knowledge is a unique kind of resource, in that it is not consumed in use but grows more valuable and more productive as it is shared and reused:

> Economic theory has a problem with knowledge: it seems to defy the basic economic principle of scarcity. Knowledge is not scarce in the traditional sense—the more you use it and pass it on, the more it proliferates. It is different from traditional goods in that it is, as economists put it, "infinitely expansible" . . . meaning that however much it is used, it does not get used up. It can be replicated cheaply and consumed over and over again: if you use a software package, you are not stopping millions of other people using it too.[10]

Second, knowledge comes in different forms: "Explicit knowledge . . . can be articulated in formal language including grammatical statements, mathematical expressions, specification manuals, and so forth. Tacit knowledge is . . . embedded in individual experience and involves . . . such factors as personal belief, perspective and values." Explicit knowledge can be easily replicated and widely distributed but is often outdated before the ink is dry. Tacit knowledge is personal, shared only with the consent and participation of the individual who possesses it.[11]

Third, knowledge has a number of distinct characteristics and social and political connotations that influence—and often inhibit—its creation, sharing, and distribution within organizations. New knowledge is continually being created through complex processes of social interaction that link the tacit knowledge embodied in individuals and the explicit knowledge resources that the organization possesses.[12] But the creation of knowledge is only part of the story. How knowledge is applied, shared, and preserved for future use has significant implications for organizational effectiveness. Researchers have observed that knowledge is fuzzy—that is, its categories and meanings change frequently. Knowledge is intimately and inextricably bound with the egos and occupations of the individuals who hold it. Because knowledge is closely linked to power in organizations, changes in the way knowledge is managed can have significant implications for a company's power structure.[13]

Competing in the Knowledge-Based Economy

How will organizations compete in a knowledge-based economy? Will the sources of competitive advantage be totally new, or extensions of what managers have been doing for years? Increasingly, leading companies are recognizing that creating knowledge, stimulating invention and innovation, and building organizational know-how are the primary means by which they create economic value. The management of intellectual resources has become the focal point of the strategies of these companies. Knowledge-based businesses—in health care, consulting, software development, design and engineering services, and biotechnology—are typically driven by rapid, continuous, and overlapping cycles of invention and innovation. Johnson & Johnson's CEO, Ralph Larsen, competing in the health care industry, asserts that "we are not in the product business. We are in the knowledge business. New products are our lifeblood." New products, defined as those introduced within the past five years here and abroad, accounted for 36 percent of Johnson & Johnson's sales in 1996, up from 26 percent in 1988.[14]

Recruiting and retaining top-quality talent is clearly one of the prerequisites for success in the knowledge economy. *Fortune*'s 1997 survey noted that the "most admired" companies, in industry after industry, had one thing in common: "a knack for finding, nurturing and keeping smart employees."[15]

Attracting and retaining the "best and brightest" employees is only part of the equation, however. The organization's ability to access and leverage the skills and capabilities of its employees by encouraging individual and organizational learning, and facilitating the sharing and application of their collective knowledge and expertise, must also be developed and then strengthened. Coca-Cola's 1996 Annual Report emphasized the importance of its workforce and the development of the organization's capability to learn and apply their talents: "Everything we do begins with the hard work of our people—we're developing new ways to help them help our business, as we focus on building not just our financial capital, but our 'human capital'—the intelligence, learning, dedication and focus of our people."[16]

The ability to harness an organization's talent and focus its collective efforts on innovation is also critical. *Fortune* singled out the Disney Company as "the world's best innovator." "We create a new product—a book, a movie, something—every five minutes, and each one has to be superb. Our goal is to do it better every time out," says CEO Michael Eisner. "But our real product is managing talent. That's what we really do here, and we never lose sight of that—because without that, what have you got?"[17]

Although superior human capital resources may sometimes be "acquired" by hiring more capable employees, it is generally not sufficient simply to employ the best and the brightest and apply their talents within the framework of existing processes, systems, and procedures. Organizations must also focus on developing a culture and creating an infrastructure that supports and reinforces individual capabilities and collaborative efforts. In a 1992 interview, Paul Allaire, Xerox's newly appointed CEO, described how he intended to remake Xerox. He envisioned "a company that combined the best of both worlds—the speed, flexibility, accountability and creativity that come from being a part of a small, highly focused organization; and the economies of scale, access to resources, and strategic vision a large company can provide." He set out to reconfigure the three key components of organizational architecture: the *hardware*—organizational structure and formal processes; the *people*—skills, personality, and character; and the *software*—"the informal networks and practices linking people together, the value system, the culture."[18]

The idea that internal networks and practices are the critical glue that holds organizations together and helps them to work effectively is echoed by Hamel and Prahalad. They maintain that "the real sources of [competitive] advantage are to be found in management's ability to consolidate corporate-wide technologies and production skills into competencies that empower individual businesses to adapt quickly to changing opportunities."[19] John Peetz, the chief knowledge officer of Ernst and Young, suggests another important dimension: the relationships that exist between an organization and its customers, and the value they place on each other's abilities.[20]

A Framework for Understanding

It has been broadly observed that the difference between the market value reflected in an organization's stock price and the book value reflected on its financial statements is steadily widening. The difference between market and book value is significantly greater for knowledge-intensive corporations than for organizations whose competitive positions are based primarily on tangible assets. Exhibit 1-1 shows the ratios of market-to-book value for selected examples (sales and book value as of latest fiscal year; market value as of June 1998). In organizations in which knowledge and the management of knowledge workers are relatively important contributors to the production of goods or services, and physical resources are relatively less critical, the ratio of market to book value tends to be considerably higher.

EXHIBIT 1-1.

Ratio of market value to book value for selected companies.

Company	Annual Sales ($ millions)	Market Value ($ millions)	Book Value ($ millions)	Ratio of Market to Book Value
America Online	1,685	24,323	128	190:1
Amazon.com	147	4,661	29	164:1
Yahoo! Inc.	67	6,882	118	58:1
Microsoft Corporation	11,358	257,343	10,777	24:1
Intel Corporation	25,070	135,256	19,295	7:1
Sears, Roebuck & Co.	41,296	23,439	5,862	4:1
NationsBank Corporation	17,333	74,895	21,337	3.5:1
General Motors Corp.	178,174	47,584	17,506	2.7:1

Key Definitions

The term *intellectual capital* generally has been used to describe all of the intangible factors that contribute to the gap between the book and the market values of an organization. This broad definition includes everything other than tangible assets that contributes to the market value of the company: human brainpower, employee commitment, company values, brand names, trademarks, technology leadership, business relationships, market position, customer loyalty, and internal systems and processes. *Human capital* is generally understood to consist of the individual capabilities, knowledge, skill, and experience of the company's employees and managers, as they are relevant to the task at hand, as well as the capacity to add to this reservoir of knowledge, skills, and experience through individual learning. Everything else— the organization's core value-creating activities, organizational knowledge, and information resources, and the organization's structure, systems processes, and culture—are lumped into the broad category of *structural capital*. Leif Edvinsson, the corporate director of intellectual capital at Skandia AFS, describes it this way: "Structural capital might best be described as the embodiment, empowerment and supportive infrastructure of human capital—in a word, everything left at the office when the employees go home."[21]

Understanding the Relationships

Exhibit 1-2 illustrates the principal relationships of an organization's resources (human, information, and physical and financial), its core value-creating activities, and its organizational structure, systems, processes, and culture.

Human capital consists of the individual capabilities, tacit knowledge, skills, and experience of the organization's managers and employees.

Organizational knowledge and information resources contains three broad categories. Intellectual property consists of the organization's documented and legally protected information, including patents, trademarks, and proprietary processes. Explicit organizational knowledge and information is also found in technical and financial data, engineering drawings and libraries, sales catalogs, customer lists, sales collateral, advertising copy, and so forth stored in files, databases, and other forms. Finally, management, process, and industry know-how is

EXHIBIT 1-2.
Organizational resources and structural capital.

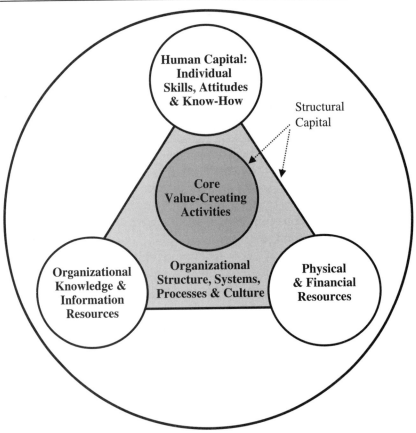

embodied in organizational routines, policies, procedures, forms, maintenance and operating manuals, and other implementations of management practice and policy.

Physical and financial resources are all of the organization's physical assets (land, buildings, equipment, inventories, leaseholds, etc.) and its financial resources (cash, accounts receivable, etc.).

Structural capital is the multidimensional framework that integrates all of the resources and capabilities of the organization into the core activities through which the organization creates value for its customers. Think of structural capital as the plumbing or the wiring that ties the organizational system together and helps it to function as a coordinated whole.

Structural Capital

The principal role of structural capital is to link the resources of the organization together into processes that create value for customers and sustainable competitive advantage for the firm. The organization's core business processes—product development, sales and marketing, order fulfillment, and the like—are key elements of structural capital. Equally important are the organization's structures and task designs, information and communications infrastructures, internal support functions and processes, incentives, controls and performance measurement systems, culture, values, and leadership. Structural capital also captures dynamic internal processes: organizational learning, the development and sharing of knowledge, and the ongoing development of collective and shared values, culture, and philosophy. Following are the key components of structural capital:

Core Value-Creating Activities
- Core business processes
- External relationships with customers, suppliers, and alliance partners
- Reputation, brand loyalty, image, and legitimacy

Organizational Structure, Systems, Processes, and Culture
- Organizational and reporting structures
- Operating systems, processes, procedures, and task designs
- Information and communications infrastructures
- Resource acquisition, development, and allocation systems
- Decision processes and information flows

- Incentives, controls, and performance measurement systems
- Mechanisms to promote sharing, collaboration, and organizational learning
- Organizational culture, values, and leadership

It is not any one factor or element of structural capital by itself that is likely to create a sustainable competitive advantage. Rather, sustainable advantages depend on complex interactions and interdependencies among multiple processes and resources. Management's challenge is to structure, link, and blend human and other organizational resources into unique capabilities that maximize individual productivity and organizational performance in ways that create real advantages in the marketplace yet resist imitation. While the objective of these efforts must necessarily be the ongoing development and leveraging of the knowledge, skills, and know-how of the organization's workforce, successful implementation will depend to a considerable extent on how effectively the organization designs, implements, and uses the key elements of its structural capital.

Human Capital

Our definition of human capital focused primarily on capabilities, knowledge, skills, and experience, all of them embodied in and inseparable from the individual. In order to address the opportunities for effective leverage of an organization's human capital resources, it is important to understand these skills and capabilities fully. We begin by drawing a parallel to the resource-based view of the firm. A growing number of management researchers have come to view the organization as a collection of resources and capabilities.[22] It is useful to extend this perspective to the individual level and consider the separate elements that contribute to the unique capabilities, knowledge, skill, and experience of the individual employee. Exhibit 1-3 identifies eight key categories, or elements, of human capital:

1. Motor skills: The ability to grasp, place, move, and manipulate objects in coordinated movements
2. Information-gathering (perceptual) skills: Sensory, perceptual, and interpretative capabilities
3. Information-processing (cognitive) skills: The ability to reason, analyze, and make decisions
4. Communication skills: The ability to listen, communicate, and share information and ideas

5. Experience: Know-how (and perspective) from having done the task before
6. Knowledge: Knowledge of self, the job, the organization, and the environment
7. Social skills: The ability to interface, coordinate, and collaborate productively with others
8. Values, beliefs, and attitudes: Personal values that shape perceptions, performance, and attitudes.

Each individual brings to the workplace a rich and varied collection of skills and capabilities, ranging from knowledge gained through formal education to everyday street smarts based on a unique set of

EXHIBIT 1-3.
Elements of human capital.

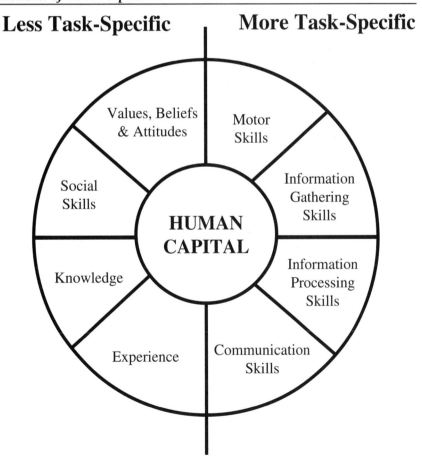

personal experiences. These elements are highly interdependent. Values, attitudes, and beliefs have deep roots, but are based largely on each individual's knowledge (what he or she has been taught) and experience (what he or she has done or seen). An individual's values and beliefs, knowledge and experience influence the kinds of information the person gathers (perceives) about events in the environment and how that information is processed and interpreted.[23]

Some of these skills and capabilities are general in nature, while others are more task specific. In many cases, an individual's ability to perform a task that uses motor, information-gathering, information-processing, and communications skills can be improved or redirected over relatively brief periods of time through education, training, and practice (the learning-curve effect). An individual's values, beliefs, and attitudes; knowledge; experience; and social skills are usually less task specific, deeply embedded and more difficult to change through education, training, and practice. The opportunities for leverage and the approaches that will be most effective will depend, to a considerable extent, on which skills and capabilities are to be addressed.

Individuals relate to organizations in multiple ways—for example, as employees, team members, and shareholders. The relationship of the individual to his or her assigned responsibilities is most important to this discussion of leverage. The assigned position may require the performance of a single, well-defined task, or multiple interrelated tasks, each of which may be more or less structured and defined. For jobs involving manual or clerical labor, employers are primarily interested in motor skills, job-related knowledge, and task-relevant experience. Information-gathering, information-processing, communications, or social skills are of little consequence. Service industry or customer contact positions, on the other hand, typically require a much broader range of experience and capability, with an emphasis on information gathering, communications, and social skills.

Task performance depends, to a considerable extent, on how well individual skills and capabilities are matched with the requirements of the task environment. If the requirements exceed the skills or the motivation of the individual assigned, performance will fall short, and the organization will suffer a loss of effectiveness. If the individual's skills and capabilities exceed the task requirements, task performance may be satisfactory, but the utilization of the organization's human capital will be inefficient. Values, attitudes, and commitment to the task and the organization are also critically important.[24]

Because individual tasks are aggregated into the larger organizational processes through which the company does its work and creates value for its customers, the relationship of the individual to others performing related tasks is also an important consideration. The relationships between tasks are usually defined by their input and output: the output of one task becomes the input for the next, and so on. Less frequently considered, however, are the linkages between the knowledge, skills, and capabilities of the individuals performing the separate tasks that collectively make up one or more of the larger organizational processes. To the extent that different kinds of knowledge, experience, and skills can be shared, considerable synergies may often be realized through collaborative efforts. On the other hand, poor individual communications skills, conflicting values, or differences in attitudes, knowledge, experience, or other abilities can affect the relationships between workers in ways that adversely affect task performance.

In this changing environment, the key management challenge will be to develop new approaches and master a new set of management techniques. Managers must learn how to recruit and retain the best talent, and to design organizations, tasks, and processes that leverage the individual and collective skills and capabilities of the workforce in ways that create significant and sustainable competitive advantages for the company.

Leveraging Human Capital

What do we mean by *leveraging* human capital? What are we trying to accomplish, and how do we go about it? According to *Webster's*, *leverage* refers to mechanical advantage—a lever is "a rigid bar used to exert a pressure." This definition is not much help when applied to human resources; most management theorists would frown on the notion of using a rigid bar to improve the motivation and performance of a group of workers. The secondary definitions of *leverage* as "effectiveness" or "power" are more useful for our purposes. In economic terms, the more effective use of a resource is closely aligned with the notion of productivity—more output with the same input, or the same output with a smaller input—but productivity is really more a measure of efficiency than a measure of effectiveness. The difference is important, and parallels the distinction Warren Bennis made between leadership (doing the right things) and management (doing things right).[25] When we think about leveraging human capital, it is important that these resources be used both effectively (focused on doing the right things) and efficiently (maximum output for a given input).

Hamel and Prahalad have argued that resource leverage is an essential component of any successful strategy and suggest that leverage can be achieved in five fundamental ways:

1. by more effectively concentrating resources on key strategic goals
2. by more efficiently accumulating resources
3. by complementing resources of one type with those of another to create higher-order value
4. by conserving resources whenever possible
5. by rapidly recovering resources—minimizing the time between expenditure and payback[26]

Concentrating resources on key strategic goals deals with the effectiveness issue: doing the right things. *Complementing* resources addresses the opportunities for synergy when different resources are combined into higher-order capabilities. The remaining categories—*accumulating, conserving,* and *recovering*—deal with matters of efficiency.

Although many of these concepts can be also be constructively applied to leverage an organization's human capital resources, they do not fully address the unique characteristics of human capital. First, the knowledge and capabilities embodied within an organization's human resources cannot be "owned" by the organization in the same way as other assets. Second, they do not depreciate (in the traditional sense). Third, although human capital is not, like knowledge, "infinitely expansible," in many respects the resource is a work in progress. Except as bounded by disease, age, or fatigue, the skills and capabilities of the individual can be developed or improved throughout the employee's working life. Further, because synergies are created when individuals work together in teams or other structures, we must consider opportunities to leverage human capital resources at both the individual and the organizational levels. Exhibit 1-4 summarizes, within the framework Hamel and Prahalad proposed, some of the ways we have identified that companies are leveraging human capital resources at the individual level and organizational levels.

Exhibit 1-4 identifies a number of leverage opportunities that were not explicitly addressed within Hamel and Prahalad's framework. At the organizational level, companies can accumulate knowledge resources at minimal cost by sharing knowledge, experience, and know-how with customers, suppliers, and alliance partners and extend their

EXHIBIT 1-4.
Opportunities to leverage human capital.

At the individual level, opportunities exist to leverage human capital by:

- *Concentrating* resources by
  —Setting performance targets
  —Designing tasks, incentives and controls to focus efforts on firm priorities
  —Shaping employee values and attitudes in ways that enhance motivation and performance
- *Accumulating* human capital resources efficiently through well-designed selection and hiring practices
- *Complementing* individual skills and capabilities with complementary resources
  —Designing tasks to make the best use of employee skills and capabilities
  —Matching employee skills to the requirements of the job
  —Multiplying and extending individual capabilities through the effective application of technology
- *Enhancing* individual knowledge, skills and capabilities by encouraging and facilitating individual learning and providing opportunities for training, skill development and practice
- *Conserving* resources through the implementation of well-designed safety and retention programs
- *Recovering* resources by minimizing the lag between hiring and full productivity

At the organizational level, opportunities exist to leverage human capital by:

- *Concentrating* resources by:
  —Building consensus on strategic goals
  —Using incentive and control systems to focus collective efforts on organizational priorities
  —Designing organization structures to concentrate resources on the highest priority activities
- *Accumulating* knowledge and experience at reduced costs by sharing knowledge, experience and know-how with customers, suppliers and business partners
- *Complementing* resources by:
  —Designing organizational structures and processes, communications infrastructures, and support systems that integrate individual tasks into efficient, flexible and responsive organizational processes
  —Combining individual and organization skills in new ways to create higher-order organizational capabilities
  —Using organizational mechanisms and communications technology to improve internal coordination and collaboration
  —Multiplying the capabilities of the organization with advanced processes, systems and technology
- *Extending* organizational capabilities by using technology to improve communications and coordination with customers, suppliers and business partners
- *Enhancing* the knowledge, skills and capabilities of the organization by encouraging and facilitating organizational learning and the widespread sharing of knowledge and market intelligence
- *Conserving* resources by implementing standard processes and routines, accomplishing the same results with less skilled labor

capabilities—reduce requirements for other resources (inventories, for example)—by using technology and other processes to improve communications and coordination with customers, suppliers, and alliance partners.

Although the unique characteristics of human capital provide a number of opportunities, there is a downside: the resource is highly mobile: "Knowledge workers, unlike manufacturing workers, own the means of production: they carry their knowledge in their heads and therefore can take it with them."[27] This mobility and control of the means of production contributes to a new sense of independence among knowledge workers that changes the rules of the game for employers: "the only employees worth having are those with many other choices of employment." Because the resource is highly mobile, retention strategies will assume increasing importance as organizations look for opportunities to leverage their investments in human capital.

A New Perspective

Our research has suggested an alternative framework that provides useful perspectives for identifying opportunities to improve the performance and productivity of an organization's human capital resources. We begin with the assumption that management faces two challenges in leveraging an organization's human capital resources:

1. To address the quality and the capabilities of the resource itself—to recruit, develop and retain the best talent available
2. To design and configure the organization's structural capital so as to maximize the potential and performance of its human capital

If we accept the premise that, all things being equal, each company has the same opportunity to compete for the best and the brightest, it becomes evident that the search for leverage opportunities must focus primarily on the organization's structural capital resources.

Structural capital plays an important role in the creation of competitive advantage: linking organizational resources into the processes and capabilities that create value for the customer. Exhibit 1-5 points out how structural capital links the organization's resources to each other and to its core value-creating activities. Understanding these linkages will help us to identify the opportunities for leverage that are found in every organization.

EXHIBIT 1-5.

How structural capital links an organization's Resources.

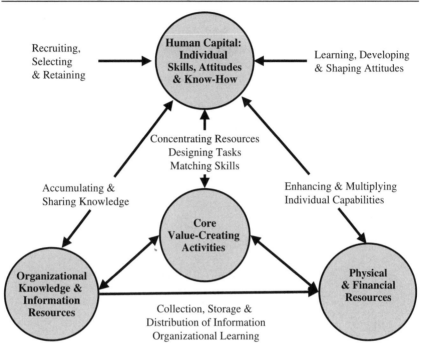

Because this will serve as the organizing framework for the rest of the book, it is important that each of the opportunities for leverage illustrated in this exhibit be fully appreciated and understood. In the sections that follow, we briefly provide illustrative examples from our research. Each of these examples is developed in the chapters that follow.

Recruiting, Selecting, and Retaining Human Capital

Attracting and retaining top-quality talent is a key strategic priority for most organizations. The systems, processes, procedures, and practices that support the acquisition and retention of human capital resources are critical elements of an organization's structural capital, and many leading companies place a high priority on these activities. Cisco Systems has a simple philosophy: "If you get the best people in the industry [and] motivate them properly, then you're going to be an industry leader." The following examples illustrate what some of the other leading companies are doing to ensure that they attract the best and the brightest:

■ GE Medical Systems has found referrals from its own employees to be the most effective recruiting source.

■ Southwest Airlines and Silicon Graphics live by the adage, "Hire for attitude, train for skill," placing greater emphasis on general knowledge and experience, social skills, and attitudes than on job-related training, experience, and skills.

■ Microsoft's recruiters look for flexibility, problem-solving ability, and creativity.

■ Cooper Software screens applicants through the company's web site.

■ USWeb handles 75 to 80 percent of its recruitment electronically. The entire process is virtually paperless, and it's fast, shortening hiring cycles from weeks to days.

Retention is a key element of human resources strategies for many leading organizations. Compensation and benefits play a key role, but other factors are also important:

■ Medtronic and Whole Foods Market work hard to foster employee identification with company values.

■ The intrinsic motivation of challenging work and a stimulating environment is an important factor at Hewlett-Packard, Motorola, and Gillette.

■ Flexibility and valued amenities are important tools for retention at USAA, Progressive Insurance, and Trilogy Systems.

Learning, Developing, and Shaping Attitudes

The knowledge, skills, and task-related experience of human capital resources can be strengthened through individual learning, training, development, and practice. Increasingly, training and development opportunities at leading organizations are being offered to all employees, not just those on professional or managerial career paths:

■ Cinergy, a Cincinnati-based utility, has replaced executive and leadership development with "talent development," available to everyone.

■ Employee development is a key priority at Solectron, where the CEO estimates that "20 percent of an engineer's knowledge becomes obsolete every year."

■ Intensive orientation programs get employees off on the right foot at Intel and UPS; FedEx and Greet Street have developed innovative approaches in this area.

■ General Electric, Motorola, and Merck emphasize widespread involvement, with managers at all levels involved in developing and conducting training.

■ Citibank and Arthur Andersen have sophisticated career tracking systems to monitor the development progress of their employees.

■ Sabbaticals are used effectively at McDonald's, Intel, and Hallmark Cards.

■ Sophisticated 360-degree evaluation systems are used effectively at GM's Saturn Division, Warner-Lambert, and General Electric.

Technology is playing an increasingly important role in the development of more efficient and more flexible employee training and development programs:

■ Arthur Andersen has saved millions of dollars by replacing classroom training with self-paced computer programs that permit new employees to complete required training in their own offices.

■ FedEx employees take computer-based job competency tests every six to twelve months. The tests highlight areas of weakness, which are then addressed through a series of self-paced training programs, also implemented on the computer.

Organizational culture, a key element of structural capital, can facilitate or impede efforts to leverage an organization's human capital resources by the way it shapes employee values, attitudes, and behaviors. The dominant values of some organizations help to focus and ensure the effective implementation of their strategies; others focus on storytelling and rituals, humor and fun, or formal mechanisms for gathering employee feedback:

■ A commitment to customer service is the centerpiece of FedEx's culture; innovation drives the 3M Corporation; efficiency is the dominant value at Wal-Mart.

■ A major component of the culture at Southwest Airlines and Sun Microsystems is fun and foolishness, an effective counterbalance to the stresses of competition.

■ Reinforcing its core value of customer service, Roadway Express publishes letters from satisfied customers in its quarterly employee newsletter.

■ Northwestern Mutual Life Insurance's CEO uses company stories to communicate the central values of his organization's traditions and culture.

■ Effective role modeling by the CEO reinforces organizational values at Nucor, Dallas Semiconductor, Intel, and Xerox.

■ Washington Mutual Savings and AES, a Virginia-based utility, use employee surveys and an electronic "Voting Booth" to keep managers in touch with the pulse of employee morale and attitudes.

Concentrating Resources

Concentrating and focusing resources on key organizational priorities is an important element of strategic leverage. Individual skills and know-how can be focused and concentrated more effectively on the organization's core value-creating activities in several ways:

■ Employee orientation programs, such as those used by UPS and Intel, are an effective starting point for many companies.

■ Strong cultures, such as those at 3M, Hewlett-Packard, and Wal-Mart, are powerful tools for aligning individual goals with organizational objectives.

■ Performance targets and incentives can be used to focus attention and direct resources toward the achievement of organizational objectives.

■ Boundaries, such as Lockheed Martin's criteria for diversification or Eli Lilly's narrowed focus for medical research, effectively focus strategic efforts.

Technology can also be used to focus resources on key objectives or organizational priorities:

■ By automating order processing, PSS World Medical, Inc., has realized 30 percent productivity gains, as sales representatives spend more time with customers.

■ A statistical database helps the New York Police Department allocate resources to the areas of highest need; serious crime is down 37 percent in three years.

■ A new prescription management system implemented by Walgreen's automates administrative tasks, freeing pharmacists to do patient counseling.

At the organizational level, outsourcing noncritical activities can free up management time and physical and financial resources, allowing managers to attend to higher-priority core business processes and value-creating activities:

■ Dell Computer outsources most of its manufacturing and customer service activities, freeing up internal resources, and continuing to grow at more than 50 percent per year.

■ Nike and Reebok focus on design and marketing, outsourcing virtually all of their manufacturing to low-labor-cost countries.

■ Monorail, a fast-growing PC manufacturer, outsources all but management, product design, and marketing, relying on partnering relationships with key suppliers.

Designing Core Business Processes

Designing core business processes and value-creating activities to utilize the skills and capabilities of the organization's human capital resources most effectively is critically important. Individual task performance can be improved through the thoughtful design of tasks and organizational structures and the careful matching of individual skill sets with job requirements. Technology has been used in many organizations to leverage the skills of employees:

■ Sears, Roebuck and Co. uses speech recognition systems to route customer calls, improving customer service and freeing up nearly three thousand employees for other assignments.

■ A new scheduling system at Digital Equipment Corporation's worldwide services division is expected to respond to customers' needs in a more timely fashion, with the right person assigned to the right problem at the right time.

■ A computer network configuration system recently installed by Danish network systems distributor Oilcom, Inc. has shortened selling cycles and reduced pricing and configuration errors.

■ L. L. Bean's new Order Fulfillment Center combines "what people do best with what technology can do better" in a totally new system.

Accumulating and Sharing Knowledge

The relationships between human capital and organizational knowledge and information resources provide opportunities for leverage in both directions. Individual knowledge, skills, and capabilities can be enhanced by encouraging and facilitating individual learning and providing opportunities for training, skill development, and practice. Individual task performance can be leveraged by providing ready access to the knowledge and resources required for the job, whether the source is internal or external to the organization. The capabilities of the organization can be broadened by encouraging and facilitating organizational learning and the widespread sharing of individual knowledge, collective know-how, and market intelligence. Technology can facilitate communications and collaboration, knowledge sharing, and the gathering and integration of external information. Technology plays an increasingly important role in the internal communications and information-sharing activities of virtually every individual and organization in the workforce today:

- David Pottruck, CEO of Charles Schwab, calls himself a "champion of executive computing." He relies heavily on his laptop computer and e-mail to keep in touch with both the markets and his organization from wherever he happens to be.
- John Quain, a contributing editor for *Fast Company*, works in cyberspace, relying on virtual partnering. He claims, "Most of the people I work for, I never see."
- Groupware is increasingly used in many organizations to facilitate internal communications and collaborative efforts.

The World Wide Web has created a new forum, the virtual meeting, recently used by British Petroleum to involve thousands of workers around the world in a three-day Innovation Colloquium. Bell & Howell has held its last two shareholders' meetings on the web, with excellent results.

Many organizations are using technology to share information and achieve closer coordination with their suppliers and customers:

- Online procurement systems designed to take the purchasing department out of the loop by using Internet-based communications links have been installed by Los Angeles County, Chevron Corp., and General Electric Information Services.
- Roadway Express has developed a number of innovative systems to provide timely information through network-based links to its agents and customers.
- Audio Adventures' Internet-based system allows audio books rented from any of 450 truck stop–based kiosks to be returned at any other kiosk across the country.
- Ambitious efforts linking complex manufacturing, procurement, and production scheduling systems directly with those of their customers and suppliers are underway at Marshall Industries, Basset Furniture, and Colgate-Palmolive.

It is widely acknowledged that much of what is valuable in the collective expertise of an organization is generally inaccessible because it is "owned" by individuals and exists only in the form of their personal know-how and expertise. Numerous barriers exist to the open sharing of this valuable reservoir of personal knowledge and experience. Some companies have, however, made remarkable progress:

■ Buckman Laboratories, a manufacturer of specialty chemicals, has an internal network accessible to each of its twelve hundred employees in eighty countries, and they use its industry-focused forums to share their knowledge and expertise in real-time with their colleagues around the world.

■ Xerox's Field Information Research Systems Team researches queries from customers for the company's field sales reps. Posted on a web site, the responses are widely shared, with over 3,000 users averaging 75,000 hits per month to review the 1,500 documents on file.

Another real challenge for most organizations is gathering, filtering, and distributing information from external sources. Understanding the environment is critical for competitive advantage in a rapidly changing marketplace. Personal news services such as *The Wall Street Journal*'s Personal Journal and PointCast's targeted information service provide valuable help.

Multiplying Individual and Organizational Capabilities

The strength and precision of individual motor skills can be multiplied many times by the appropriate application of technology resources, such as machine tools and transportation equipment. Technology can also leverage communications and information-gathering capabilities by extending the scope and range and reducing the time and effort expended in these activities:

■ General Motors recently began the rollout of a new technology architecture designed to improve collaboration and cooperation across the organization. The system will ultimately link 175,000 users through common financial, human resources management, and manufacturing systems.

■ Welch's Foods, Inc.'s sales representatives can now design their own account management reports. Available on demand, customized data sets are updated daily.

■ Sun's Java is being used to create a whole new class of software capabilities—for example, estimating health insurance benefits for consumers at the time of filing and allowing travel agency customers to plan and price their own itineraries.

Analysis and decision making, the key information-processing skills, can be improved and made more productive by the use of a wide range of analytical and decision-support tools and technologies:

■ Institutional traders on Wall Street use sophisticated computer programs and advanced communications technologies to make complex trading decisions in real time, performing calculations so complex and handling volumes of data so massive that this work could not be done without the technology.

■ Volvo's truck plant in Dublin, Virginia, uses a new system based on genetic algorithms to solve scheduling problems too complex to be addressed with conventional methods. The man-machine interface is critical, as a twenty-one-year veteran scheduler adds his experience and judgment to help the system reach a solution.

Encouraging and Facilitating Organizational Learning

Organizations adapt to a changing environment by learning from experience and outside influences how to use their resources more effectively and manage their core value-creating activities. Successful learning organizations encourage a proactive, creative approach to the unknown, actively solicit the involvement of employees at all levels, and enable everyone to use their intelligence and apply their imagination. According to former Citibank CEO Walter Wriston, "The person who figures out how to harness the collective genius of the people in his or her organization is going to blow the competition away."

■ British Petroleum recognizes the importance of having everyone involved in the process of learning and adapting. A recent Innovation Colloquium was made available to nearly twenty thousand employees worldwide over the corporate intranet.

■ Xerox Business Systems has an executive called the "learning person" within the organization. Her responsibilities include the creation of an environment in which everyone is willing and able to challenge the status quo.

■ Springfield ReManufacturing Corporation in Springfield, Missouri, is a pioneer of "open book" management, where individual productivity statistics are maintained and the books are open to all employees.

■ Hewlett-Packard's CEO, Lew Platt, includes some time each day for management by walking around, which keeps him in touch with the pulse of the organization and alert to the need for change.

■ Cisco's John Chambers has quarterly meetings with five hundred top managers and regular "birthday breakfasts" with a cross section of employees during their birthday month. Any question is fair game at either event.

■ Many organizations are using the Internet as a rich source of timely information about their suppliers, customers, and competitors. Others encourage active networking among industry peers as an important source of business intelligence or use benchmarking on a regular basis.

■ Dana Corporation relies on its employees to identify improvements to business processes through a well-designed suggestion system; 70 percent of the ideas are used.

■ Motorola has institutionalized a "culture of dissent." By filing a "minority report," an employee can officially challenge business decisions made by others.

Recipes for Success in a Changing Environment

As we enter the knowledge age, the rules of the game are changing rapidly. Leading companies in industries as diverse as health care, beverages, entertainment, office products, and professional services have begun to focus increasingly on their intellectual capital resources as a key source of competitive advantage.

The management of knowledge and knowledge workers presents a whole new set of challenges. People have always been important to organizations, but in the machine age, the attributes that mattered most for nonmanagerial jobs were the individual's task-specific skills and experience: motor skills and job-related knowledge and experience. In the knowledge age, information-gathering, information-processing, and communications skills have become increasingly critical.

Enabled by technology and driven by global competition, organizations have been forced to become flatter and more flexible, and new organizational forms have evolved; the barrier-free, modular, virtual, and cellular forms are increasingly common. These forms demand a much higher level of communications and coordination across boundaries, placing a premium on the social and communications skills—and the values and attitudes—of workers at all levels.

Finally, because much of the knowledge critical to competitive success is not owned by the firm, but rather is embodied in the individuals who make up the organization, the key resources themselves are mobile. And as knowledge—and knowledge workers—become increasingly important to success, the best talent is becoming scarce and in high demand, placing a premium on the organization's ability to retain, motivate, and continuously enhance the skills and capabilities of its workers.

Our investigation of nearly two hundred organizations has concluded that organizations seeking competitive advantage and superior performance by leveraging their human capital resources face two key challenges. They must (1) recruit, develop, and retain the best talent available and (2) design and configure the organization's structural capital so as to maximize the potential and performance of their human capital. Based on our investigation of the best practices of these leading organizations, the recipes for success in this new environment appear to be as follows:

- Recruiting, developing, and retaining the best talent available
- Optimizing the efficiency and effectiveness of core value-creating activities
- Creating a flexible and responsive organizational infrastructure
- Facilitating individual and organizational learning
- Encouraging the sharing of knowledge and know-how throughout the organization
- Fostering an environment that values collective effort and cooperation, but also encourages risk taking, innovation, and initiative
- Building strong and mutually reinforcing relationships between an organization and its employees, customers, and suppliers.

It is not any one factor by itself that makes a significant difference. Rather, sustainable competitive advantage depends on complex interactions and interdependencies among multiple initiatives. Management's challenge is to blend human and other organizational resources into unique capabilities that maximize individual productivity and organizational performance in ways that create real advantages in the marketplace yet resist imitation. And the focal point of these efforts must necessarily be the ongoing development and leveraging of the knowledge, skills, and know-how of the organization's workforce.

Notes

1. *Triumphs, Blunders and Bitter Pills*—No. 6 in a Series: Offensive Ideas. 1997. From an advertisement for CSX Intermodal.

2. Stephen B. Shepard, "The New Economy: What It Really Means," *Business Week*, November 17, 1997, pp. 38–40.

3. Philip B. Evans and Thomas S. Wurster, "Strategy and the New Economics of Information," *Harvard Business Review* 75(5) (September–October 1997): 71–82.

4. "An Acknowledged Trend: The World Economy Survey," *The Economist*, September 28, 1996. © 1996 The Economist Newspaper Group. Reprinted with permission. Further reproduction prohibited.

5. Peter F. Drucker, "The Future That Has Already Happened," in "Looking Ahead: Implications of the Present," *Harvard Business Review* 75(5) (September–October 1997): 20–24.

6. Gary Hamel and C. K. Prahalad, "Competing in the New Economy: Managing out of Bounds," *Strategic Management Journal* 17 (1996): 237–242. Copyright John Wiley & Sons Limited. Reproduced with permission.

7. Ibid. Reproduced with permission.

8. Drucker, "Future."

9. Thomas A. Stewart, "Yikes! Deadwood Is Creeping Back," *Fortune*, August 18, 1997, pp. 221–222.

10. "An Acknowledged Trend." Reprinted with permission.

11. I. Nonaka and H. Takeuchi, *The Knowledge Creating Company* (New York: Oxford University Press, 1995).

12. I. Nonaka and N. Konno, "The Concept of 'Ba': Building a Foundation for Knowledge Creation," *California Management Review* 40(3) (Spring 1998): 40–54.

13. Thomas H. Davenport, David W. De Long, and Michael C. Beers, "Successful Knowledge Management Projects," *Sloan Management Review* (Winter 1998): 43–57.

14. Howard Rudnitsky, "One Hundred Sixty Companies for the Price of One," *Forbes*, February 26, 1996, pp. 56–62.

15. Anne Fisher, "The World's Most Admired Companies," *Fortune*, October 27, 1997, pp. 220–240.

16. Coca-Cola Company, Annual Report, 1996.

17. Fisher, "World's Most Admired Companies."

18. Robert Howard, "The CEO as Organizational Architect: An Interview with Xerox's Paul Allaire," *Harvard Business Review* 70(5) (September–October 1992): 107–121.

19. C. K. Prahalad and Gary Hamel, "The Core Competence of the Corporation," *Harvard Business Review* 90(3) (1990): 79–91

20. Thomas A. Stewart, "Is This Job Really Necessary?" *Fortune*, January 12, 1998, 154–155.

21. Leif Edvinsson and Michael S. Malone, *Intellectual Capital: Realizing Your Company's True Value by Finding Its Hidden Roots* (New York: HarperBusiness, 1997).

22. Jay Barney, "Firm Resources and Sustained Competitive Advantage," *Journal of Management* 17(1) (1991): 99–120.

23. D. C. Hambrick and P. A. Mason, "Upper Echelons: The Organization as a Reflection of Its Top Managers," *Academy of Management Review* 9(2) (1984): 193–206.

24. Dave Ulrich, "Intellectual Capital = Competence X Commitment," *Sloan Management Review* (Winter 1998): 15–26.

25. Quoted in M. Loeb, "Where Leaders Come From," *Fortune*, September 19, 1994, p. 241.

26. Gary Hamel and C. K. Prahalad, *Competing for the Future* (Boston: Harvard Business School Press, 1994), p. 175.

27. Drucker, "The Future."

2

FINDING AND KEEPING THE
BEST AND THE BRIGHTEST

Max DePree, the former CEO of Herman Miller, Inc., recently shared an amusing family experience:

> Our grandson once locked himself in the bathroom. Despite his mother's best efforts to get the door open, she failed. She called in the police, who also failed to open the door. Finally his mother called the fire department. By the time the fire trucks arrived, there was quite a scene on the front lawn. The firemen promptly broke down the door with their axes, tools they certainly know how to use.
>
> When our son Chuck arrived, at the height of the suspense, he could not figure out what was happening. There was no fire or smoke, but his bathroom door and its frame were in shambles.
>
> At the office the next day, he was complaining to a colleague about the damage. The colleague observed that there might be a management lesson in the story. "A fireman has two tools, an axe and a hose. If you call him, you're going to get one."[1]

This story highlights the essential character of labor in the industrial age: the need for specialization of tasks, lack of discretion, and mass production technologies. Performing more than two tasks would be anathema to production efficiency.

The rise to prominence of the knowledge worker and the salience of intangible assets as the vital source of competitive advantage is changing the balance of power in organizations. The traditional hierarchy and rules do not motivate knowledge workers; instead, managers must constantly work to develop a supportive atmosphere of openness and trust to leverage their workers' knowledge for competitive advantage.

Today's knowledge workers place professional development and personal enrichment, tangible and intangible, above company loyalties. And they have more options than ever before. In April 1998, according to Department of Labor statistics, the overall jobless rate was 4.3 percent, but a microscopic 1.7 percent for college graduates. Moreover, the department pegs unemployment among professional specialty workers at 1.7 percent, a figure so low that some assert that most of the "unemployed" are simply stuck in Silicon Valley traffic jams enroute to higher-paying jobs! Another revealing statistic, according to an American Management Association survey, is that six out of ten companies indicated that it takes longer to fill professional and technical positions than it did three years ago.[2]

A *Fortune* writer recently painted a picture of the new reality for today's highly educated, high-in-demand "gold-collar" workers:

> Loyalty. Gratitude. Fortitude. They're dead, man. And who's the culprit? Maybe corporate America. After all, it was big companies that in the late 1980s and early 1990s ended the traditional employment contract. That whole loyalty-in-exchange-for-lifetime-employment-and-a-gold-watch thing no longer made sense. So they got rid of it. Hundreds of thousands of workers were fired. Now employees would be self-sufficient and responsible for their own careers. That new deal worked fine when there weren't a lot of jobs. But now that there are too many jobs, it's a disaster. Changing jobs every two years is no longer frowned on; gosh, it's encouraged. How else do you expect to get a huge raise?[3]

Doesn't it provide a sharp contrast to the 1956 imagery of William H. Whyte's Organization Man? He was bound to his company, wearing his gray flannel suit, briefcase in hand and fedora on head, waiting on the train platform for the 7:37 to take him downtown. Clearly, now it is a seller's market, especially for the highly talented people most likely to add value for the organizations fortunate enough to hire them.

The first challenge for organizations seeking to leverage their human capital resources is to address the resource itself. In order to compete, organizations must have top-quality talent—employees with the right sets of skills and capabilities and the right kinds of values and attitudes. These skills and attitudes must be continually developed, strengthened, and reinforced, and each employee must be motivated and his or her efforts focused on the organization's top priorities. Exhibit 2-1 shows how these activities relate to the overall framework introduced in Chapter 1.

Attracting, recruiting, and hiring the best and the brightest is a critical first step in the process. In a May 1997 symposium for CEOs, Bill Gates said, "The thing that is holding Microsoft back . . . is simply how [hard] we find it to go out and recruit the kind of people we want to grow our research team."[4]

But hiring is only the first of three vital processes in which all successful companies must engage to build and leverage their human capital. They must also develop employees, at all levels and in all specialties, to their full potential in order to maximize their joint contribution. And, finally, the first two processes are for naught if organizations can't provide the working environment and the intrinsic and extrinsic rewards to retain their best and brightest. As the visionary Charles Handy, author of *Beyond Certainty* and *The Age of Paradox* puts it:

EXHIBIT 2-1.

Finding, developing, and retaining the best employees.

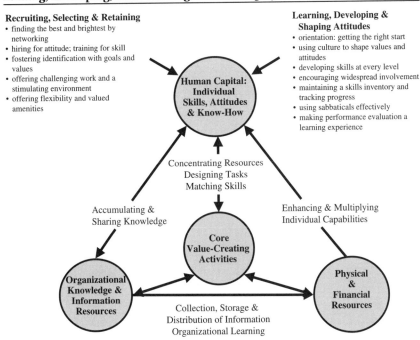

Recruiting, Selecting & Retaining
- finding the best and brightest by networking
- hiring for attitude; training for skill
- fostering identification with goals and values
- offering challenging work and a stimulating environment
- offering flexibility and valued amenities

Learning, Developing & Shaping Attitudes
- orientation: getting the right start
- using culture to shape values and attitudes
- developing skills at every level
- encouraging widespread involvement
- maintaining a skills inventory and tracking progress
- using sabbaticals effectively
- making performance evaluation a learning experience

Human Capital: Individual Skills, Attitudes & Know-How

Concentrating Resources
Designing Tasks
Matching Skills

Accumulating & Sharing Knowledge

Enhancing & Multiplying Individual Capabilities

Core Value-Creating Activities

Organizational Knowledge & Information Resources

Physical & Financial Resources

Collection, Storage & Distribution of Information
Organizational Learning

Nowadays the organization cannot demand the loyalty of its people: it has, instead, to earn their loyalty. There is no logical or economic reason why those assets should not go to a better hole if they can find it. As my boss once said to me when I told him of a tempting offer from a rival for my services: "We expect our best people to be wanted by others; we just hope that they won't be persuaded, and certainly not by mere money." This is the newest challenge to leadership—to make your hole the preferred hole for the best people.

In this chapter we address the hiring and selection, development, and retention of human capital—highly interrelated activities. We like to think of them using the image of a three-legged stool (see Exhibit 2-2). If one leg is weak or broken, the chair collapses. For example, poor hiring can impede the effectiveness of development and retention processes, and ineffective retention efforts place additional burdens on hiring and development. The colorful, but blunt, warning of David Pritchard, head of Microsoft's recruiting operations, captures some of the flavor of these interrelationships: "If I hire a bunch of bozos, it will hurt us, because it takes time to get rid of them. They start infiltrating the organization and then they themselves start hiring people of lower quality. At Microsoft, we are always looking to hire people who are better than we are."[5]

There are no simple, easy-to-apply answers, but we can all learn from what leading-edge organizations are doing to attract, develop, and retain human capital.

EXHIBIT 2-2.
Human capital: Three interdependent activities.

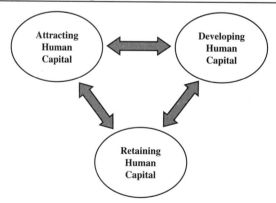

More Effective Hiring Practices

"All we can do is bet on the people we pick. So my whole job is picking the right people."
—Jack Welch, CEO, General Electric, Fortune (October 27, 1997)

The first step in the process of building superior human capital is input control: hiring the right person. Emphasizing the importance and value of effective hiring practices, Jack Welch of GE takes an active role, personally interviewing all candidates for GE's top five hundred positions—a rather dramatic investment of his time and effort.

Many human resources professionals still approach employee selection from a "lock-and-key" mentality. That is, they seek to fit a key (a job candidate) into a lock (the job). Such an approach requires a thorough analysis of both the person and the job. Only then can the right decision be made as to how well the two will fit together. How can you fail, the theory goes, if you get a precise match of knowledge, ability, and skill profiles? Within the framework of our model of human capital as a bundle of skills and capabilities, the precise-matching approach emphasizes task-specific skills—motor skills, information-gathering and -processing capabilities, and communication skills—and places less emphasis on the other elements.

Many have questioned the precise-matching approach. Instead, they argue that companies can identify top performers by focusing on key employee mind-sets, attitudes, or general orientations that lead to success in nearly all jobs. This approach emphasizes an employee's values, beliefs, and attitudes and the person's more general knowledge, experience, and social skills. These companies reason that if they get these elements right, the new employee can learn the task-specific skills in relatively short order. (This does not imply, however, that task-specific skills are unimportant. Rather, it suggests that the requisite skill sets must be viewed as a necessary but not sufficient condition.)

Consider an example from the world of professional sports. In major league baseball, the basic agreement states that a player cannot sign with another team until he has played for his original team for at least six years in the major leagues. In this era of lucrative free agent contracts, the key assets (the players) are highly mobile. From the team's perspective, it makes economic sense to "grow your own" and develop minor league teams. How does an organization build a strong minor league system? According to Charlie Blaney, the Los Angeles

Dodgers' vice president for minor league operations, "It's good scouting, first and foremost." The criteria used include the five physical tools that are relatively easy for scouts to determine: hitting, hitting with power, fielding, running, and throwing. But these are not the most important criteria. Instead, Blaney argues, "There's a sixth tool called general makeup. Makeup encompasses work habits, desire, drive, attitude, discipline—all those things that a player learns from his family or his coaches in growing up. *Makeup, for me, is number one* [emphasis added]."[6]

Hire for Attitude, Train for Skill

In the business world, leading-edge companies live by the adage, "Hire for attitude, train for skill."[7] Essentially they are emphasizing the employee's general knowledge and experience, social skills, and values, beliefs, and attitudes—the individual attributes on the left-hand side of Exhibit 1-3. Consider Southwest Airlines' (SWA) hiring practices, with its strong focus on employee values and attitudes. Given its strong team orientation, SWA uses what could be best described as an indirect approach in hiring. The interviewing team asks a group of candidates to prepare a five-minute presentation about themselves. During the presentations, the interviewers observe which candidates are enthusiastically supporting their peers and which are focused on polishing their own presentations while the others are presenting. The former are, of course, favored.

Social skills are also important. You need to be pleasant and collegial to be hired by Rosenbluth International, a Philadelphia-based travel management company with 1997 revenues estimated at $3.5 billion. Here, job applicants are asked to play a trial game of softball with the company team. Potential executives are frequently flown to the firm's North Dakota ranch to help repair fences or drive cattle. Do athletic ability or ranching skills matter? Not at all. According to Keami Lewis, Rosenbluth's diversity manager, "You can teach a person almost anything. But you can't teach them how to be nice."

Silicon Graphics Inc. (SGI) also places a premium on a prospective employee's mind-set and attitude. Although the company needs highly skilled chip designers and software programmers, technical virtuosity alone is seldom the determining factor. According to Eric Lane, director of worldwide staffing:

It's the kind of place where the main mode of transportation between cubicles is the skateboard. In interviews I give people an opportunity to be fun, to show their sense of humor. We look for people's passions, what they've done with their lives—the guy who took a year off after his MBA to play the violin or travel the world.

Many leading companies look for creativity and flexibility in problem solving—broadly applicable information-gathering and -processing skills—during the interview process. For example, Microsoft asks offbeat questions such as, "How much water flows through the Mississippi River each day?" and for a reason. According to Pritchard:

> We're not looking for the "right" answer. We're looking for the method. . . . We want to see what information they ask for, like the length of the river or the flow rate at certain measuring points. It's a learning process. One of the things we look for is smarts and experience, but we also want to know what they will bring here over the long term. Are they flexible? Can they learn new concepts? In this industry, thing are changing on a daily basis, and if you're not capable of learning new things, you won't be successful.

Alan Cooper, president of Cooper Software, in Palo Alto, California, cleverly uses technology to hone in on his applicants' problem-solving ability—and on their attitudes. Prospects are given a test based on his company's business: designing user interfaces for companies such as Microsoft, Oracle, and Prodigy. He contends the test can be applied in any industry: before you spend time figuring out whether job candidates will work out, find out how their minds work. According to Cooper, "Hiring was a black hole. I don't talk to bozos anymore because 90 percent of them turn away when they see our test. It's a self-administering bozo filter." How does it work?

> Cooper directs job applicants to the web site and asks them to complete the test. A key question asks the prospective software engineer to design a new table creation interface for Microsoft Word. Candidates are requested to provide pencil sketches and a description of the new user interface. A question for design communicators asks them to develop a marketing strategy for a new touch-tone phone—directed at consumers from 1850! Candidates submit their entries by

e-mail. Cooper forwards the answers around the company to solicit feedback, and only candidates with the highest marks get interviews.

Jonathan Korman, a design communicator, suggests that the test "told me more about real job duties than any description could." Josh Seiden, a software designer, is even more positive: "It was a fun puzzle—much more engaging than most of what I was doing at my previous job."

That's exactly the kind of attitude Cooper wants. "We get e-mail from some people saying, 'Before I take this test, is the position still open?' I say no, because I don't want anybody who sees it as an effort," claims Cooper. "People who really care take the test and love it. Other people say it's hard. We don't want those people."

The central point of this section is the suggestion to, in essence, heed the "Popeye Principle": "I y'am what I y'am." Many have argued that the most common—and fatal—hiring mistake is to select someone with the right skills but the wrong mind-set under the theory that "we can change them." According to Alan Davidson, an industrial psychologist in San Diego whose clients include Chevron, Merrill Lynch, and the Internal Revenue Service, "The single best predictor of future behavior is past behavior. Your personality [largely reflecting values, beliefs, attitudes, and social skills] is going to be essentially the same throughout your life."

Companies that ignore the Popeye Principle do so at their own peril. Consider the recent experience of Ann Rhodes, executive vice president of Doubletree Hotels Corp., based in Phoenix, Arizona. She has excellent credentials—having spent most of her career at Southwest Airlines—and had become the person most identified with SWA's innovative approach to hiring. But look at what happened when she recently trusted her gut feeling:

At Doubletree, she was charged with remaking the culture to stress freedom, creativity, informality, and flexibility. She had developed an acid-test interview question: "Tell me about the last time you broke the rules." A long silence or noncommittal response indicated that a candidate was trying to manufacture the desired response, whereas, she claims, "The good ones don't care." Rhodes recently hired a senior financial executive who bombed the acid test. However, his credentials were so impressive that Rhodes "went with her heart" and hired him anyway, hoping that he would change. The result was unfortunate: "He was so by-the-book, he read from the book. Literally! 'It says here on page 10 that I can't do that,' " claims Rhodes. He quit before Rhodes could fire him.

Network, Network, Network!

Companies that take hiring seriously must also take recruiting seriously.[8] The number of jobs that today's successful, knowledge-intensive companies must fill is astonishing. IBM's Global Services Division tried to hire 15,000 software engineers last year; Andersen Consulting wants to hire 3,500 graduates off college campuses and an additional 6,500 elsewhere; Electronic Data Systems is trying to fill 10,000 jobs; and so on. The competition (and resultant poaching) for qualified professionals is so intense that Microsoft Corporation hired bouncers to keep headhunters at bay during a recent training session for programmers in Holland. And a recruiter trying to fill IBM's voracious need introduces himself as James R. Bunch, "as in 'bunch of jobs.' "

Many of the most attractive companies still have no shortage of applicants. Southwest Airlines typically gets 150,000 resumes a year yet hires only about 5,000. Netscape reviews 60 resumes for every person hired.[9] The challenge becomes having the right job candidates, not the most.

Many companies are finding that their most effective recruiting efforts start closest to home: referrals from their own employees. It makes sense. After all, people who thrive at one company are likely to associate (both personally and professionally) with people similar to themselves. And, as suggested by Susan Loker, senior vice president of human resources for Boston-based Cambridge Technology Partners (CTP), "Referrals are a good indicator of how people feel about working for us. If people are happy, they'll refer other people to us." Incentives never hurt: Any employee who refers a candidate who is ultimately hired by CTP gets a $1,000 bonus, which grows to $3,000 when times get particularly tight.

GE Medical Systems has also found that current employees are the best sources for new ones. The GE unit has a few impediments to overcome. Located in Milwaukee, Wisconsin, employees must endure ice and snow over a long winter. And because this is not a start-up, the chance for becoming a multimillionaire with a one-hit wonder is clearly out of the question. However, this company does have some drawing power: it invents and produces products such as CT scanners and magnetic resonance imagers that can be life saving, thus appealing to employees' social consciousness.

Recently, Steven Patscot, head of staffing and leadership development, made a few simple changes to double the number of referrals. First, he simplified the process to do away with complex forms and the usual bureaucracy. Second, he increased incentives. Everyone referring a qualified candidate received a gift certificate at Sears. For referrals who were hired, the "bounty" was increased to $2,000 ($3,000 if the referral was a software engineer). It sounds like a lot of money, but not compared to the $15,000 to $20,000 fees GE typically pays to headhunters for each new person hired.

When it comes to networking, few can match the rigor and originality of high-flying Cisco Systems. The San Jose networking equipment company had fiscal 1997 sales of $6.4 billion and profits of $1.4 billion, up 53 percent over 1996. The company has it all together in its approach to recruiting and provides a good summary example:

> Cisco's rapid growth has fueled its voracious appetite for new knowledge workers. During a recent eighteen-month period, it doubled its workforce to 10,000, resulting in the hiring of nearly 300 new employees per month. During that period, Cisco was responsible for roughly 10 percent of the total net job gains in the Silicon Valley.
>
> Drawing top talent is a vital strategic weapon. According to CEO John Chambers, "Cisco has an overall goal of getting the top ten to fifteen percent of the people in our industry. Our philosophy is very simple—if you get the best people in the industry to fit your culture and you motivate them properly, then you're going to be an industry leader."
>
> Key to Cisco's success is its effectiveness in going after passive job seekers: people who are happy and successful where they are. Barbara Beck, Cisco's vice president for human resources, says, "The top ten percent are not typically found in the first round of layoffs from other companies, and they usually aren't cruising through the want ads."
>
> Four mechanisms are central to Cisco's efforts to lure them. First, it holds focus groups with prime recruitment targets, including senior engineers and marketing professionals from competitors to find out how they spend their free time (lots of movies), what web sites they visit (Dilbert Zone is popular), and how they feel about job hunting (they hate it). Based on such useful information, Cisco goes to work reaching poten-

tial applicants through a range of innovative approaches: activities such as art fairs, microbrewery festivals, and Silicon Valley's annual home and garden show. Cisco recruiters work the crowd, collect business cards from prospects, and talk informally about their careers.

Second, Cisco has dramatically changed the way it uses newspaper help-wanted ads. Instead of listing and describing specific job openings, the ads feature Cisco's Internet address (http://www.cisco.com/jobs) with an invitation to apply.

Third, directing all job seekers to the web site has a significant benefit for Cisco. The company can post plenty of information about each of its hundreds of job openings inexpensively on its web site. The site also enables Cisco to tap extremely useful information. It can tell where prospects work as well as "customize" responses. For example, people visiting the site from 3Com, Cisco's arch rival, were once automatically greeted with the message, "Welcome to Cisco. Would you like a job?" The company advertises in cyberspace as well, which enables it to reach a self-selected set of candidates (those able to navigate the Internet) from around the world. The company can easily monitor and measure important aspects of its recruiting, such as the number of visits to its site.

Last, the company uses insights gained from its focus groups to entice happily employed people into the fold. As a result of one response it got—"I'd do it if I had a friend who told me he had a better opportunity at Cisco than I have at my current employer"—Cisco launched the Friends program. The method is straightforward: "If you have a friend at Cisco, give them a call—there might be a job waiting for you! If you don't have a friend at Cisco, visit our website and we'll find you one. Your new friend will teach you about the company, introduce you to the right people, and guide you through the hiring process."

Although the program is advertised only in local movie theaters, Cisco still gets 100 to 150 inquiries each week. A thousand Cisco employees have volunteered for the program, drawn by its generous referral fee (starting at $500 and a lottery ticket for a free Hawaii trip) for each referral eventually hired.

It's not surprising that Cisco's referral rates are twice the industry average. That creates a performance edge because referrals tend to lead to qualified employees with long tenures; people are putting their reputations on the line. CEO Chambers tracks the referral rates as a vital performance indicator. Overall, referrals and the Friends program account for an impressive 50 to 60 percent of all newly hired employees.

Clearly, selecting and developing individuals for the top positions is critical to the organization's long-term viability. Hiring the right people makes things a lot easier: fewer rules and regulations, less need for monitoring and hierarchy, and a greater internalization of organizational norms and objectives. But building superior human capital also involves transforming the inputs into resources that add real value and help to create sustainable advantages in the marketplace.

Leveraging Human Capital Through Employee Development

It is not enough just to hire superior talent and expect the skills and capabilities of those employees to remain current and competitive throughout the duration of their employment.

Solectron assembles printed circuit boards and other components for its Silicon Valley clients. Its employees receive an average of 95 hours a year of company-provided training. Chairman Winston Chen observes, "Technology changes so fast that we estimate 20% of an engineer's knowledge becomes obsolete every year. Training is an obligation we owe to our employees." The return on training may be hard to calculate, but most experts believe it is real and essential. Chen observes, "If you want to have high growth and high quality, then training is a big part of the equation." Motorola calculates that every dollar spent on training returns thirty dollars in productivity gains over the next three years.[10]

According to Patrick Kelly, CEO of PSS World Medical, Inc., of Jacksonville, Florida, "We don't hire truck drivers or computer specialists. We hire CEOs—people who want to develop a broad-based knowledge of the business and who are prepared to act on that knowledge."[11] Similarly, Cinergy, the $3.2 billion Cincinnati-based gas, electric, and energy services company, has changed how it develops people to recognize that all employees must be the prime investors and beneficiaries in learning. The past focus on executive and leadership development has been replaced by "talent development," which is available to everyone. According to Elizabeth Lanier, the legal chief of staff, "The premise is that we want to have the smartest people in every layer of every job. If it's a janitor in a power plant, I want him smarter than any other janitor." Lanier is convinced that if you only recruit and train your best talent you run the risk of having that talent take your investment to the competition. Colorfully, she adds, "You get a high piss off factor. You tick off all existing employees. Our ability to respond to opportunities is not a function of how well we recruit MBAs but of how many smart people we have that we can lateral to and say run with it."

If this sounds too egalitarian, recall the old adage, "A chain is only as strong as its weakest link." And keep in mind that the business press is replete with examples of companies that have benefited tremendously from ideas and contributions at all levels. Can a business really afford to write anyone off?

Making Orientation Work

In a sense, the old saw, "You don't get a second chance to make a good first impression," embodies the importance of orienting new employees to a company's mission, culture, and objectives. It is here that expectations must be set regarding both style and substance: how you conduct yourself and what is expected, which begins with the critical process of aligning employee values with those of the organization. Clearly there is no "one best way": the approach must reflect an organization's underlying values and mission. Consider how the highly structured orientation programs of UPS and Intel contrast with the informal and creative approach used by Greet Street, a three-year-old San Francisco–based company that offers personalized greeting cards and other multimedia products.[12]

At UPS, the foundation of training is a classroom orientation that immerses new employees in the firm's culture. Every employee must develop a strong service orientation and learn why each step in the process is a vital link in the satisfaction of each UPS customer. The brief orientation is followed by a twenty-two-day period of intensive, one-on-one training with the new employee's immediate supervisor. This graduated, results-oriented instruction on proper methods steadily raises performance levels, reinforcing consistency and attention to detail. Additionally, special sessions devoted to customer focus train employees to put themselves in the customer's place.

Intel has experienced soaring growth recently. Over two-thirds of its 65,000 employees have joined in the past five years, and the company has added 31,000 employees over the past two years alone—

which works out to about 300 employees per week. Its approach to new employees has been described as an "orientation boot camp." To leverage its high rate of recruitment, it has created a six-month "integration" curriculum.

Day One at Intel begins *before* the first day on the job. "We send you a packet that reaches you before you even come in the door," states Mike Fors, manager of new employee integration. "We want to introduce you to our culture and values, get you some practical forms that you'll need, and reconfirm that Intel is a good choice to be your employer." The Pre–New Employee Orientation packet uses an international theme, titled "Welcome to the World of Intel," and includes a passport that doubles as a workbook.

The first day on the job features a video starring Chairman Andrew Grove with a briefing on Intel's strategy, mission, and objectives. This is followed by what has been described as a no-nonsense meeting with the employee's direct manager. Fors explains, "It's important to get clear on what we call 'deliverables.' These are the tangible results that you'll be held accountable for during your first performance-review period."

A month later, new employees attend a class called "Working at Intel," a formal, eight-hour introduction to the company culture. Says Fors, "After about one month on the job, you're starting to settle in and to do some work. But you need help in learning how to do your work within our culture." To add a sense of cohesiveness, a manager's annual bonus is impacted if all his or her new employees don't complete the course.

Finally, after six months with Intel, the new employees have a question-and-answer session—with the executives asking all the questions. At the end of the structured two-hour session, the executive asks a long-term question: "What do you think it will take to succeed at Intel?"

Fors knows that each response to that question—and there are as many as 10,000 a year—contributes to Intel's overall success. He claims, "We believe our culture has played a major role in Intel's success. We also know that new employees come in with their own experience and expertise to contribute. It's a two-way street."

The informal and creative nature of the orientation at Greet Street is diametrically opposed to the structure provided in the orientation programs at UPS and Intel. And it reflects the nature of this business.

> When the new employee shows up the first day at Greet Street, there's no human resources manager, no personnel office, and no title waiting for her. All thirty people in the company work in the same large, open room, and everybody has the same first assignment: "You walk in, and your job is in the box," according to Elizabeth Cox, who joined the company as a promotions manager on January 2, 1997. "Your desk is in a box. Your computer is in a box. Your phone is in a box. The first thing you do is set it all up."
>
> There's no manual, making the second phase of the orientation ritual very important: Recruits talk to every other employee in the company. They are expected to learn about the organization by sitting in on meetings, talking with new colleagues, and observing how things work. Claims Cox, "It's not like there's a mold to fit into. Things change so quickly in this business that it's important to establish connections."
>
> The third phase reflects the company's creative nature: You think up your own unique job title. The tradition started with the company's two cofounders: Tony Levitan, Creator of Chaos, and Fred Campbell, Creator of Substance. Recalls Cox, "They told me I was going to be a promotions manager but they said not to put that title on anything. I came up with ten titles, including 'Minister of Propaganda' but Tony vetoed them all. I finally picked 'Pied Piper of Promotion' because I want to lead people to the site."

Successful orientation programs such as these reflect each organization's core values and mission. Ideally, it sets the tone for how new employees can quickly become key contributors to the organization's mission.

Finally, orientation programs can help to provide a mechanism for assessing whether candidates have the attributes that are critical for succeeding in a particular career endeavor. Thus, poor selection (or poor self-selection) decisions are reversed; new employees don't become frustrated and unproductive, and the redirection (or even retention) of valued employees is facilitated. Consider FedEx's orientation program for managers.

> FedEx has developed a program that it uses to turn rank-and-file employees into middle managers (and senior leaders) with as much creativity and attention as the process used to sort packages in its Memphis hub. The company has developed nine core attributes for leadership success, as well as a fourteen-month-long FedEx Leadership Curriculum.

Because more than 10 percent of first-time managers were leaving the company within just fourteen months of taking on their new assignment, FedEx's leadership decided to incorporate an eight-hour orientation class, "Is Management for Me?" (IMFM). Senior management has taken responsibility for teaching the course.

By providing a "realistic job preview," the eight-hour IMFM class changes a lot of minds. A full 20 percent of the management candidates drop out of the leadership program after the class. According to George Pollard, a senior official in human resources, applicants leave after the three major frustrations of being a manager are driven home: increased workload, an unrelenting sense of obligation, and responsibility for other people.

One "happy ending" of a candidate who dropped out after IMFM is Mary Smith, a high performer in the company's logistics division. After realizing that management wasn't for her, she decided to make a contribution in a nonmanagerial role by transferring to human resources, where she develops training materials for customer service agents. She explains, "I realized how tough a manager's job is. I certainly have more sympathy for my manager today."

Getting Widespread Involvement

The successful development of human capital requires the active involvement of leaders at all levels of the organization.[13] It can't be successful if it is just viewed as a human resources function. Recall Jack Welch's involvement in personally interviewing candidates for the top 500 managerial positions at GE; he not only evaluates prospective managers, but uses this opportunity to share the organization's knowledge, values, and accumulated experience with each candidate. Furthermore, each year two hundred facilitators, thirty officers, thirty human resources executives, and many young managers participate in the orientation program at GE's impressive Crotonville training center outside New York City. Topics include global competition, what it takes to win on that global playing field, and personal examination of the new employees' core values in relation to GE values. As a senior manager once commented, "There is nothing like teaching Sunday school to force you to confront your own values." Welch himself likes to get into the action. At least three times a month, his helicopter delivers him to the Crotonville campus, and he drops in unexpectedly on a classroom with the line, "Ask me whatever questions you like." Welch adores the exercise.

In mid-1996 Merck, the giant pharmaceutical company, introduced a leadership model to serve as a foundation for its training and development programs and for other business processes such as performance appraisals, employee development, succession planning, and hiring. The model, developed by Merck's management committee (the top eleven company officers), is built around four leadership principles that describe how the management committee expects employees to achieve results:

- Know and develop yourself.
- Know and develop our business.
- Know, support, and develop our people.
- Communicate.

Based on these principles, human resources worked with employees from several Merck divisions, as well as with senior executives, to develop a series of programs for Merck managers and executives. In 1996, more than twenty-seven hundred managers, or 37 percent of eligible employees, attended one of the sessions. Managers and employees from all of Merck's divisions attended the programs, facilitating learning about other Merck businesses and sharing best practices across the company.

Many members of the management committee have played an active role in constructing and facilitating the sessions. According to Bill Mullin, senior director of quality planning in Puerto Rico, "It was clear to me throughout the entire session that this was not just another program. Mr. Gilmartin [the CEO] and his team are placing a very high degree of emphasis on this issue and its potential benefits to Merck and individual employees."

The cascade approach is another way that managers at multiple levels in an organization can become actively involved in developing human capital. For example, Robert Galvin, former chairman at Motorola, requested a workshop for over one hundred senior executives to help them understand the market potential of selected Asian countries. However, rather than bringing in outside experts to explain the situation, participants were asked to analyze the existing competition and to determine how Motorola could compete in these markets.

After researching their topics, the executives traveled around the world to observe local market developments directly. Then they taught the concepts of globalization to the next level of three thousand Motorola managers. In this way, they not only verified their impressions with firsthand observations but reinforced their learning, sharing it by teaching it to others.

Tracking the Development of Human Capital

Whether a company uses on-site formal training, off-site training (such as at universities), or on-the-job training, tracking individual progress and sharing this knowledge with both the employee and key managers become essential.[14] Consider Citibank and Arthur Andersen. At Citibank, a talent inventory program keeps track of roughly ten thousand employees worldwide: how they're doing, what skills they need to work on, and where else in the company they might thrive. Larry Phillips, head of human resources, calls the program critical to the company's global growth. Arthur Andersen too has developed a career tracking system for every employee throughout the world. Complementing the system is a carefully designed career ladder with courses required at each stage in an employee's career.

Many leading-edge companies have also developed systematic and detailed approaches to identifying and tracking key executive talent in their organizations. Three noteworthy examples are Whirlpool Corporation, Corning, Inc., and SmithKline Beecham. At Whirlpool, a "bunker" has been created to track the progress of its top five hundred managers. The four walls of the fifteen-by-twenty-five-foot room are divided by regions of the world and contain the names, titles, and photos of the company's key talent. The only topic discussed in this room is management development. Ed R. Dunn, corporate vice president for human resources, believes that "it's really made us much more focused during succession discussions."

The CEO and the board of Corning, Inc., meet every February to discuss only officer-level succession issues. Prior to the session, directors are given books that detail candidates for the key jobs: those ready now, good possibilities three years out, and the long shots who may need a decade more of seasoning. Asserts chairman and CEO Roger G. Ackerman, "The more time you spend on succession planning and having the board involved, the better."

Like many other leading-edge organizations, SmithKline Beecham places increasingly greater emphasis on broader experiences over longer periods of time. Dan Phelan, senior vice president and director of human resources, explains, "We ideally follow a two-plus-two-plus-two formula in developing people for top management positions." The formula reflects the belief that their best people should gain experience in two business units, two functional areas such as finance and marketing, and two countries. When vacancies occur among the firm's top three hundred positions, the company does consider looking outside for talent. According to CEO Jan Leschly, "A little new blood doesn't hurt. If you're not the best person for the job, we'll show no hesitancy to go outside."

Using Sabbaticals Effectively

Many organizations use sabbaticals as a means of enabling professionals to recharge their batteries as well as looking at their job from the perspective of a new set of experiences.[15] Sabbaticals are not a new concept, but they have gained increasing popularity in our knowledge-intensive economy. (Harvard was the first university to offer sabbaticals in 1880. Corporate sabbaticals were first proposed in 1946 to combat high postwar unemployment. Sabbaticals became popular in the Silicon Valley in the early 1970s.)

Examples are abundant: Apple's employees can take six-week sabbaticals every five years, McDonald's offers employees eight weeks of sabbatical leave every ten years, and Intel employees get a two-month sabbatical every seven years. In some organizations, the opportunity is open-ended: "take some time off to recharge your batteries"; in others, the development or enhancement of job-related skills is expected. Taking time off to reflect and ponder is a critical step in converting a stream of experiences into useful knowledge and perspective.

Hallmark, the Kansas City–based greeting card giant, has a unique approach to sabbaticals. According to Marita Wesley-Clough, creative strategy director, "We're in the business of creativity. We need to give people the space to create." "Creative renewal" is thus the central objective behind Hallmark's approach. The company has two distinctive categories of sabbaticals, which it calls "rotations." One focuses on artistic development, where teams of approximately ten people spend four months exploring a new skill, such as stitchery, engraving, papermaking, glassblowing, or ceramics. They leave their day-to-day duties and cubicles and relocate full time to Hallmark's 180,000-square-foot innovation center.

The second category of rotations involves smaller teams of three or four people who spend six months in an intensive mission learning about a specific social trend. Hallmark has sponsored nine of these sabbaticals over the past five years on issues ranging from computer technology to angels, from masculinity to spirituality. One of the early sabbaticals in 1992 explored ethnicity in society. Jan Bryan-Hunt found her artistic calling in the course of this rotation. In fact, she developed a new jewelry line, Symbolic Notions, based on multicultural symbols she discovered during the rotation. Hallmark has test-marketed the line in forty stores.

Silicon Graphics recently discovered an unintended benefit of sabbaticals: they can be stimulating as well for those who remain behind to pick up the slack. Since almost everybody takes the six-week sabbatical every four years, there's a constant need for people to fill in. But rather than feeling overworked, many professionals feel recharged by trying new assignments. It helps avoid burnout, and the risk is rather low since the job is only temporary. Consider the following example:

Denise Espinoza recently made a permanent job change from payroll manager in the finance department to compensation analyst in the human resources department. Since she had spent the previous year filling vacancies in the human resources department, the move was virtually risk free. By the time she transferred, she knew the new job was right for her. Staffing director Eric Lane had this insightful comment: "It's like playing a new job while using training wheels. I don't know if it's a cure for burnout, but it certainly creates a longer fuse."

Evaluating Human Capital

Years ago in the days of tall hierarchies with many levels of managers, evaluation was rather straightforward. Managers would rate their subordinates on job performance and task-related skills; except for unusual outlier cases, that would be the end of it. Feedback, and the opportunity for the employee and the organization to learn from the experience, was generally limited.

Collaboration and interdependence have since become much more vital to organizational success. Successful organizations recognize that jobs, as well as product and service outputs, are becoming highly complex. The ability of individuals to work constructively in groups and strive for collective, not just individual, goals becomes vital to success. But traditional evaluation systems evaluate performance from a single perspective (top down) and generally don't address the softer dimensions of communications and social skills, values, beliefs, and attitudes.

In order to address the limitations of the traditional approach, many organizations have begun to use 360-degree evaluation and feedback systems: superiors, direct reports, colleagues, and even internal and external customers rate a person's skills. Managers also rate themselves in order to have a personal benchmark.[16]

The 360-degree feedback system complements philosophies such as teamwork, employee involvement, and organizational flattening. As organizations continue to push responsibility downward, traditional top-down appraisal systems become insufficient. For example, a manager who previously managed the performance of three supervisors might now be responsible for ten, and less likely to have the in-depth knowledge needed to appraise and develop each sufficiently and fairly.

In addition to being more accurate, companies are also adopting multirater feedback systems because the evaluation shortens the process for developing human capital. "What might have taken four or five years for people to realize about themselves before can happen in much less time," claims Stella Estevez of Warner-Lambert Corp., an organization that uses 360-degree feedback.

Jerry Wallace of Saturn (a division of General Motors) recently told *Fortune* magazine that he learned that although he viewed himself as flexible, his subordinates did not. Instead they felt he was using excessive control. Wallace says he "got a strong message that I need to delegate more. I thought I'd been doing it. But I need to do it more and sooner."

At UPS, supervisors and managers agree that multirater feedback improves the review process. Seventy percent of the 414 UPS people surveyed said that the feedback from multiple sources gave them useful insight that they would not have received from their managers alone.

What does a 360-degree evaluation system look like? Exhibit 2-3 contains an excerpt from General Electric's managerial evaluation form. The system evaluates each of ten characteristics with respect to four performance criteria. The rating scale for each criterion ranges from 1 to 5, anchored by "Significant Development Need" at one end and "Outstanding Strength" at the other end. The raters are the individual's manager, peers, subordinates, and others (generally internal and external customers).

Robert Higgins, a partner at Goldman Sachs, reinforces the importance of teamwork and the role of development inherent in the 360-degree process:

EXHIBIT 2-3.
Excerpt from GE 360-degree evaluation form.

Vision	<ul><li>Has developed and communicated a clear, simple, customer-focused vision/direction for the organization.</li><li>Forward-thinking, stretches horizons, challenges imaginations.</li><li>Inspires and energizes others to commit to Vision. Captures minds. Leads by example.</li><li>As appropriate, updates Vision to reflect constant and accelerating change affecting the business.</li></ul>
Customer/Quality Focus Integrity Accountability/Commitment Communication/Influence Shared Ownership/Boundaryless Team Builder/Empowerment Knowledge/Expertise/Intellect Initiative/Speed Global Mind-Set	

In the investment banking division, I evaluate my peers and junior people, and they evaluate me. In the case of team-work, you're judged as to whether you avoid political behavior, whether you share information and credit, whether you're a resource to others. The goal is to learn the business, not to get advice on your career.

Finally, evaluation systems must ensure that a manager's success does not come at the cost of compromising the organization's core values. Behavior that leads to short-term wins at the expense of morale, turnover, and productivity is unacceptable. Reinforcing this point, Merck chairman Ray Gilmartin recently told his employees, "If someone is achieving results but not demonstrating the core values of the Company, at the expense of our people, that manager does not have much of a career here."

Jack Welch, GE's CEO, is even more straightforward. In his view, there are four categories of employees. The first shares GE's values and achieves good results. Fine. The second ignores them and performs poorly. Employees in this category have to go. The third group shares the values but does not achieve good results. Employees in this group are encouraged and get a second chance. In the fourth category, the ones who achieve good performance but renounce the values, are also fired. Every year, the staff learns of the surprise departure of bright young managers. What did they do wrong? They did not respect the spirit of the company. They kept to the targets but at the expense of heavy sacrifices made by their subordinates. Welch doesn't tolerate the "bully" approach to management.

Retaining Human Capital

It has been said that talented employees are like "frogs in a wheelbarrow."[17] That is, they can jump out at any time. You can focus on either forcing the frogs to stay in the wheelbarrow with a metal grid across the top, or try to decide how to keep them from wanting to jump out.

Similarly, today's leaders can either provide the work environment and incentives to keep productive employees and management from wanting to bail out, or rely on legal means such as employment contracts and noncompete clauses. Clearly, companies must provide mechanisms that prevent the transfer of valuable and sensitive information across organizational boundaries. Not to do so would be, among other things, the neglect of a leader's fiduciary responsibility. Obviously, we believe the greater effort should be directed at the former, but as we all know, the latter also has a place.[18]

Without a doubt, financial rewards have their place in the retention of human capital. We address the use of rewards, both financial and nonfinancial, as a vital organizational control mechanism in Chapter 5. Money—whether in the form of salary, bonus, stock, grants, stock options, restricted stock, and so forth—can mean many different things to people. For some it might mean security, to others recognition, and to others a sense of freedom and independence. Consider the unique form of compensation at Viewpoint DataLabs International, a Salt Lake City–based company that makes 3-dimensional models and textures for film production houses, video game companies, and car manufacturers.

> Walter Noot, head of production, was having trouble keeping his highly skilled Generation X employees happy with their compensation. Each time one was lured away for more money, everyone would want a raise. "We were having to give out raises every six months—30 percent to 40 percent—then six months later they'd expect the same. It was this big struggle to keep people happy."

Then he hit on a solution that worked: eliminate all salaries. Full-time employees would still receive benefits but were paid like contract workers. Every project team would split 26 percent of the money that Viewpoint expects from the client. Almost overnight, incomes jumped 60 percent to 70 percent, and productivity almost doubled. Additionally, there are no set hours. One fellow works marathons lasting from twenty-four to thirty-six hours and keeps a blanket under his desk for catnaps. Some employees only work at night. Claims Noot, "Now life is bliss. It has totally changed attitudes. I never hear complaints."

Clearly, money was a motivator here—but probably not the only motivator. Consider the working relationships both personal and professional among team workers, freedom to set hours, flexibility in the work environment, "superior-subordinate" relationships, feelings of achievement and accomplishment, and so on. Although the motivators are difficult to assess and no doubt vary by employee, chances are good that retention rates have also increased.

Without strong retention mechanisms, organizations can commit time and resources to helping the competition develop their human capital base. And given the importance of networking, teams, and the scarcity of talent in today's tight job market, losses tend to multiply and intensify. Few would argue that the mobility of talent can erode (or for the fortunate recipient organizations, enhance) competitive advantages in the marketplace.

Let's look at what some leading-edge companies are doing.

Identification With Organizational Goals and Values

People who identify with and are more committed to the core mission and values of the organization are less likely to stray or bolt to the competition.[19] Consider Medtronic, a medical products company in Minneapolis. CEO Bill George states, "Shareholder value is a hollow notion as the sole source of employee motivation. If you do business that way, you'll end up like ITT." What motivates its workers goes well beyond Medtronic's average 34 percent total return to shareholders. Simply put, it's helping sick people get well. The company's motto is, "Restoring patients to full life," and its symbol is an image of a supine human rising toward upright wellness. There is more to it, however, than resurrection imagery.

Each December at the company's holiday party, patients, their families, and their doctors are flown in to tell their survival stories. It's a session for employees only (not journalists), and year after year they are moved to tears. Recalls president Art Collins, a strapping guy with a firm handshake who is not prone to crying fits, "I remember my first holiday party and someone asked me if I had brought my Kleenex. I assumed I'd be fine, but then these parents got up with their daughter who was alive because of our product. Even surgeons who see this stuff all the time were crying."

So much for the usefulness of a total emphasis on shareholder value . . .

Along the lines of improving human health but in a different industry, consider Whole Foods Market. The successful chain of natural food grocery stores has grown from a dozen stores in three states in 1991 to forty-three stores in ten states, with 1998 revenues expected to reach $1 billion and net profits that double the industry average. The clearly stated mission of improving human health has helped the organization attract motivated employees who are better educated than the average grocery employee. Listen to thirty-year-old Lisa Shaw, a Wellesley College graduate who works for one of the organization's Bread and Circus stores: "I remember going to a wedding after I graduated and seeing the looks on people's faces when I told them what I was doing. I just hang on to the fact that my job is good in some larger sense. If people buy the sprouts, they're eating healthier foods, the farmer is doing well, and it's good for the planet because they're grown organically."

Employees can also form strong allegiances to organizations that create simple and straightforward missions, or "strategic intents," that channel efforts and generate intense loyalties. Examples include Komatsu's goal to "encircle Caterpillar," Canon's passion to "beat Xerox," and Honda's quest to become a second Ford. Similarly, leaders can arouse passions and loyalty by reinforcing the firm's quest to "topple Goliath" or by constantly communicating a history of overcoming adversity and life-threatening challenges. For example, CEO Richard Branson constantly uses the David and Goliath imagery, pitting the Virgin Group against such powerful adversaries as British Airways and Coca-Cola. And a key part of Southwest Airlines' folklore is its struggle for survival in the Texas courts against such entrenched (and now bankrupt) rivals as Braniff and Texas Air. After all, Southwest does not exist because of regulated or protected markets but in spite of them. During its first three years of existence, red tape and regulatory squabbles ensured that no planes left the ground.

Offering Challenging Work and
a Stimulating Environment

Arthur Schawlow, winner of the 1981 Nobel Prize in physics, was once asked what he believed made the difference between highly creative and less creative scientists. His reply: "The labor of love aspect is very important. The most successful scientists often are not the most talented. But they are the ones impelled by curiosity. They've got to know what the answer is."[20]

Such insights highlight the importance of intrinsic motivation: the motivation to work on something because it is interesting, involving, exciting, satisfying, or personally challenging.[21] Consider the perspective of Jorgen Wedel, an executive vice president in Gillette's international division, on the relative importance of pay versus the meaningfulness of work: "I do get calls from headhunters who offer bigger salaries, signing bonuses, and such. But the excitement of what I am doing here is equal to a 30 percent pay raise."

Richard Henderson, a contract attorney at Motorola's space technology group in Scottsdale, Arizona, points out the dual importance of exciting work and relationships with colleagues. He is now working on the Iridium low-earth orbiting communications satellite program, which will soon make telephone service available for the first time in remote corners of the world. He says, "Of course the pay and benefits matter. But lots of places have those. And I really like working at a place where you have as many friends as colleagues or superiors. This is my third group within Motorola, and with each move I've gotten more of the two things that matter most to me."

Given the interdependent nature of tasks and the importance of teams, the relationships among coworkers become an increasingly important vehicle for motivating and retaining top talent. Howard Stevenson, a Harvard Business School professor, has noted the importance of what he calls "tribal loyalty" as one of the key integrative control mechanisms in today's organizations. The tribe is not the organization as a whole (unless it is quite small) but rather teams, communities of practice, and other small groups within the company or one's occupation.

Relationships go beyond "soft organization behavior issues." According to Stevenson, "We have to know each other, know how we work together, so that when a crisis comes, we don't have to spend a lot of time coordinating." At Hewlett-Packard, for example, tasks change constantly; more than 50 percent of the company's orders derive from products that did not exist two years ago. HP's attrition rate is far below industry norms, and much of the magic lies in the primacy of relationships over tasks. According to Sally Dudley, a twenty-four-year HP veteran and a manager of human resources, "I've done 14 different jobs here. Those who have spent most of their careers at HP—and most of us have—don't identify with doing the same thing."

Finally, especially for knowledge workers, learning is a key motivational and retention device. At a large consulting firm, leaders talk about "knowledge handcuffs": people often remain because they feel bound to the knowledge of the firm—the networks, electronic and human, of information and expertise on which they rely. And this is in spite of the lure of big bonuses from fast-growing competitors seeking to poach others' talents.

Providing Valued Amenities, Including Flexibility

USAA, the San Antonio–based insurance and financial services company, demonstrates the value of attracting and retaining employees with an impressive plethora of amenities.[22]

> If you're not keen on driving to work, the company sponsors a van pool. A run in your hose? Pick up a pair at the on-site store. There are also a dry cleaning service, a bank, and several ATMs on site. And the cafeteria food is so tasty that several years ago employees began demanding dinner to go. It started a trend. For example, at Thanksgiving, employees bought 5,620 pies and 188 turkeys to take home to their families.
>
> The athletic facilities are striking. The three gyms rival those of many upscale health clubs, and one is open twenty-four hours a day. Outside, employees compete in intramural leagues in basketball and tennis as well as on softball and tennis courts. Into golf? There's a driving range.
>
> Many return to campus on weekends with their families. Says Donna Castillo, a sales manager in consumer finance and auto service, "There are playgrounds where they [children] can run around, and it's nice to take pictures when the bluebonnets come out in the spring."
>
> USAA also scores high on the emerging trend for on-site child care. The San Antonio facility can handle three hundred children. In Tampa, where the company has a huge presence,

industrial-strength fencing surrounds the kiddie playground
to ward off marauding alligators. Claims Raul Navarez, a security officer, "My wife and I visited ten or twelve day-care
facilities all over town. There was no competition at all."

Coping with the conflicting demands of family and work is a challenge for virtually all employees at some point. Women represent 44
percent of today's workforce, and mothers of children under age 6 represent the fastest-growing segment.[23] It is projected that 61 percent of
working-age women will be employed outside the home by the year
2000. And according to a recent study, 13 percent of women with pre-
schoolers said they would work more hours if additional or better child
care were provided.

Flexibility in various employment practices has thus become an
important mechanism in retaining employees. Progressive Insurance, a
rapidly growing insurance company based in Mayfield, Ohio, increased
its employment by 38 percent, to 13,600, in 1997. To maintain such
employment growth, it realized the need to make certain concessions.
Every day is now "casual Friday." Work schedules are more flexible;
and telecommuting is permitted. According to Linda Pantaleano, head
of recruiting, "Now it's a daily negotiation with employees. The worst
nightmare is a manager who hasn't replaced anyone in a while. They
don't realize that things have changed. It's a painful process. First
they're horrified, then they turn around and say, 'You must not be
sourcing right; there must be better people out there.' "

Hewlett-Packard is also experimenting with job and process redesign in several units, with 16 percent of employees involved in telecommuting, part-time jobs, or compressed schedules. It recognizes that it
needs to integrate such options better into the business to allay employees' fears of "career death" if they take part. First Chicago NBD Corporation now requires all managers to submit written plans for expanding
job flexibility. First Tennessee Bank goes one step further: teams of
workers decide how and when their jobs get done.

Increasingly companies are discovering that they must go to rather
extraordinary lengths when it comes to retaining top performers. In
the Silicon Valley's hotly contested market for high-tech labor, offering
fantastic food is not merely another perk. There's even a business model
for lunch: in return for free space and utilities (and sometimes direct
payments), expert service providers offer great food at low prices. In
ten years, Bon Appetit, the Netscape of an industry dominated by "one

sandwich fits all" food service giants, has grown from a tiny catering company to an organization with more than four thousand employees and $120 million in annual revenues. In essence, the company provides the finest gruyere and camembert to "bait" the recruiting mousetraps of Cisco Systems, Hewlett-Packard, and Claris. Says Fedele Bauccio, Bon Appetit's CEO, "In the Silicon Valley, everyone knows everyone, and they're competing for employees like crazy. So if someone has a great mousetrap for an employee benefit, then everyone will want it too."

At Trilogy, in Austin, Texas, Joe Liemandt, the twenty-nine-year-old cofounder and CEO, has a dreary five-by-five-foot cubicle. Although his stake in the still-private company is worth close to $500 million, he doesn't need amenities to remain focused. The corner office instead goes to Paul Rogers, one of Trilogy's star performers. There's a breathtaking view of the hills, a 20-gallon aquarium stocked with exotic fish, and a full-size Yamaha keyboard that Rogers plays when he takes a break. Explains Liemandt, "It's all about keeping top performers happy."

That sums it up. In today's marketplace for the type of scarce and valuable human capital that provides sustainable competitive advantages, do whatever it takes.

Putting It All Together

PSS World Medical, Inc. (PSSI), is an organizational success story that illustrates the importance and benefits of consistency and focus in an organization's approach to the recruitment, development, and retention of its human capital resources.

> Patrick Kelly and two partners started (what they then called) Physician Sales and Service, Inc. on May 2, 1983. Kelly had hit on a unique strategy. They would offer local physicians what competitors couldn't match: next-day delivery of any common item (the industry standard was three or four days), with a premium charge for its wares. And all of this with one warehouse and a sales rep or two. It worked immediately.
>
> The "virtuous circle" had begun. The huge margins enabled Kelly to invest in computer systems and his own fleet of delivery trucks (whereas his competitors relied on UPS or simply tacked the physicians' orders onto the larger hospital orders). The margins also helped Kelly attract, develop, and

retain top-flight salespeople, the heart of his business. Whereas other distributors' reps typically just took orders, Kelly made sure that doctors were made aware of the latest advances, such as the then-revolutionary ten-minute pregnancy test.

From their modest beginning—a total of $100,000 in start-up money—PSSI has fulfilled the mission that Patrick Kelly boldly set in 1988: to become the first national physician supply company. Sales soared to $1.3 billion for fiscal 1998. Based in Jacksonville, Florida, PSSI now has four thousand employees, sixty-one core service centers spread throughout America, sixteen imaging division service centers, and three European operations service centers.

Many factors have been identified that help to explain PSSI's success, including these:

- A dynamic and charismatic founder—Patrick Kelly.
- A highly motivated, knowledgeable, and well-paid sales staff, with no limits placed on income potential.
- An outstanding training program, including sixteen weeks of training at PSSI University for all new salespeople.
- State-of-the-art technology, including the notebook computers that all sales reps use. The associated gains in productivity translate into an additional $10,000 in sales for each of the company's five hundred sales reps every month.
- Mechanisms for keeping everyone focused on the bottom line: the open sharing of performance information, the company's Employee Stock Ownership Program, and other financial incentives.
- An aggressive acquisition program, including both core medical supply and equipment distributors, as well as local and regional diagnostic imaging equipment and supply distributors.
- A culture that has been described as "a cross between the U.S. Marine Corps and *Animal House.*" On the one hand, PSSI's mission has instilled an esprit de corps and a single-minded mission. The typical PSSI salesperson is responsible for two hundred to three hundred accounts and is expected to make about thirty sales calls a day. On the other hand, there are exhortations to have fun and party to a degree that is not expected in a $1 billion firm.

We interviewed Kelly in March 1998, seeking to understand the principles and practices used to recruit, develop, and retain an extraordinarily loyal and productive sales force.[24]

Recruiting is the first step in the process. PSSI's sales and distribution strategies are unique in the industry. The company wants to start from scratch with raw talent and then develop a set of skills and capabilities that fits its business strategy. Kelly gave this description of what his recruiters look for when they go to college campuses:

> We look at what they've accomplished, their work ethic, kids who've worked and had to pay part of their tuition. That's the first thing. Then we look at what they did: sports, fraternities, and clubs where they had a leadership role in a social setting. We don't really care what their degree is in. We're looking for the kids who feel that if they work hard, they can gain something and be motivated by levels of achievement they've not gotten before.

Sounds a lot like "hire for attitude, train for skill," doesn't it? But starting salaries at PSSI are a meager $24,000 per year. How does PSSI compete in a job market where the best undergraduate talent is being offered $50,000 a year or more to start? Kelly's response suggests a combination of a challenging environment, financial incentives, and self-confidence: "We've got to find someone who asks the next logical question; 'That's fine; you'll pay me $24,000; but what am I going to be making in three years?' And it's the kid who understands that they'll be making $100,000 for us . . . if they're successful."

Because they deliberately start out with raw talent, an effective training and development program is essential. PSSI University, as it is known, is a rigorous and intensive sixteen-week indoctrination program designed to weed out anyone who doesn't fit the mold—and prepare the rest to hit the ground running. This initial training and indoctrination is followed by an internship under the supervision of a branch manager before the new salesperson is assigned to a territory. Why the lengthy training program and internship? According to Kelly, "We try to cull them out while they're in the training mode, not in the actual customer calling mode, because that is extremely disruptive to our customers." The company also wants to be sure that they will be successful—well on the way to that $100,000 salary—right from the start.

Once the company has invested that much time and energy in training a new salesperson, retention becomes a critical issue, and PSSI's turnover rate has historically been very low. Kelly claims that "it's very, very rare for us to lose a person to a competitor. I know of only five times that's happened in our history." Pretty impressive in a company with more than four thousand employees! We asked Kelly to tell us the secret of his success:

> Well, I think the number one reason is because our people believe that the people they work for really care about them. This is an extraordinarily hands-on organization. We spend 80 percent of our time traveling. I see every employee a minimum of twice a year. We do annual picnics at each of twelve branches. We bring our employees in. We do a national sales meeting, and I'm at every one of those picnics in the month of September. Number one, we really come through for our people, listen to them. They really believe we care about them, and we sincerely do.
>
> Second, they've got a career in which they can provide for their families and do extraordinary things. if they want to stay in sales, they have unlimited income because we don't put a cap on what they can earn. And if they want to become a CEO, we can really encourage them. We're growing 40 percent a year and we promote from within. There are extraordinary opportunities.

PSSI recognizes that its success is in the hands of its sales force, and it invests heavily in the tools and technology required to leverage the skills and talents of each and every employee. At the same time, culture plays a pivotal role. Right from the start, the message is "unlimited opportunity." The company aggressively recruits the kind of employee who responds to that kind of challenge, prepares them thoroughly, provides the resources necessary to help them succeed, and then rewards them handsomely. Management is highly visible, with a distinctly personal touch, and reinforces the message at every opportunity.

Each of the three key elements—recruiting, development, and retention—is in place, and each is consistent with and reinforces the others. The bait is the prospect of challenge, independence, and unlimited income potential. Candidates are carefully screened to identify those most likely to succeed, and a rigorous training and indoctrination program weeds out any candidates not up to the challenge. Once they are in the field, the company provides a high level of support designed to ensure individual and organizational success. All of this is reinforced by a committed top management group and a culture that consistently echoes the themes of challenge, opportunity, individualism, and "we care about your success." Is it any surprise that retention is not a major problem?

A Checklist: Recruiting, Development, and Retention

Recruiting Top-Notch Human Capital

☐ Does the organization assess attitude and general makeup instead of focusing primarily on skills and background in selecting employees at all levels?

☐ How important are creativity and problem-solving ability? Are they given appropriate importance in hiring decisions?

☐ Do people throughout the organization engage in effective networking activities to obtain a broad pool of worthy potential employees? Is the organization creative in such endeavors?

Enhancing Skills and Capabilities by Employee Development

☐ Does the development and training process inculcate an organization-wide perspective?

☐ Does the orientation process effectively emphasize core organizational values?

☐ Is there widespread involvement, including top executives, in the preparation and delivery of training and development programs?

☐ Is the development of human capital effectively tracked and monitored?

☐ Are there effective programs for succession at all levels of the organization, especially the top levels?

☐ Does the organization have a sabbatical program? If so, is it effectively used and related to strategic goals and objectives? How do sabbaticals affect those left behind to take up the slack?

☐ Does the organization effectively evaluate its human capital at all levels? Is a 360-degree evaluation used? If not, why not?

☐ Are mechanisms in place to ensure that a manager's success does not come at the cost of compromising the organization's core values?

Preserving Resources: Retaining the Best Employees

☐ Are mechanisms in place to prevent the inappropriate transfer of valuable and sensitive information across organizational boundaries?

☐ Are there appropriate financial rewards to motivate employees at all levels?

☐ Do people throughout the organization strongly identify with the organization's mission?

☐ Are employees provided a stimulating and challenging work environment that fosters professional growth?

☐ Are valued amenities offered (e.g., flextime, child care facilities, telecommuting) that are appropriate given the organization's mission, strategy, and how work is accomplished?

☐ Is the organization continually devising strategies and mechanisms to retain top performers?

Notes

1. Max DePree, *Leadership Is an Art* (New York: Doubleday, 1989), pp. 91–92.

2. T. A. Stewart, "In Search of the Elusive Tech Workers," *Fortune*, February 16, 1998, p. 171.

3. N. Munk, "The New Organization Man," *Fortune*, March 16, 1998, pp. 68–72.

4. G. Dutton, "Are You Technologically Competent?" *Management Review* (November 1997): 54–58.

5. R. Lieber, "Wired for Hiring: Microsoft's Slick Hiring Machine," *Fortune*, February 5, 1996, p. 123.

6. A. M. Webber, "He Breeds Dodger Blue." *Fast Company* (April–May 1997): pp. 110–112.

7. The examples that follow are drawn from a variety of sources, including: J. Martin, "So, You Want to Work for the Best . . . ," *Fortune*, January 12, 1998, p. 77; P. Carbonara, "Hire for Attitude, Train for Skill," *Fast Company* (August–September 1997): 66–67; Lieber, "Wired for Hiring"; R. Cardin, "Make Your Own Bozo Filter," *Fast Company* (October–November 1997): 56.

8. The examples that follow are drawn from a variety of sources, including: S. Baker, G. McWilliams, and M. Kriplani, "Forget the Huddled Masses: Send Nerds," *Business Week*, July 21, 1997, pp. 110–116; Carbonara, "Hire for Attitude"; B. Birchard, "Hire Great People Fast," *Fast Company* (August–September 1997): 132–143; Martin, "So, You Want to Work for the Best"; "Hiring Smart—and Fast," *Fast Company* (August–September 1996): 88; and Stewart, "In Search of the Elusive Tech Workers." The Cisco Systems example draws on P. Nakache, "Cisco's Recruiting Edge," *Fortune*, September 29, 1997, pp. 275–276; Birchard, and J. Greenwald, "Where the Jobs Are,"*Time*, January 20, 1997, pp. 54–61.

9. Carbonara, "Hire for Attitude"; Birchard, "Hire Great People Fast"; and Martin, "So, You Want to Work for the Best."

10. Ronald Henkoff, "Companies That Train Best," *Fortune*, March 22, 1993.

11. The examples that follow draw on several sources, including: P. Kelly, "My Struggle With Wall Street," *Fast Company* (December–January 1997): 67; and T. A. Stewart, "Gray Flannel Suit? Moi?" *Fortune*, March 18, 1998, pp. 80–82.

12. The examples that follow draw on a variety of sources, including: *UPS Stan-*

dards of Quality: A Grassroots Commitment (company document): 2; K. Mieszkowski, "Get With the Program," *Fast Company* (February–March 1998): 28, 30; M. Jarman, "Employee Networks Are Working: Firms Recognize Diversity," *Arizona Republic*, March 8, 1998, p. D1; J. Rumler, "Intel Inside Umpqua Brings Rewards," *Oregon Business* 21(2) (February 1998): 52; and S. Eng, "Building Teamwork," *San Diego Union-Tribune*, April 6, 1998, p. D1; L. Jaffee, "Betting That the Future Is in the Cards," *DM News*, March 11, 1996, p. 19; T. Seideman, "Multimedia Is the Message," *Inc.*, September 17, 1996, pp. 82–83; H. Row, "Is Management for Me? That Is the Question," *Fast Company* (February–March 1998): 50–51; and P. A. Galagan, "Training Delivers Results to Federal Express," *Training and Development* 45(12) (December 1991): 26.

13. The examples that follow are drawn from a variety of sources, including: N. M. Tichy, "GE's Crotonville: A Staging Ground for Corporate Revolution," *Academy of Management Executive* 3(2) (May 1989): 103; M. Nexon, "General Electric: The Secrets of the Finest Company in the World," *L'Expansion*, July 23, 1997, pp. 18–30; M. Watts, "It's New and It's Now, " *Merck World* (November–December 1996): 8 (internal company publication of Merck); and R. Fulmere, "The Evolving Paradigm of Leadership Development," *Organization Dynamics* (Spring 1997): 59–72.

14. The following examples are drawn from several sources, including: "Keys to Success: People, People, People," *Fortune*, October 27, 1997, p. 232; Fulmer, "Evolving Paradigm"; and J. A. Byrne, J. Reingold, and R. A. Melcher, "Wanted: A Few Good CEOs," *Business Week*, August 11, 1997, pp. 64, 66–68, 70.

15. The examples in this section draw on a number of sources, including: A. Grove, "Only the Paranoid Survive," *Forbes ASAP*, December 1, 1997, p. 22; E. W. Book, *Working Woman* (March 1998): 29–34; and C. Fishman, "At Hallmark, Sabbaticals are Serious Business," *Fast Company* (October–November 1996): 44, 46; G. Robertson, "Firms Go to Free Form to Promote Creativity," *Richmond Times Dispatch* , December 9, 1996, p. D6; and E. Lane, "We Try Softer!" *Fast Company* (December–January 1997): 143.

16. The discussion of the 360-degree feedback system draws on: "360-Degree Feedback: Coming From All Sides," *Vision* (March 1997): 3 (internal company publication from UPS Corporation); R. Slater, *Get Better or Get Beaten: Thirty-One Leadership Secrets from Jack Welch* (Burr Ridge, IL: Irwin, 1994); Nexon, "General Electric"; and D. Smith, "Bold New Directions for Human Resources," *Merck World* (October 1996): 8 (internal company publication).

17. The examples in this section are drawn from various sources, including: M. F. R. Kets de Vries, "Charisma in Action: The Transformational Abilities of Virgin's Richard Branson and ABB's Percy Barnevi," *Organizational Dynamics* (Winter 1998): 20; and N. Munk, "The New Organization Man," *Fortune*, March 16, 1998, pp. 62–74.

18. One has only to consider the most celebrated case of industrial espionage in recent years wherein Jose Ignacio Lopez was indicted in a German court for stealing sensitive product planning documents from his former employer, General Motors, and sharing them with his executive colleagues at Volkswagen. The lawsuit has been dismissed by the German courts, but Lopez and his colleagues are still under investigation by the U.S. Justice Department. Also consider the recent litigation involving noncompete employment contracts and confidentiality clauses of International Paper versus Louisiana-Pacific, Campbell Soup versus H. J. Heinz Co., and PepsiCo versus Quaker Oats' Gatorade. In addition to retaining valuable human resources and, often, their valuable network of customers, companies must also protect proprietary information and knowledge. For interesting insights, refer to W. M. Carley, "CEO Gets Hard Lesson

in How Not to Keep His Lieutenants," *Wall Street Journal*, February 11, 1998, pp. A1, A10; R. Lenzner and C. Shook, "Whose Rolodex Is It, Anyway?" *Forbes*, February 23, 1998, pp. 100–103.

19. The examples in this section draw on a variety of sources, including: R. B. Lieber, "Why Employees Love These Companies," *Fortune*, January 12, 1998, pp. 72–74; C. Fishman, "Whole Foods Is All Teams," *Fast Company* (December–January 1997): 102–109; S. Lubove, "New Age Capitalist," *Forbes*, April 6, 1998, pp. 42–43; Kets de Vries, "Charisma in Action"; and J. Pfeffer, "Producing Sustainable Competitive Advantage Through the Effective Management of People," *Academy of Management Executive* (February 1995): 55–69. The concept of strategic intent is generally credited to G. Hamel and C. F. Prahalad, "Strategic Intent," *Harvard Business Review* 67(3) (1989): 63–76.

20. T. M. Amabile, "Motivating Creativity in Organizations: On Doing What You Love and Loving What You Do," *California Management* (Fall 1997): 39–58.

21. The examples in this section draw on the following sources: Stewart, "In Search of the Elusive Tech Workers,"; and A. Fisher, "The 100 Best Companies to Work for in America," *Fortune*, January 12, 1998, pp. 69–70.

22. Fisher, op. cit.

23. The statistics on child-care trends are drawn from S. E. Bubbar and D. J. Aspelin, "The Overtime Rebellion: Symptom of a Bigger Problem?" *Academy of Management Executive* 12(1) (February 1998): 68–76. The other examples in this section are drawn from various sources, including: Munk, "New Organization Man"; K. H. Hammonds, R. Furchgott, S. Hamm, and P. C. Judge, *Business Week*, September 15, 1997, pp. 96–104; and E. Ransdell, "Silicon Valley's Best Bites," *Fast Company* (December–January, 1997): 29–30.

24. This information is based on the authors' personal interview with Patrick Kelly on March 3, 1998. Other sources include: M. Basch, "PSS Chief Isn't Hiding Secrets of His Success: Book Is a Fast Read on Kelly's Company," *Florida Times Union*, February 18, 1998, p. B6; J. Case, "The 10 Commandments of Hypergrowth," *Inc.* 17(14) (October 1995): 32–34; P. Kelly, "My Struggle With Wall Street," *Fast Company* (December–January 1997): 66–67, and PSSI's 1997 Annual Report, p. 14.

3

TECHNOLOGY: BUILDING BRIDGES AND LEVERAGING CAPABILITIES

I think, in the long run, technology makes us what we are already, only more so. Lazy people will be lazier, smart people will be smarter. Moving data faster doesn't really enter into it. It's like speeding up in a car when you're lost; the result usually just enables you to get lost over a wider area.

—Arno Penzias, Forbes ASAP (December 1, 1997)

Arno Penzias, who won the Nobel Prize in physics in 1978 and recently retired as vice president of research at AT&T's Bell Laboratories (now Lucent Technologies), makes a couple of important points about technology and leverage in the opening quotation of this chapter. Technology is, first and foremost, about leverage: what we are already, only more so. When we think about leverage, we tend to think about getting more output with less input, in other words, increased productivity. And leveraging human capital generally means making human capital more productive. But Penzias also makes the point that more output is not necessarily better output—not necessarily smarter, higher quality, or more useful. We need to keep this point in mind as we begin to explore the ways that technology can be applied to leverage human capital resources—we are looking for opportunities to create more value—in terms of quality and usefulness, and not just more volume.

When most people think about technology, they tend to think first of information technology—bits and bytes, networks and computers and the Internet—all of it new, innovative, and a bit difficult to understand. But technology is far more than this. In its broadest definition, technology is *a technical method of achieving a practical purpose* or, in even simpler terms, *how we get things done.*

Since the days of the Neanderthal, technology has been about extending and leveraging human skills and capabilities. When a cave man first fashioned a crude stone ax, he was using a tool (technology) to leverage his individual capabilities. The stone ax was harder, sharper and more effective at cutting or breaking tree limbs, or bones, or whatever it was used against, than human hands. Technology *made the caveman more powerful.* And when we focus on leveraging human capital, we are primarily interesting in how we can make the individual more powerful: how we can leverage his or her skills and capabilities by the application of technology.

In Chapter 1 we described eight key elements of the human capital resource. Of these, motor, information-gathering, information-processing, and communications skills are the most likely to be task specific, and the most easily developed and leveraged in the context of a specific task environment. The others, the individual's values, beliefs, and attitudes and his or her knowledge, experience, and social skills—are usually less task specific and tend to be developed over a longer period of time and in a variety of settings, not necessarily related to any specific job context. This chapter looks primarily at the task-specific capabilities and how technology can be applied to leverage and enhance an individual's motor, information-gathering, information-processing, and communications skills.

- *Motor skills* deal with the individual's ability to grasp, place, move, and manipulate objects in coordinated movements. Most of the technological progress made over the past two hundred years has focused on extending and enhancing the motor skills of the individual. Tools of all kinds represent technology applied to multiply and extend the strength, speed, and precision of the individual's motor skills. Transportation systems—from the invention of the wheeled cart to trucks and automobiles, planes, railroads, and ships—are technological improvements that extend our human ability to move over the surface of the earth and increase the loads we can carry with us.

- *Information-gathering skills* include the individual's sensory, perceptual, and interpretative capabilities. Technology has long been used to enhance and extend individual sensory capabilities. Optical technology, in the form of eyeglasses and telescopes, improves the clarity and extends the range of visual perception. Arrays of sensitive microphones on the bottom of the ocean allow technicians in remote facilities to listen for and "hear" submarines beneath the surface of the ocean thousands of miles away. Temperature and pressure sensors, monitored by microchips, "touch" and "feel" the systems of our automobiles to warn us about actual or potential problems.

■ *Information-processing skills* have also been progressively enhanced by technology over the years. Thousands of years ago, the Chinese invented the abacus as an aid to numerical calculations. The engineer's slide rule was designed to aid in the performance of certain repetitive calculations. Electronic calculators and computers have extended the speed and precision with which individuals can manipulate data. Today, personal computers and software have significantly extended the potential information-processing capacity and capabilities of individual employees.

■ *Communications skills* refer to the individual's ability to listen to, communicate, and share information and ideas with others. For centuries technology has been at work to leverage and extend our ability to communicate. The printing press, telegraph, telephone, radio, television and the Internet have all extended the scope and reach of our ability to share and communicate our ideas with others. Unfortunately, however, these technological advances have had little impact on our willingness or ability to listen attentively to others.

■ *Attitudes, knowledge, experience, and social skills* have also been influenced by technology. Whether for better or worse, the mass media have shaped our values, beliefs, and attitudes and influenced social norms about the ways individuals should act and interact with each other and with the institutions of our society. Individuals who spend their days (and nights) interacting with computers, video games, and television screens sometimes fail to develop the social skills needed to work effectively with others. Television and the Internet have made information and learning resources widely available to the masses, but the virtual experience of television or the World Wide Web is usually a poor substitute for the personal experience of witnessing or participating in an activity or event.

Clearly technology is a two-edged sword. While it provides the means to leverage and extend the capabilities of our human capital resources in a variety of ways, it can also undermine and devalue knowledge and experience and erode values, beliefs, and social skills. The key for managers seeking to leverage their human capital resources is to understand the potential and the limitations of technology and to clearly define the objectives and expectations before changes are made.

For the next several decades, the world of business and commerce will be driven by the rapid evolution of information and communications technologies. In industry after industry, these technologies are changing the rules of the game forever.

The Changing Competitive Landscape

Jack Welch, CEO of the General Electric Company, began a speech in 1997 by declaring that "the Information Age . . . has been the longest running disappointment in business history. For thirty years, countless CEO's have waited for the promised productivity that information technology was to bring, only to be sorely disappointed." The time, he said, has come for action: "Today, information is understood as a competitive necessity, from resolving internal organizational issues to addressing market-based competitive realities. Today . . . information management is at the heart of everything we do!"[1] In industry after industry, the rapid evolution of information and communications technologies is driving change and rewriting the rules of the game.[2]

J. P. Morgan & Co.'s 1996 Annual Report claims that its clients "are the world's most active and sophisticated users of financial services" and observes that "in a business dependent on the rapid, constant, global flow of information, fast-changing technologies are both the basic tools and sources of competitive advantage."

According to a recent article in *The Wall Street Journal*, information technology is the driving force behind the recent consolidation of the banking industry. Noting that "technology has transformed everything banks do," the article quotes Jim Dixon, president of technology and operations at NationsBank Corp.: "Customers want to do their banking any time of day and by using whatever 'appliance' they choose, be it a phone, home computer, automatic teller machine or other device. The race is on to put that in place." The head of IBM's banking consulting team argues that "there are virtually no business or strategic decisions that are not either driven by technology or have immediate massive implications for technology."

FedEx figured out a long time ago that being in the package delivery business also meant being in the information business. Knowing everything about a shipment—where it originated, where it was headed, where it was right now, and its cost, price, and anticipated arrival time—was as important as its safe and reliable delivery. FedEx's sophisticated data network—and the information it shares with its customers about their shipments—is a formidable source of competitive advantage. In the process, FedEx retains records of the shipping habits of millions of customers in a huge "data warehouse." By mining this information, it can evaluate the profitability of individual customers and adjust pricing and discount structures as required to maximize profits.

Data warehousing—gathering information about customers and records of transactions from the hundreds of separate databases maintained by most large corporations and making it accessible in one location—is a booming business. MicroStrategy, Inc. is a leader in the field, building software that analyzes these data and helps companies target their markets with pinpoint accuracy. MCI, for example, uses Micro-Strategy's software to analyze detailed records on more than 100 million current and potential customers, permitting it to target marketing strategies down to the individual consumer.

Big companies with big databases aren't the only ones using information to advantage. Consumers are tapping into the vast array of information available on the Internet. Electronic commerce is booming, and business buyers can access a company's web page in seconds to comparison shop—checking prices, specifications, and deliveries offered by suppliers around the globe. Consumers are using the Internet to gather information and place orders for airline tickets, cars, insurance, stock brokerage services, and other items. Suppliers of goods for which such comparisons are easy and reliable are rapidly being forced to compete primarily on price. And in a global marketplace, excess capacity in one market rapidly drives prices down around the world.

The way we communicate with each other is changing rapidly as well. E-mail is exploding. Hotmail Corp., a free Internet e-mail service supported by advertising, captured 6.5 million customers in its first fourteen months, and in the fall of 1997 was adding customers at the rate of 40,000 a day. Analysts estimate that by 2005, the United States will have more than 170 million e-mail users, sending as many as 5 million messages a day.

The external changes we described as the new economy in an earlier chapter have also triggered profound changes in the nature of work and in the relationships of employers and employees. When most employees worked in large companies and competed in internal labor markets, jobs were well defined; a career meant climbing the ladder within a single organization; and compensation and advancement were based on individual performance. As organizational boundaries become fuzzy, hierarchies are flattened, and the traditional power base of senior executives is eroded, the definition of the "job" is changing as well. As internal opportunities for advancement are reduced in a flattened organization, building a career increasingly means moving from company to company. As organizations emphasize teamwork, cooperation, and flexibility, individual performance is less visible, and compensation and reward systems are being adjusted to conform. As organizations demand that their workers become more flexible, employees are demanding more flexible employment arrangements—working hours, the allocation of tasks, and where work is performed—in return. These changes have significant implications for both employees and employers. *Forbes ASAP* recently made this observation:

> In the 1960's, almost everyone dream[ed] of a job that [was] meaningful, challenging, and . . . fulfilling. They got their wish. Today, in the information age, the world of work is now so intellectually challenging, meaningful, and compelling that we are never bored. But neither is there much time for dreams. Workers are now their own bosses—and what tyrants those bosses can be. Today's work doesn't end when the whistle blows. It follows us into the evenings, the weekends, and to every corner of the world.*

For employers, the changing nature of the employment relationship may mean a loss of control over the organization's most important resources: its most highly skilled and capable employees. The implications are clear. Organizations must become increasingly sensitive to the needs and priorities of its most valuable resources—its employees—and carefully balance the anticipated benefits of new technologies against the risks of alienating or demotivating their employees.

Leveraging Human Capital With Technology

In Chapter 1, we developed a framework that illustrated how organizations could enhance their stock of human capital resources by recruiting, developing, and retaining the best and brightest. We described how organizations could leverage their investments in human capital by designing their structural capital to link their human resources more effectively to the organization's core value-creating activities, its knowl-

---

*Rich Karlgaard, "The Chip, the Net and Us," *Forbes ASAP,* December 1, 1997, p. 1. Reprinted by permission of FORBES Magazine © Forbes Inc., 1997.

edge and information resources, and its physical and financial resources. Exhibit 3-1 details some of the ways that technology can be
used both to support the organization's efforts to enhance its human
capital resources and to develop and strengthen the key elements of its
structural capital.

Chapter 2 focused on how organizations could increase the quality of their investments in human capital resources through more effective recruiting, selection, and retention efforts, and on how the
performance of human resources could be developed and strengthened
through orientation, training, and skill development. Technology can
play an important role in improving the effectiveness and efficiency of
these processes, as the examples of Cooper Software and Cisco Systems
illustrated in Chapter 2. In this chapter, we turn to the relationships
and linkages between human capital and the organization's core value-
creating activities, human capital and the organization's knowledge
resources, and human capital and the organization's physical and financial resources. These relationships and linkages—including the organization's structure, systems processes, and culture—are the essence
of structural capital.

EXHIBIT 3-1.
Leveraging human capital with technology.

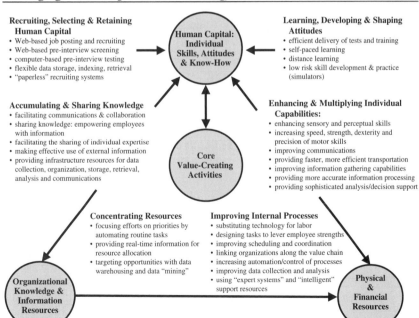

Linking Human Capital to Core Value-Creating Activities

In terms of opportunities for leverage, the relationships that exist between human capital and the core value-creating activities of the organization are probably the most important. These core processes, including the organization's external relationships with its customers, suppliers, and alliance partners, are central to the creation of value and the development of sustainable competitive advantage. Over time, the way an organization performs and conducts itself in the marketplace determines its reputation, the loyalty of its customers, and its image and legitimacy.

The principal function of the organization's structural capital is to link its human capital resources to its internal processes and key external stakeholders, and to link its internal processes to each other. Through these structural linkages, human capital resources can be leveraged by concentrating them on the most important tasks, designing tasks and interfaces to draw on individual capabilities most effectively, and carefully matching individuals with the right mix of skills to each task. Technology can play a key role at each of these points of leverage in the following ways:

- Focusing resources on the most critical priorities
- Automating routine tasks to allow individuals to focus on the most critical activities
- Making processes more efficient so that less human capital is required
- Designing systems, processes, and tasks to use employee skills and capabilities well
- Linking the organization effectively to its customers, suppliers, and alliance partners.

Focusing Resources on Critical Priorities

One of the hallmarks of successful organizations is their ability to effectively focus and concentrate their human capital and other resources on the problem at hand. The use of technology can help to accomplish this objective in a number of ways.[3]

When William J. Bratton was hired in 1994 as the police commissioner for New York City, the criminals seemed to be gaining the upper hand. To focus his resources more effectively, Bratton developed a four-step process: develop timely, accurate intelligence; respond rapidly; use effective tactics to deal with identified problems; and follow-up regularly to see how you're doing. He began to make real headway when he geared up the department's computer systems to gather and consolidate daily crime statistics from throughout the city. Bratton empowered the local precinct commanders by giving them the same daily information so they could respond rapidly and deploy their resources most effectively. The system focused attention not only on problems, but also on the performance of each precinct. The new system provided Bratton the objective data he needed to evaluate personnel—and he replaced more than half of the precinct commanders in the first year. Between 1993 and 1996, serious crime dropped by 37 percent. Bratton gives much of the credit to his system, which provided the real-time information needed to target his resources to the problems at hand.

The processing of credit card transactions seems like pretty mundane work, but the economics are interesting. The cost to process a $1,500 credit card transaction is not much greater than the cost of processing a $15 transaction, but the processing institution earns much higher fees with the larger transaction. One of the by-products of credit card processing is the wealth of information available about the purchasing and payment habits of consumers. MBNA, the huge credit card bank, has mined these data to identify its best potential customers. By concentrating its marketing efforts on this group, the company has effectively leveraged the skills and capabilities of every employee and, from 1994 to 1996, improved its expense-to revenue-margin by 15 percent. In 1996, MBNA had the highest return on equity of any bank listed on the Fortune 500.

Automating Routine Tasks

Most jobs consist of multiple tasks and activities. Some of these tasks are inherently more productive (create more value) than others. The use of technology to automate routine and repetitive tasks can free up an employee's time to focus on tasks that require greater skill or judgment or create greater value for the customer. The following examples illustrate this point:[4]

■ In 1996, Walgreen's pharmacies introduced Intercom Plus, a new computer-based prescription management system. Linked by computer to both doctors' offices and third-party payment plans, the system automates telephone refills, store-to-store prescription transfers, and drug reordering; provides information on drug interactions; and, coupled with a revised work flow, frees the pharmacist from administrative tasks to focus on patient counseling.

■ Auto dealers are finding ways to use technology to leverage the productivity of their employees—and making car buying a more pleasant experience for their customers at the same time. At some dealerships, the salesperson no longer has to flip through yesterday's computer printout only to find that the car his customer wanted was sold two hours ago. Customers can check the inventory directly at automated computer kiosks. One Michigan dealer has equipped each salesperson with a wireless phone, fax, and personal computer, creating a one-stop shopping experience and "empower[ing] our people to be the definitive answer for every customer that walks through the door."

■ In 1996, Roadway Express implemented a document imaging system to manage shipping documents. Every day, more than 160,000 freight documents are scanned with digital imaging technology and stored in a data warehouse. The manual paper shuffling that used to occupy hundreds of clerks has been largely eliminated. The system allows Roadway to transmit documents directly to customers without delay, automatically attaching the required documentation to customer invoices. The result has been more timely invoicing, reduction of human error, and significant cost savings (through the more efficient use of personnel).

PSS World Medical, Inc. (PSSI), is a nationwide distributor of supplies and equipment to physicians, clinics, and nursing homes. Its marketing and sales strategies have evolved rapidly over the past five years as changing market requirements and the availability of technology have reshaped its entire approach to the marketplace. Prior to 1993, PSSI's marketing strategy was built on superior service at premium prices: a broad line of standard products, frequent deliveries, and a direct sales force that built relationships with the physicians' office staffs. Because the product line was composed primarily of standard commodities, the company needed little more than an order taker. But as the company added new products, including a line of sophisticated diagnostic equipment, the role of the salesperson changed. Patrick Kelly, PSSI's founder and CEO, described it this way in a recent interview with us:

> We had to free up the sales reps' time to do more consultative selling. We did that by automating them with computers.

That had a major impact in increasing their productivity by freeing up some of the time they used to spend in taking orders—we're estimating approximately 30 percent. Now they have time to take the order quickly, check the inventory, check the pricing, get it done in front of the customer, and then say, "Oh, by the way, can I spend a few minutes talking to the physician about a new procedure he should be doing here in the practice?" And that has made a dramatic impact. I've watched our equipment sales go from about 6 percent a couple of years ago to 25 percent of our sales last quarter. Technology has been a major factor both in our tremendous growth and in the added value we have been able to bring to our customers. Over the next few years, we'll be automating more and more of the order-taking functions; about 10 percent of our customer base is now ordering through the Internet. We're going to have to continue to find ways to free up our salespeople. We see a lot of new medical technologies coming, and we want to be able to sell them. If we haven't invested in the information technology to make our workforce more efficient, then we're not going to be able to capture the opportunities.

Investing in technology to improve sales force productivity is not without its challenges, as Kelly notes: "I've got to tell you. It's very hard to do when you have a sales force that's somewhat suspicious of why you're trying to do something like that. The fear, of course, is that they are being taken out of the loop—and ultimately out of the pay—for servicing that customer. Probably more than anything else, the barrier to getting our customers to sign on to this new Internet-based order process is the salesperson's reluctance to introduce them to it."

Improving Internal Processes

Just as technology can be used to automate routine tasks, and thus free up the organization's human capital resources to spend more time on core value-creating activities, it can also be used to improve the efficiency of an organization's core processes.[5] And in today's competitive environment, efficiency means more than just accomplishing the same task with a smaller input of resources. Andy Grove, chairman of Intel, recently made the following observation: "In all businesses, to provide value, you've got to do whatever it is you do fast and with immense efficiency. Why do you think everyone is buying computers? It's not that they render you more productive, in the sense of more physical output per hour. They permit you to make decisions and produce results *faster.*"

Organizations competing across a wide range of industries are using technology to improve the efficiency of their core business processes. Consider how such diverse organizations as retailer Sears, Roebuck and Co., the worldwide services division of Digital Equipment Corporation (recently acquired by Compaq Computer Corp.), Danish network equipment distributor Oilcom, Inc., regional automobile club AAA of Minnesota/Iowa, public utility Baltimore Gas & Electric, and Internet start-up USWeb have each used technology to improve the efficiency of their key business operations.

Sears, Roebuck is a broad-line retailer. Each of its stores has multiple departments, stocked with goods ranging from appliances to jewelry, from automotive tools and services to underwear. When customers call, they are usually looking for a product or service that can be found on the shelves of competing retailers. If they can't get through to the right department quickly, the sale may be lost. During peak calling hours at some locations, the phone may ring thirty to forty times before it is answered. Sears is currently deploying speech-recognition systems in seven hundred stores nationwide. The computer-based systems will answer the telephone on the first ring, ask the customer what department he or she would like to be transferred to, confirm the response ("Did you say shoes?"), and transfer the call to the appropriate extension. If the system doesn't recognize the name of the department, the call will immediately be routed to a live operator at one of two national call centers. Sears expects that 60 to 70 percent of the 120,000 calls each day will be routed successfully by the system. In addition to improved customer service, Sears expects to be able to reassign almost three thousand operators to other functions, saving more than $80 million annually.

Digital Equipment's worldwide services division provides contract product and technical support for more than 14,000 products from 1,300 different suppliers. The division's 23,000 staffers handle 5 million service calls annually in support of more than 12 million users in 113 countries around the world. Scheduling is a key business process, critical to the efficient utilization of its human and physical capital resources. Digital is testing a new scheduling system in Europe, with plans for a worldwide rollout in late 1998. The system is fully integrated with Digital's proprietary customer service database and tracks such information as the skill sets and qualifications of field service engineers, their location and availability, and the terms and requirements of the service agreement for each customer. The system will automatically schedule resources and field engineers and dispatch them to appropriate calls. According to Jean Hoxie-Wasko, vice president of product management and engineering development, the system is expected to improve both productivity and customer service; it will make sure that the division responds to customers' needs in a more timely fashion, with "the right person assigned to the right problem at the right time."

The Danish distributor Oilcom, Inc. sells network equipment and services to major corporations through a network of resellers throughout Europe and North America. The company maintains a line of nearly 10,000 different network system components. The technical configuration of a communications network is a key business process for Oilcom's resellers. The company recently installed a secure, web-based system that allows its resellers to configure, quote, and then order entire communications network systems on-line. Resellers can now configure and price a typical system in 15 to 20 minutes, as compared to 2 to 3 hours to design, configure, and price a system manually. Not only is the system more efficient for the reseller, but configuration and pricing errors have virtually been eliminated, saving time for both Oilcom and its resellers and increasing satisfaction levels for the end customer.

Regional auto club AAA of Minnesota/Iowa is in the information business. Its members contact the service organization for advice and emergency service when they run into trouble on the highways. The winter storms of 1996, with thousands of stranded motorists and nearly 10,000 calls a day, overloaded AAA's telephone system and nearly brought it to its knees. Customers were stuck on hold, and AAA had no way to differentiate between urgent calls from a stranded motorist needing a tow or a jump start, and routine inquiries from individuals who wanted travel information for next month's trip. When members did get through, they frequently had to provide their name, address, and account information to an agent multiple times, because every service offered required a separate computer program. Frustrated customers were hanging up in droves, and many threatened to cancel if service didn't improve. Faced with a major loss of revenue, AAA responded by upgrading the technology of its incoming call center.

Members now call AAA's call center on a toll-free 800 number and provide a member number and reason for their call. They are then routed to an agent who has their account information displayed on a screen. The agent can access multiple applications on the same screen and address the member's needs promptly and efficiently. Customer service has improved considerably—hangups are down by 20 percent—and errors and callbacks have been reduced. Agent productivity is up too; agents are handling 10 percent more calls per hour on the new system than on the old. Plans are underway to provide work-at-home access for agents during future winter emergencies.

In 1992, the Federal Energy Regulatory Commission ordered utility companies to let natural gas marketers sell gas through their local distribution systems. Baltimore Gas & Electric (BGE), a $3 billion local gas distributor, has recently implemented an Internet-based electronic bulletin board to link suppliers, third-party natural gas marketers, and industrial customers to manage the use of BGE's pipes to deliver natural gas to industrial customers in the Baltimore area. Fully integrated with BGE's billing systems, the bulletin board is an important link to the key business process of managing the supply and demand for natural gas, providing both suppliers and customers with detailed historical information about supplies, consumption, and pricing. Before BGE implemented the system, two full-time employees received data by fax and manually entered it into BGE's computer systems. The system has replaced these manual processes and improved customer service and billing.

For fast-growing companies in a tight labor market, recruiting, screening, and selecting new employees is a key business process. A number of technology-based solutions have recently become available to help overworked human resources managers efficiently sort through the thousands of inquiries and resumes that pass across their desks. Over the past two years, USWeb, a technology company based in Santa Clara, California, has grown from 20 to 650 employees (with a couple of acquisitions along the way). USWeb handles 75 to 80 percent of its recruitment electronically, using software that helps compose the ad, post it on the web sites specified by the company, track the progress of the recruiting effort, and automatically remove the posting when the job is filled. Hard-copy resumes are scanned into the computer and routed electronically to the hiring managers, who can make notes on the copies electronically. The entire process is virtually paperless and it's fast, shortening hiring cycles from weeks to days. Other software allows recruiters to scan the database of electronic resumes with key word searches to locate a pool of candidates for new postings.

These examples have shown how the application of technology can leverage an organization's human capital investments by making core business processes more efficient: replacing labor with more efficient technological solutions, improving scheduling and resource allocation, eliminating the barriers to more effective human performance, or accelerating paper-intensive processes. These jobs are being done more efficiently, but the jobs themselves have not changed much. In the following section, we look at an example in which technology and job design have interacted to change the nature of the work itself.

Designing Systems, Processes, and Tasks to Leverage Employee Strengths

In most cases, technology is used to improve existing work processes incrementally by automating parts of processes, providing better information for management and control, or providing tools to enhance the motor skills of the human capital involved. Rarely is a process totally redesigned to combine what people do best with what technology can do better in a totally new system. L. L. Bean's new Order Fulfillment Center is an exception to the rule:

> L. L. Bean is the nation's largest outdoor catalog company, with 1996 sales of $1.2 billion. More than 3,000 customer service representatives take orders by phone 24 hours a day, 365 days a year. The distribution center stocks 16,000 items and ships 12 million packages each year to Bean's customers in 150 countries. FedEx has its own shipping facility inside the warehouse; it's FedEx's third largest operation. And Bean does so much business with the post office that it has its own zip code. For years, Bean's distribution center in Freeport, Maine, was a mandatory stop on the corporate benchmarking tour; Nike, Disney, Gillette, and Chrysler all studied Bean's approaches to fulfillment and customer service.
>
> Bean's old system, designed in the late 1970s, was fairly traditional. Orders came in by telephone, the operators entered them into a computer, and a batch of orders was issued to the warehouse every 12 hours. Pickers would pull carts, each with twenty-five compartments, from bin to bin throughout the warehouse until all twenty-five orders were filled. They would then deliver the completed orders to the packers, who would pack the orders for shipment. The system worked well until the mid-1990s, when increasing volume (up to 150,000 orders per day during the peak season) and complexity (product line diversity and growing international sales) had stretched the system to the breaking point.
>
> Rather than duplicate the existing process in a new and

larger facility, Bean's managers decided to reinvent the process. The widespread participation of the people who did the work was considered essential, and hundreds of employees participated in the research and investigation, benchmarking similar operations around the world. The result is a radically different facility that uses state-of-the-art technology and a totally redesigned work flow built around order fulfillment teams. The batch system is gone. Orders now flow to the warehouse as they are received. The system breaks the order down into its component parts and assigns each part of the order to a picker specializing in one type of merchandise. As the orders are pulled, they are placed on a conveyor system that moves the merchandise to the packing area, automatically sorting it into completed orders by reading the bar codes on the merchandise. The completed order is delivered to the next available packer.

Productivity is up. Efficiency has increased, and errors have been reduced as the pickers have become more familiar with the merchandise in their respective areas. Worker fatigue is lessened—no longer pushing fully loaded carts around the warehouse, pickers have less walking from station to station— and more productive work gets done. Peak loads are easier to manage, and delivery performance has improved dramatically. Five years ago, customers routinely received their orders within two weeks. Today, many orders are shipped within two hours after receipt. Bean is approaching its goal of filling 100 percent of its orders within 24 hours. The facility has been called "a working model of a sociotechnical system, where the design of the work supports the community of workers." According to Lou Zambello, Bean's senior vice president for operations, "The technology here is very simple. The innovative part is adapting it to create a new sociotechnical norm in a new facility. What we did before was like individual swimming in a relay race. Now we do synchronized swimming."[6]

Linking Organizations Along the Value Chain

Many organizations are using technology to enable closer coordination with their suppliers and customers.[7] Of course, electronic data interchange (EDI) has been around for a decade or more, processing orders and invoices between producers and their customers over private data networks, with smaller suppliers coming on board through dial-up connections to the larger partner's host computers. But EDI is cumbersome, limited in the range and scope of the transactions that can be processed and the kinds of information that can be shared, and managed exclusively by the purchasing departments of most organizations. Today many organizations, large and small, are going beyond EDI and moving toward broader-based solutions that coordinate core business processes between the organizations and their supply chain partners. On-line procurement systems that use Internet-based communications links to take the purchasing department out of the loop are becoming increasingly popular.

Los Angeles County has recently replaced its paper-based purchasing system with a paperless system that links more than 10,000 internal users in thirty-six different departments directly to vendors by a secure extranet. Using a web browser, authorized buyers order computer, office, and janitorial supplies (80 percent of its current purchases) directly from approved vendors, who upload their catalogs directly into the system. Billing and payment transactions are also automated within the system. The county reports that it cannot estimate savings—which are nevertheless expected to be huge—because no one knows how much the existing system costs to operate and maintain.

Chevron Corp. recently began the deployment of a web-based purchasing system. By the end of 1998, $2.7 billion of purchases from 200 national suppliers will have been moved to the Internet. Eventually the company hopes to move the majority of its $9.9 billion of annual purchases, including capital equipment and major maintenance services, onto the system. Chevron anticipates substantial savings in terms of reduced administrative costs.

Collective electronic commerce efforts are also underway. General Electric Information Services has developed a trading process network (TPN) that links more than twenty big industrial companies—including Hewlett-Packard, 3M, and Textron—to a large group of pre-approved industrial suppliers. General Electric already buys over $1 billion of goods each year through TPN and expects the system to grow significantly over the next few years.

Roadway Express has developed a number of innovative systems to provide timely information through network-based links to its agents and customers, including these:

- QUIKTRAK Online, which allows customers to track their shipments anytime through Roadway's web site
- E*Z Rate Online, which provides quotes for specific shipment classes and weights, or complete rate tables through Roadway's web site

- ExpressWORKS, a complete, PC-based transportation management system available to customers, enabling them to manage their shipping functions and communicate electronically with carriers
- Agent-Net, an intranet that enables international agents to access Roadway's full suite of information capabilities quickly

Web-based systems are also being used internally to link the far-flung retail operations of some companies, with both headquarters and their customers. Audio Adventures, Inc. is a small specialty distributor with fifty employees that leases audio books. It's a niche market with a unique group of customers and one that probably couldn't exist without web-based technology. Like many other companies, Audio Adventures publishes a catalog and maintains a web site for use by individual customers and libraries nationwide, but its retail outlets are unique: staffed kiosks located in travel centers and truck stops across the United States. All are linked together through Audio Adventures' web site. The customer base is highly mobile, and tapes picked up at one kiosk may be returned at any one of the company's 450 kiosks down the road. When customers rent tapes using their Audio Adventures cards, bar code scanners record the identification of the customer and the tapes and forward the information electronically to the web site. Returns are handled in a similar fashion. Customers can also visit the web site to browse through thousands of titles and place orders on-line. According to Dan Conser, Audio Adventures' direct sales manager, "The Web is the perfect answer [for this unique business]; it couldn't be done with paper."

One of the most successful organizations doing business on the web is Amazon.com, a company that has developed a unique relationship with its customers. This success story points out that just "being there" is not the whole story:

> An old saying goes something like this: "There are three things you need to succeed in retailing: location, location, and location." So if location is the answer, can you imagine owning a bookstore in every major city in the world? In every town or village? On every corner in every city and every village in the world? Not likely, you say. But Amazon.com is open for business on every computer connected to the Internet, and its success story is bordering on the stuff of legends. On-line retailing is in its infancy, but in terms of location, the World Wide Web must be the ultimate extension of the range and scope of an organization's opportunities.

But location isn't the only answer. Founder Jeff Bezos lays out Amazon.com's value proposition: convenience, selection, service, and price. Bezos argues that "it is still so inconvenient to use the Web; the technology is so primitive" that the other elements of the proposition must overcome the lack of convenience. Selection is a strong suit; the company offers 1.1 million titles, all indexed and searchable (up a notch on the convenience scale), as compared to a mere 175,000 titles in the world's largest conventional bookstore. Service is informative, reliable, and quick. And because Amazon.com has a lower cost structure than conventional stores, its prices are very low. And this is just the beginning. With interactive features still on the drawing board, the web site can be tailored to the preferences of individual customers. Remember the friendly clerk who waited on you the last time you visited a retail bookstore? Amazon.com to replicate that experience with a customized "store" for you to browse through, a clerk who knows your preferences better than you do yourself, and the ability to avoid the clutter of the thousands of books you have no interest in. It's a new concept—one that Amazon.com has implemented effectively. And it demonstrates both the opportunity and the complexity of doing business on the World Wide Web.

Although the preceding examples may appear to be leading edge in many respects, they are generally limited to a well-defined series of transactions between an organization and its customers or suppliers. The kinds of information shared are limited and tightly controlled. The real leading edge involves a much broader-based sharing of information, and success requires a much higher level of trust and commitment between organizations.

Over the past decade, many organizations (mostly larger firms) have installed comprehensive enterprise resource planning (ERP) systems. ERP systems offer finance, human resources management, procurement, manufacturing, distribution, and customer management systems in tightly integrated packages linked together by large common databases that facilitate analysis and reporting across functional and systems boundaries. Now, some organizations are beginning to link their ERP systems directly with those of their major supply chain partners, enabling tighter collaboration with customers, suppliers, and, ultimately, end users around the world. Smaller partners are being included through Internet-based linkages. Companies are sharing manufacturing production schedules and inventory data with key suppliers and product specifications, pricing, availability, and delivery information with customers. Three examples of this type of integration are illustrative:

- Marshall Industries is a $2 billion distributor of electronics components. CEO Robert Rodin stresses the importance of making a broad range of business information available "at any time, at any place, and by any method" to its suppliers and customers. As a middleman in the supply chain, Marshall's systems have valuable information about both the future requirements of its customers and the product development schedules and production capabilities of its suppliers—critical information essential to meeting the needs of its customers and managing its inventories. Rodin emphasizes that "today, business is not about me versus my competitor. It is about my supply chain versus your supply chain."

- Until recently, Bassett Furniture, a $400 million manufacturer of wood furnishings, had a communications problem. Shoppers in stores might ask whether an item was in stock, what patterns it came in, and when it could be delivered. Good questions, but salespeople couldn't always answer them. The company solved the problem by creating an extranet, giving all of its retail partners access to its internal information over the Internet. Salespeople can now tap into Bassett's system to check inventory, inquire about deliveries, and place orders with the company.

- Colgate-Palmolive is another manufacturer linking its systems closely with those of its key suppliers. The goal is vendor-managed inventory, in which the vendor will monitor Colgate's inventory levels and automatically replenish stocks on a just-in-time basis. Colgate expects to make the process more efficient, reduce inventories, and shorten replenishment cycles.

Buying and selling products or leasing audiotapes are relatively structured processes that lend themselves to automation. From a systems design perspective, each transaction looks much like the one before. But how about customer service, where the problems are considerably more diverse? Consider the case of Hartness International:

> When you make a product that's at the heart of your customer's business, you'd better be able to service it fast. Hartness International, of Greenville, South Carolina, makes case packers—the high-speed machines that load bottles of soda, syrup, ketchup, or whatever else into cartons before they are

shipped to stores. For Hartness's customers, time is money. Problems with a case packer can bring the entire production line to a halt—and at a cost of up to $150 a minute. Do the math: if a machine is down for 24 hours, the cost is $216,000.

A couple of decades ago, when the company was just getting started, every service technician was also a licensed pilot. When the phone rang, the technician cranked up one of the company's four planes and flew directly to the customer's site. But today, with 5,000 customers scattered across ninety countries around the world, timely customer service is a challenge that can't be met by a flying mechanic. The answer has been videoconferencing. Working with a technology partner, Hartness developed a new video response system (VRS) that is up and running at more than fifty installations in six countries. With VRS, Hartness engineers, working with customer technicians on site, can conduct live, interactive repairs and have the machines up and running again in minutes. When the system is fully implemented, the company estimates that 80 percent of its service calls can be handled remotely. And the advantages multiply. Because the customer's own technicians make the necessary repairs on site, the chances are good that if the same failure occurs again, they can fix it without a service call. Even if they don't remember all the details, they have a videotape of the last repair to walk them through the procedure. According to CEO Bern McPheeley, "That's the ultimate form of customer service."

Linking Human Capital to Knowledge and Information

The relationships between human capital and organizational knowledge and information resources provide opportunities for leverage in both directions. These linkages are critical. Ikujiro Nonaka and Hirotaka Takeuchi, authors of *The Knowledge Creating Company*, argue that the primary source of innovation in most organizations is the creation of new knowledge. New knowledge is created through the ongoing interaction between the tacit knowledge embodied in the individual and the explicit knowledge possessed by the organization. This two-way exchange of information benefits both the individual and the organization in a variety of ways. Individual knowledge, skills, and capabilities can be enhanced by encouraging and facilitating individual learning and providing opportunities for training, skill development, and practice. Individual task performance can be leveraged by providing ready access to the knowledge and resources required for the job, whether the sources of the information are internal or external to the organization. The capabilities of the organization can be deepened by encouraging and facilitating organizational learning and the widespread sharing of individual knowledge, collective know-how, and market intelligence.

Technology, and in particular information systems, can play a number of important roles in this process. Quinn, Baruch, and Zien, in their new book, *Innovation Explosion*, emphasize the power of information technologies for leveraging knowledge and extending human capabilities:

> [Software] can extend human capacities in new ways: (1) capturing knowledge more rapidly and accurately than ever before, (2) enabling analysis of more complex problems than humans can handle alone, (3) controlling physical processes under harder conditions and more accurately than humans can, (4) allowing remote monitoring of physical and intellectual processes without human intervention, (5) searching a broader range of information sources and interconnecting far more human minds—enabling creative solutions that would otherwise be impossible, and (6) diffusing knowledge more widely, efficiently, and effectively than any other means.[8]

In the sections that follow, we provide specific examples of the ways technology can be used to lever human capital resources by linking individuals to information and knowledge:

- Facilitating communications and collaboration
- Facilitating the sharing of knowledge by empowering employees with information
- Encouraging and facilitating the sharing of individual knowledge and information
- Collecting, filtering, and distributing information from external sources
- Facilitating employee development through training, skill development, and practice.

Communications and Collaboration

Leveraging individual performance through the use of communications technologies is one of the most common and widely acknowledged applications of technology. We illustrate this point with two examples from opposite ends of the spectrum.[9]

David S. Pottruck, CEO of Charles Schwab, is a recent convert. Until three years ago, Pottruck was a casual computer user who couldn't even type. Now he calls himself a "champion of executive computing." The driving force behind Schwab's highly successful move to net-based securities trading, Pottruck uses his laptop PC to stay in touch with the markets and his organization from wherever he happens to be. He reports that he spends about 30 minutes a day on the Net, taking the temperature of the markets and skimming through the 100 or so market-related web sites to which Schwab's own site is linked. He also spends a lot of time reading and sending e-mail from his portable office. He views e-mail as a tremendous resource for personal productivity: "I hit a few keystrokes, and 400 people receive a message instantly, with no administrative overhead."

John Quain is a contributing editor for *Fast Company*, on the front lines of advanced personal productivity technology. He began a recent article about hardware and software tools for use in the brave new world of "virtual partnering" with the following observations:

> Most of the people I work for, I never see. In fact, some of the people I work for, I've never really even spoken to. How is this possible? We work together in cyberspace. Sure, I miss the frequent flyer miles, but on the Internet I can hash out ideas with an editor in the U.K., correspond with an author in Boston, kibitz with a lab researcher in Silicon Valley. Simultaneously, we can view test results, discuss their importance, and make quick decisions.

In many ways, his description of the needs a series of new products satisfied was more interesting than the products he reviewed:

- Set up a meeting with people who aren't on your company's LAN (scheduler for virtual meetings)
- Stay in sync with your teammates (contact manager)
- Share the flow of information among team members (data organizer)
- Edit documents and spreadsheets in real time (virtual meetings with concurrent text and voice; joint editing of standard documents over the Internet)
- Work together across platforms (Internet-based conferencing)

- Work together on a digital whiteboard and discuss the results through your computer (Internet-based conferencing)
- Build trust and camaraderie among virtual teammates (video-conferencing)
- Have a face-to-face meeting with your teammates when you're a hemisphere away (portable PC with built-in videoconferencing)

Videoconferencing is another way individuals can work together at a distance. Although videoconferencing has been around for a number of years, only recently has the technology become cheap enough and the quality high enough that the medium is coming into widespread use. The latest systems feature miniature PC-mounted cameras and computer dialing to make "face-to-face" meetings in your own office just a phone call away.

One of us recently conducted a market research study involving a series of focus groups in six cities across North America. Normally focus groups are conducted in special rooms with an adjacent viewing room, so the clients can observe the proceedings. In this case, the focus groups were conducted with no on-site observers. Rather, a special one-way videoconferencing hookup allowed thirty midlevel managers to see and hear the entire proceedings in real time and provide follow-up questions to the on-site moderator of the panel. The debriefing sessions used a two-way hookup, permitting the moderator to participate fully in the subsequent discussions. The study was completed in a much shorter time, and at a much lower cost, with only one individual (the moderator) having to travel to each of the cities.

Under CEO John Browne, British Petroleum has worked to become flatter, faster, and more democratic. A top-level strategy session held in mid-1997 probably deserves mention in the *Guinness Book of World Records* for employee participation. A three-day Innovation Colloquium brought together seventy of BP's top executives and an all-star cast of consultants, futurists, and other invited guests. Also invited were the 20,000 (out of 53,000) BP employees with intranet access. Employees who logged on could review presentation slides and handouts and hear a real-time audio broadcast of the proceedings. Questions could be e-mailed in from the field, and the on-site participants responded to them. The meeting was an outstanding success and stimulated tremendous interest and participation from managers and workers around the world. A second Web-based conference, a Futures Forum to explore BP's potential competitive environment over the next twenty years, is in the planning stages.

Bell & Howell has held its last two shareholders' meetings on the web. Although fewer than forty people attended the actual meeting in a conference room at corporate headquarters in Skokie, Illinois, more than 1,700 participated over the World Wide Web. During 1997 meeting, 4.5 million proxy votes—nearly 25 percent of all votes—were cast over the web rather than in person or by mail.

Sharing Knowledge: Empowering Employees with Information

The sharing of job-related information with employees—empowering employees with information—is a potent force for productivity, but it is neither easy to implement nor an effective solution on its own.[10] Coca-Cola's senior vice president and chief financial officer, James Chestnut, emphasizes the importance of timely and accurate information: "Every decision this company makes—from major acquisitions to the smallest product detail—depends on the information available at the time. [Unless the right information is available] we aren't going to make the best decisions." The sharing of organizational knowledge with employees is only half the solution; employees must also be encouraged to share their individual knowledge and experience with the organization and with each other if the full capability and potential of the organization's knowledge base are to be realized. The essence of the problem—and the solution—is participation, as GE's Jack Welch recently observed: "Today, with advanced information systems and flat organizational structures, everyone has simultaneous access to the same information; everyone can be part of the game. We believe that there is nothing more important in winning in today's global marketplace than getting everyone involved and using every brain in the organization."

Making organizational knowledge broadly accessible is possible only if the organization has appropriately provided for the accumulation, storage, and distribution of organizational knowledge. Developing and installing an appropriate infrastructure is the first essential step. General Motors Corp. recently began the global rollout of a new information technology architecture that will link 175,000 internal users to each other and to the Internet. GM OnLine will be one of the world's largest private networks. The system is designed to allow collaboration between all business sectors and will result in "lower costs, higher performance, more reliability, and more consistency [in the applications interface]." According to Dennis Walsh, GM's chief technology officer,

"Whether you're logging on in Brazil or Detroit, you shouldn't be able to tell the difference." The two-year hardware rollout will be followed by the installation of common financial, human resources management, and manufacturing systems worldwide.

Developing the right applications is next. A couple of years ago, Welch's Foods, Inc., decided that it needed to get key product and sales information to its employees more quickly and conveniently. Two new products from Cognos, Inc. are helping to make that vision a reality. These software tools help employees develop customized data sets, called "cubes." The system comes with a selection of predesigned reports; users just specify what data they want to see. More advanced users can build their own reports. Analytical support tools help employees to analyze the data. Members of the sales team are now responsible for managing their own account information. According to project leader Bill Krueger, "The bottom line for us is getting information out to people so they can react to it quicker." With the old paper-based system, "It sometimes took days to get information to users . . . .Now, all users have to do is dial in and they've got their [customized reports] up-to-date as of the previous night."

Getting the organization to use the systems and applications is a critical third step. Some employees take full advantage of the opportunities. A recent article profiled a day in the life of a "wired-for-productivity" sales manager for Hewlett-Packard. Stacey Wueste heads a sales team responsible for the sales and marketing of HP's hand-held computer products. Here are some of the highlights of her preparations for a major sales presentation in Chicago:

- Wednesday, 9 P.M.: Dinner with the account rep suggests prospect's focus tomorrow morning will be on sales force productivity—sends e-mail to product manager in Singapore (local time 11 A.M.) requesting latest materials on sales force automation solutions.
- Thursday, 8 A.M.: Receives e-mail with requested information from Singapore. Checks web for latest news about market and competitors by dialing into HP's intranet. Trade journal is reporting problems in competitor's supply chain. Incorporates news into her presentation.
- Thursday, 11 A.M.: Customer asks technical question about e-mail connectivity. Stacey is stumped—but demonstrates the capability of the product (equipped with a wireless modem) by using it to e-mail the query to her technical marketing manager in California. Quick response not only provides requested information, but also demonstrates the value and the effectiveness of technology she is trying to sell.
- Thursday, 4 P.M.: In the Red Carpet room at the airport, makes notes and prepares follow-up instructions to sales team on laptop com-

puter. Plugs in to modem connection and sends instructions to her office for distribution. Catches up on the day's events in a brief exchange of e-mail messages.

Technology designed to promote work group collaboration has facilitated the sharing of information in many organizations. Walgreen's has recently implemented a Lotus Notes–based application to better coordinate its real estate, construction, and facilities planning activities. The system will monitor and coordinate site selection, construction, opening, and maintenance of facilities nationwide. On the drawing boards is an even more ambitious project: the development of a self-serve human resources system integrating payroll, benefits, and employee data so that employees can maintain their own personnel records by kiosk.

Sun's new Java programming language is facilitating the development of a whole new class of software applications. A lot of the excitement about this new programming tool is related to its technical characteristics (object-oriented, platform independent), but the real benefit lies in the kinds of applications than can be developed for ordinary people to use in a network environment. These are just beginning to emerge, and most are relatively simple, but they have the potential to add value in large increments for both consumers and providers. Now investment companies can provide software tools that help consumers manage their retirement programs on-line. Software provided by insurance companies can help policyholders estimate health insurance benefits as they file a claim. Financial services companies are providing software to let consumers estimate payments and evaluate financing options before buying a house or a car. Travel agencies are providing software that helps customers devise an itinerary that fits their budget, taking into account airline tickets, car rentals, and hotel stays. And the benefit for the providers of these simple services is twofold. First, administrative costs are reduced as consumers or employees make the "what-if" calculations for themselves on-line, rather than working with a staff member while they review their options. Second, while engaging their customers in an interactive on-line environment, they can gather data and capture useful marketing information about consumer and employee preferences and choices.

Facilitating the Sharing of Individual Knowledge and Expertise

Much of what is most valuable in the collective expertise of an organization is generally inaccessible because it is "owned" by individuals and exists only in the form of their personal know-how and expertise. Numerous barriers exist to the open sharing of this valuable reservoir of personal knowledge and experience. Part of it is cultural. Because knowledge is power, personal know-how is often associated (at least in the mind of the holder) with organizational prestige and job security. For these reasons and others, individuals are often unwilling to share what they know with others in the organization, and they are even less willing to document this information in a manner that permits its widespread use and dissemination. Part of the problem is structural. Most organizations lack the infrastructure to allow it to happen even if the employees wanted it to work.

Buckman Laboratories, a $270 million manufacturer of specialty chemicals, appears to have made remarkable headway in creating an environment that breaks down these barriers.

Buckman Laboratories manufactures more than 1,000 different specialty chemicals in eight factories scattered around the world. Its 1,200 employees are located in eighty different countries. Its customers are involved in pulp and paper processing, water treatment, leather, agriculture, and personal care products. Buckman's business depends in large measure on its ability to solve its customers' problems. And knowing how to solve those problems is, in most cases, a matter of experience. Buckman's competitive advantage, as a relatively small competitor in a huge global market, derives from its ability to tap into the collective experience base and expertise of its employees around the world.

It wasn't always this way. Buckman used to be a much more traditional company—rigid, hierarchical, and run from the top down. But in the ten years Bob Buckman had been running the company since the death of his father in 1978, he had become increasingly dissatisfied with the way the company functioned. In 1988, Buckman was confined to bed for two weeks with a back injury. As he lay there, isolated from the day-to-day pace of business, he began to think about what was really important in his company. He recalled a comment he had recently read: "An individual without information cannot take responsibility; an individual who is given information cannot help but take responsibility." That struck a spark. Buckman thought, "If you can't maximize the power of the individual, you haven't done anything. . . . How do we take this individual and make him bigger, give him power? How? Connect him to the world." He says, "I realized that if I [could] give everybody complete access to information about the company, then I [wouldn't] have to tell them what to do all the time. The organization [would start] moving forward on its own initiative."

Over the next four years, inspired by that simple insight, Bob Buckman turned his company upside down. He built K'Netix, a customer-focused global knowledge transfer network organized around seven technical forums to provide structure for the company's on-line conversation. Building the network was the first step. Breaking down the internal cultural barriers was the most difficult (90 percent of the effort, according to Buckman). He used a combination of visible incentives, subtle pressure, and a blunt articulation of his expectations: "Those of you who have something intelligent to say now have a forum in which to say it. Those of you who will not or cannot contribute also will become obvious. If you are not willing to contribute or participate, then you should understand that the many opportunities offered to you in the past will no longer be available."

The power of the network is evident in the way the company does business. One of the company's top salesmen commented, "We used to carry around stacks of notebooks, and the trunks of our cars were full of files. Now half of that stuff isn't even necessary. We can fire up our laptops, pull up the most current data sheet, and have global real-time communications in a matter of seconds. Basically, the only thing we can't get out of the computer is the chemical itself."

And the system works. Representatives dial up the network in the middle of technical discussions with potential customers, pose a question on the appropriate forum, and within minutes receive responses from all over the world. In a recent example, Buckman sales rep Doug Yoder was pitching a $1 million order to a paper company. When he ran into a question he couldn't answer, he logged onto the system and posed the question. Within minutes, Bob Buckman was on-line from Brazil. They spent the next twenty minutes addressing and resolving the customer's specific issue. The customer, Yoder reports, was impressed.[11]

A recent study of thirty-one knowledge management projects in twenty-four companies (including Buckman Laboratories) provided insights into the kinds of initiatives underway in large organizations and the complex and difficult issues that surround the question, "How can organizations use knowledge more effectively?"[12] This study identified four broad goals of knowledge management projects:

1. Create knowledge repositories (capturing both explicit and tacit knowledge).
2. Improve access to knowledge (building networks to provide broad access to expertise).
3. Enhance the knowledge environment (addressing cultural issues).
4. Manage knowledge as an asset (capturing, quantifying, and reporting about information as an economic asset).

The study also identified eight critical success factors for knowledge management projects:

1. Clear links to economic performance or industry value
2. Appropriate technical and organizational infrastructure
3. A standardized, flexible knowledge structure
4. A knowledge-friendly culture
5. Clear definition of purpose
6. Changes in motivational practices
7. Multiple channels for knowledge transfer
8. Senior management support.

Usually small-scale initiatives are easier to implement than paradigm-shifting projects of the scope undertaken by Buckman.[13] Xerox's Dallas-based Field Information Research Systems Team (FIRST) shows how an organization can implement a smaller-scale project with similar objectives but without changing the culture of the entire organization. Headed by webmaster Scott Pennington, the team's charter is to support Xerox's U.S. field sales organization with technical documentation, feature comparisons, and product briefings. The FIRST team used to communicate with the sales force on an individual basis. A sales executive would phone in a question, and the staff would research the issue and provide the requested information. In 1995, FIRST established a web site. Now the sales force gets the information they need by accessing Xerox's intranet. As queries are addressed, both the questions and responses are posted on the web site, making them available to the entire sales force. By using the site's search engine to research a customer question, the field sales representative not only benefits from the work of the staff, but also taps into the collective experience of the rest of the sales organization. In the first half of 1997, the site averaged 75,000 hits per month, with more than 3,000 users searching the files to review over 1,500 documents. Pennington claims that activity indicators provide a sensitive barometer of sales performance. A couple of months after a spike in web site visits, U.S. sales showed a corresponding increase.

Some creative pioneers are beginning to use personal web sites as an effective communications tool and as a small-scale venue for global information sharing. You can't always be available for a personal meeting; you're not even accessible by telephone all the time; and e-mail works only when you access it. But a personal web site can communicate on your behalf 24 hours a day, 7 days a week. John Patrick, vice president of Internet technology at IBM, maintains a personal site that indexes his papers and speeches and contains a personal page, called Reflections, where he "humanizes" his site with personal thoughts and reflections. He gets frequent feedback and values the on-line interaction with his customers and colleagues.

Andy Oram, acquisitions editor at O'Reilly & Associates, a publisher of computer books, maintains a web site targeted at new authors. On the site he provides detailed instructions and guidelines, with tips on communications and pointers on style, all from the perspective of an experienced editor. Prospective authors benefit from his experience, the books they write are more often "on target," and Oram saves valuable time by not having to go over the same material dozens of times.

Making Effective Use of External Information

One of the real challenges for most organizations is gathering, filtering, and distributing information from external sources. Understanding what is going on in an organization's environment is critical to the development and maintenance of competitive advantage—even its survival—in a rapidly changing marketplace. Most organizations, however, don't do a very good job of systematically gathering important information about competitors, economic trends, legislative proposals, and the hundreds of other events and factors in the outside world that affect and influence their organizations. In fact, our research suggests than many organizations don't even make an attempt. The result is a haphazard, hit-or-miss approach to collecting and analyzing external information.

Personal news services are now available to do a lot of this hard work.[14] The Dow Jones Personal Journal, for example, allows you to specify the kinds of information you want to monitor (topics or companies) and then provides a customized daily e-mail version of *The Wall Street Journal*, focusing on only the items in which you have expressed interest. IBM's InfoSage is an electronic clipping service that provides a twice-daily digest of news headlines gathered from more than 2,000 sources.

Some organizations are using this kind of service to monitor their competitors. Launched in 1996, the PointCast Network signed up nearly 2 million subscribers in its first year of operation. The advertiser-supported network offers more than twenty-three channels, including CNN, major newspapers, and sports scores, and operates in the background on a desktop computer. Like a screen-saver, when the keyboard is idle for a specified interval, PointCast pops up and displays the latest news in e-mail format on the screen. Mercury Mail provides a similar service, but in an HTML (web page) format.

Facilitating Individual Learning and Employee Development

The effective and innovative use of technology plays an important role in the delivery of training and the facilitation of experiential learning at leading companies around the world.[15] According to *Fortune*, "the companies that train best deliver instruction when the employee needs it, sometimes in a classroom, sometimes by satellite TV, sometimes on a personal computer. Effective training is concise and interactive, interspersed with group projects, role-playing and hands-on experiments." Many leading companies are finding that high-tech training has dual benefits: it delivers more effective training and saves costs at the same time.

■ Several years ago, Andersen Consulting, which spends 6 to 7 percent of its annual payroll on employee training, replaced 40 hours of classroom training (and 60 to 80 hours of homework) with interactive video. The computer-based technology reduces the training time by half, and because the course is now taken in the employee's own office, Andersen saves over $4 million annually on travel and lodging expenses.

■ Workers at FedEx take computer-based job competency tests every six to twelve months. The 90-minute, computer-based tests identify areas of individual weakness and provide input to a computer database of employee skills, which is used in promotion decisions. Training programs are packaged on interactive videodisks, which permit self-paced learning available when it best fits the employee's schedule.

John Chambers, CEO of Cisco Systems, was recently asked what forces would drive the future growth of computer networking. His somewhat surprising answer was "the training video." He argues that employee training is a universal need and that distance learning, with video on demand, is the most efficient way to deliver the necessary training. The Public Broadcasting Service apparently agrees. The launching of an entirely new service, captioned "PBS The Business Channel," is underway. PBS TBC will draw on the resources of more than 300 public television stations across the country, many of which offer educational services to local businesses, colleges, and schools. These resources will be made available to businesses through on-demand access to video training at the computer desktop. This new service will use a variety of technologies that are commonplace in businesses—desktop PCs, intranets, small satellite dishes, and video servers—to bring a broad portfolio of training and educational resources to the employees of subscriber companies.

The benefits of technology really stand out when it comes to providing opportunities for low-risk skill development and practice. Training pilots to fly high-performance military or commercial aircraft is a complex and difficult process. Using real aircraft for such training is expensive (it costs $30,000 or so in fuel and maintenance for every hour a typical fighter aircraft is in the air, not including the $30 million to $50 million acquisition cost). And mistakes can be even more expensive! That's why so much training takes place in aircraft simulators. Simulators use sophisticated computer technology to represent a broad range of conditions realistically, many of which might be encountered only once in a lifetime of actual flying. Often costing more than the aircraft they represent, simulators provide the low-risk skill development and practice required to develop and test pilot proficiency. Crashes are frequent—but not fatal—and the technology provides the opportunity to review with the student exactly what he did wrong before he straps in to try it again. The cycle is repeated over and over again: encounter the situation, react, evaluate what works and what doesn't, and try it again until you get it right. Most training environments don't involve the same degree of risk or consequence, but computer simulation—in the form of interactive problem-solving exercises on computers—is providing similar benefits in progressive training programs in multiple industries.

Linking Human Capital to Physical and Financial Resources

The linkages between human capital and the organization's physical and financial resources provide numerous opportunities to leverage human capital by enhancing and multiplying individual capabilities. These linkages can be broadly grouped into three categories: leverage relationships, custodial relationships, and complementary relationships. *Custodial relationships* are of limited interest. A night watchman patrolling the perimeter of a warehouse or manufacturing facility is exercising a custodial relationship over the organization's physical resources. A banker locking the vault at night (aided by the physical resources of the vault) is exercising a custodial responsibility over the bank's financial assets. Although these functions are clearly important, they are of limited interest for our purposes, because the opportunities to leverage human capital resources are limited.

Leverage relationships are considerably more common and significantly more important. Leverage relationships are those in which physical assets (such as computers or machine tools) are used to perform more efficiently tasks that, at least in theory, could be accomplished by human capital alone. The use of computers to maintain accounting records is an example of a leverage relationship. Given enough trained accountants, any accounting task could be performed without the aid of computer technology, although at a great cost in efficiency and effectiveness (timeliness and quality of reporting). Leverage relationships are of interest to us because they enhance the utilization and performance of human capital resources. The preceding sections have provided numerous examples of how such relationships have been used to leverage the productivity of human capital resources.

Complementary relationships are those in which both human and tangible resources are required to perform an activity. For example, both aircraft (physical capital) and pilots (human capital) are required to accomplish the movement of passengers and cargo by air. In banking, the principal resources are financial assets, but these cannot be productively employed except through the actions of lending and investment officers. In both cases, the role of the human capital resource is to manage and control the utilization of the physical or financial resource. Neither is capable of performing the service without the other. In another example, institutional trading of securities on Wall Street is managed, to a considerable degree, by a relatively small number of skilled individuals using sophisticated computer models and state-of-the-art communications technologies. At first glance, this appears to fit the definition of a leverage relationship. It is fairly clear, however, that the human-software partnership is complementary, in that neither could accomplish the task without the other, and the resulting level of sophistication and performance far exceeds that which could be achieved by either alone. Complementary relationships are particularly interesting because, if properly designed and managed, the performance of both the human and the physical or financial capital resources can be leveraged by the relationship. Technology frequently plays an important, and sometimes defining, role in complementary relationships.

Complementary Relationships

The examples that follow illustrate the nature of complementary relationships in which both the individual and the technology are critical to the successful performance of the task.[16]

> Gus Riley, a twenty-one-year veteran, is responsible for the weekly scheduling of production in Volvo's million-square-foot truck factory in Dublin, Virginia. Volvo recently installed a new scheduling system, based on genetic scheduling algorithms, to help Riley do what used to be a full-time job. Genetic scheduling algorithms are a new approach to the optimization of complex problems that defy solution through the use of conventional techniques of analysis. The system must cope with hundreds of constraints, most of them unique to this particular factory. The man-machine interface is critical, with each doing the part of the job he or it does best. Each week, Riley feeds in the data to create another weekly schedule. Based on the mix of production moving through the plant, he tinkers with the criteria, loosening some constraints and tightening others. A heavy dose of experience and judgment comes in at this point. The system then takes over and does the heavy number crunching, randomly generating 100 feasible solutions and ranking them according to criteria such as costs, labor constraints, material availability, and productivity. Once this set of alternatives has been generated, the system cuts and pastes the better parts of the original pool together to generate better schedules. The system proceeds through five iterations in about 15 minutes. At the end of each iteration, the best schedules (according to the criteria) are retained in the "gene pool," and the poorest are discarded. The process is not unlike breeding cattle, but the results are impressive: what used to be a full-time job now takes less than a day.

One of the ways technology can extend the reach and range of human resources is to help them do their jobs while staying out of harm's way. British-born engineer Graham Hawkes describes his work as "extending human capabilities into hazardous environments" After more than twenty-five years of designing undersea robots, Hawkes has come up with a land-based invention. His telepresent rapid aiming platform (TRAP) is a remotely operated rifle that practically never misses. Equipped with a videocamera telescopic sight, range finder, and remote control unit, the gun can be aimed and fired from around a corner or other remote site, so that police need not be exposed to return fire.

Facilitating Organizational Learning

The final set of linkages illustrated in Exhibit 3-1, labeled organizational learning, represent the processes by which the organization learns by experience about how to more effectively manage its core value-creating activities and use its physical and financial resources. The processes of organizational learning are addressed in detail in Chapter 6. Although learning processes certainly involve an organization's human capital resources, the results of organizational learning do not leverage human capital directly. Rather, cumulative learning influences human capital through the application of knowledge and the improvement and enhancement of the structures, systems, and processes of the organization's structural capital. We must continue to be aware that the organizational environment is dynamic and that the relationships that exist today between human capital and the structures and systems of the organization will be different tomorrow.

A Checklist:
Using Technology to Leverage Human Capital

Linking Human Capital to Core Value-Creating Activities

☐ Can technology be used to help focus the organization on key value-creating activities?

☐ Could you automate (or eliminate) some routine tasks to free up employees to focus more effectively on higher-priority efforts?

☐ Could technology be used to make core processes more effective or more efficient?

  ■ Reduced resource requirements?
  ■ Faster cycle times?
  ■ Improved yields?
  ■ Better customer service?

☐ Could business processes (both core and support activities) be redesigned to use the skills and capabilities of human capital resources better?

☐ Can technology help to achieve closer integration with the value chains of customers or suppliers?

Linking Human Capital to Knowledge and Information

☐ Are there ways that information or communications technologies could facilitate communications or collaboration in the organization?

☐ Does the organization empower employees by broadly sharing organizational knowledge?

- Are infrastructures in place for accumulation, storage, and distribution?
- Do applications exist to facilitate the effective use and analysis of data?
- Are employees encouraged to use the information available? Are incentives provided?

☐ Does the organization encourage the sharing of individual knowledge and expertise?

- Are communications infrastructures in place to facilitate knowledge sharing?
- Does the organizational culture value teamwork and encourage sharing of information?

☐ Does the organization make effective use of external information?

- Have you identified the kinds of information required?
- Do you know where to find it?
- Are effective systems in place to gather, analyze, and share key external information?

☐ Does the organization use technology to facilitate individual learning and employee development? Are there opportunities that could be exploited more effectively?

Linking Human Capital to Physical and Financial Resources

☐ Are there unexploited opportunities to leverage human capital resources by using existing physical or financial resources more effectively?

☐ Are there opportunities to leverage human capital resources significantly through relatively small investments in capital equipment, software, or services?

☐ Do complementary relationships exist in the organization? Have you effectively matched the physical and human resources to optimize the performance of both?

Notes

1. Jack Welch, "The Information Age: Finally" (speech at the World Economic Forum, Davos, Switzerland, January 30, 1997).

2. The examples in this section are based on the following sources: Matt Murray and Raju Narisetti, "Bank Mergers' Major Engine is Technology," *The Wall Street Journal*, April 23, 1998, p. B1; Linda Grant, "Why FedEx Is Flying High," *Fortune*, November 10, 1997; J. William Gurley, "When Software is More Than Just Software," *Fortune*, December 8, 1997, pp. 222–226; Geoffrey Colvin, "The Changing Art of Becoming Unbeatable," *Fortune*, November 24, 1997, pp. 299–300; and Paul M. Eng, "E-mail: Fast, Fun and Now It's Free," *Business Week*, September 15, 1997, pp. 68–72.

3. The examples in this section are drawn from: William J. Bratton, "Blood, Sweat and Databases," *Forbes ASAP*, December 1, 1997, p. 56; and Ronald Henkoff, "The Fortune 500: A Year of Extraordinary Gains," *Fortune*, April 28, 1997, pp. 193–197.

4. These examples are drawn from the following sources: Walgreen Co., *Information Technology and Walgreen's: Opportunities for Employment* (January 1996); John Hughes, "Auto Dealers Focus on Pleasing Customers," *Lexington Herald-Leader*, November 24, 1997, p. 13; Roadway Express, Inc., 1996 Annual Report, p. 7; and the authors' personal interview with Patrick Kelly, March 3, 1998.

5. The examples in this section are drawn from: Stratford Sherman, "Andy Grove: How Intel Makes Spending Pay Off," *Fortune* February 22, 1993; Mary Thyfault, "Sears Adds Speech Recognition," *Information Week*, April 6, 1998, p. 32; Richard Adhikari, "Scheduling Solution," *Information Week*, April 20, 1998, pp. 154–156; Clinton Wilder, "Online Configuration," *Information Week*, March 30, 1998, p. 82; Mary Thryfault, "Midwest AAA Upgrades Call Center," *Information Week*, April 27, 1998, pp. 150–152; Justin Hibbard, "Internet Pipeline," *Information Week*, March 30, 1998, pp. 79–80; and Jenny McCune, "A Few Good Employees," *American Management Association International* (April 1998): 38.

6. Kate Kane, "L. L. Bean Delivers the Goods," *Fast Company* (August–September 1997): 104–113.

7. The examples in this section are drawn from: Clinton Wilder, "Web-Based Buying Wins More Converts," *Information Week*, April 6, 1998, p. 30; Clinton Wilder, "Chevron to Conduct Online Procurement," *Information Week*, April 27, 199, p. 30; "To Byte the Hand That Feeds," *The Economist*, January 17, 1998, pp. 61–62; "CIO Magazine Honors Roadway Express for Innovative Use of Information Systems," press release, August 12, 1997; Candee Wilde, "Internet Levels the Field," *Information Week*, June 29, 1998, pp. 64–66; William C. Taylor, "Who's Writing the Book on Web Business? (Amazon.com)," *Fast Company* (October–November 1996): 132; Tom Stein, "Extending ERP," *Information Week*, June 15, 1998, p. 75; and Chuck Salter, "This Company's Seen the Future of Customer Service," *Fast Company* (February–March 1998): 34–36.

8. J. B. Quinn, J. J. Baruch, and K. A. Zien, *Innovation Explosion: Using Intellect and Software to Revolutionize Growth Strategies* (New York: Free Press, 1997), pp. 2–4.

9. The examples in this section are drawn from: Ira Sager, "Wired to the Max," *Business Week,* November 24, 1997; John R. Quain, "Work Together, Apart," *Fast Company* (October–November 1997): 229–236; John R. Quain, "I See How to Work Together," *Fast Company* (August–September 1996): 113–118; and Heath Row, "Lights! Camera! Web action!" *Fast Company* (February–March 1998): 198–207.

10. The examples in this section were drawn from: "35 Days Hath September," *Journey* (July 1995): 20 (an internal publication of the Coca-Cola Company); Welch, "Information Age"; Justin Hibbard, "GM Prepares Rollout of Integrated Intranet Platform," *Information Week,* April 20, 1998, p. 26; Joy Russell, "Welch's Spreads Data," *Information Week,* June 15, 1998, p. 132; Michael Kaplan, "Pow! Zap! Sell!" *Fast Company* (December–January 1998): 234–245; Walgreen Co., "Information Technology"; and Stewart Alsop, "Sun's Java: What's Hype, What's Real?" *Fortune,* July 7, 1997, pp. 191–192.

11. This example is based on Glenn Rifkin, "Nothing but Net," *Fast Company* (June–July 1996): 122–127, and Thomas Davenport, David DeLong, and Michael Beers, "Successful Knowledge Management Projects," *Sloan Management Review* (Winter 1998): 43–57.

12. Davenport, DeLong, and Beers, "Successful Knowledge Management Projects."

13. The examples that follow are drawn from: Mary J. Cronin, "Knowing How Employees Use the Intranet Is Good Business," *Fortune,* July 21, 1997, p. 103; and Hiawatha Bray, "The Web Gets Personal," *Fast Company* (August–September 1997): 207–213.

14. The following examples are drawn from Steve Ditlea, "All the News That Fits You," *Fast Company* (August–September 1996): 128–134; and Gina Imperato, "The Web Is Reinventing Itself—and Television Is the Inspiration," *Fast Company* (April–May 1997): 162.

15. The examples in this section draw from various sources, including: Ronald Henkoff, "Companies That Train Best," *Fortune,* March 22, 1993; and "The Newest Member of Tech's Ruling Elite: An Interview with John Chambers," *Fortune,* November 24, 1997, p. 258.

16. The following examples are drawn from: Srikumar Rao, "Evolution at Warp Speed," *Forbes,* January 12, 1998, p. 83; and Otis Port, "Robocop Is More Than Just a Movie," *Business Week,* February 2, 1998, p. 65.

4

DESIGNING ORGANIZATIONS: ELIMINATING THE BARRIERS

We trained hard . . . but it seemed that every time we were beginning to form up into a team, we would be reorganized. I was to learn later in life that we tend to meet any new situation by reorganizing. And a wonderful method it can be of creating the illusion of progress while producing confusion, inefficiency, and demoralization.

—Petronius Arbiter

The challenge of organizational design is not new, as Petronius Arbiter, an officer in the Roman army, pointed out some two thousand years ago. One reason that organizations still have problems with how they structure and restructure themselves is due to the traditional understanding of the "right way" to structure organizations: layers of boxes, neatly stacked one atop the other and connected by solid and dashed lines. This view focuses attention on hierarchy, reporting relationships, division of labor, and accountability. As suggested by one bank CEO during a recent interview, "Organization structure creates a lot of stress because people are forced to stay in their boxes."

The architecture of an organization is one of the most critical elements of its structural capital. As the context within which human capital performs, structure has a great deal to say about power, influence, authority, decision-making processes, access to information, and formal and informal patterns of communication within organizations. Structures must not only be aligned with the purpose, objectives, processes, and capabilities of the organization and with the dynamic realities of the external environment; they must also be compatible with the skills, values, and attitudes of the individual employees. One of the key elements of structure is the scope of the organization: which value-creating activities it controls and which outsiders perform. Within the organization, the design of individual tasks and the scheme of reporting relationships—who reports to whom, what information is made available, and what kinds of decisions can be made by which managers at each level in the organization—are important structural choices. The relationships between these structural choices and the strategies the organization implements to leverage its investments in human capital are illustrated in Exhibit 4-1.

The traditional organizational form, bureaucracy, is highly structured, tightly controlled, and very formal. The bureaucratic approach to organizational design works well in simple, relatively stable environments, but it has significant limitations in dynamic environments where competitive conditions place a premium on individual initiative and organizational flexibility. A rigid and overly controlled environment works at cross purposes with most of the approaches and strategies we recommend to take full advantage of the capabilities of the organization's human capital resources.

Leaders need a new mind-set. The emphasis must be on results

EXHIBIT 4-1.
Leveraging human capital: Structural choices.

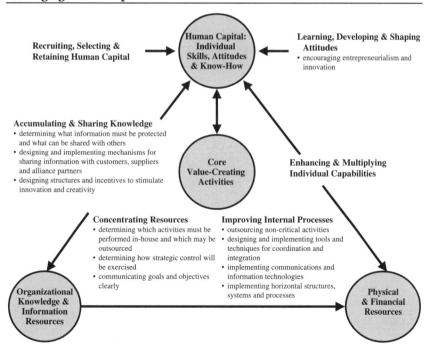

and on positioning their organizations to compete in rapidly changing global market environments. In order to develop the flexibility required to capitalize on these opportunities, many of today's leading-edge organizations are moving toward a new and innovative organization model, the boundaryless organization. Its chief architect, GE's CEO Jack Welch, describes it this way:[1]

> The old command and control structures built around military structures of the past don't engage every mind and involve every person. You have to have a boundaryless organization. . . . That means sharing ideas with each other, with suppliers, customers, and other companies. The best ideas are somewhere else. It's very difficult to flatten vertical organizational boundaries. In order to flatten the organizations, we must form teams around processes (workflow). Organizations exist only to control.

The term *boundaryless* may seem to point to a chaotic organizational reality in which anything goes. This is not the case. As Jack Welch has suggested, boundaryless does not imply that all internal and external boundaries vanish altogether. Although boundaries may continue to exist in some form, they become more open and permeable.

Several distinct types of structure may help to make boundaries more permeable and, in the process, facilitate the widespread sharing of knowledge and information across both the internal and external boundaries of the organization. We'll begin with the barrier-free type, which seeks to break down all organizational boundaries, both internal and external. We'll place particular emphasis on team concepts since we view teams as a central building block for implementation of the boundaryless organization. Then we will address the modular and virtual organization types, which focus on the need to create seamless relationships with external organizations. While the modular type emphasizes the outsourcing of noncore activities, the virtual (or network) organization focuses on alliances among independent entities formed to exploit specific market opportunities. Finally, we'll address the emerging cellular form, designed to foster entrepreneurship and facilitate information sharing and organizational learning.

The Barrier-Free Organization

The "boundary" mind-set is ingrained deeply into bureaucracies. It is evidenced by such clichés as, "That's not my job," "I'm here from corporate to help," or endless battles over transfer pricing. In the traditional company, boundaries are clearly delineated in the design of an organization's structure. These boundaries are rigid. Their basic advantage is that the roles of managers and employees are simple, clear, well defined, and long-lived. A major shortcoming was pointed out during an interview with a high-tech executive: "Structure tends to be divisive; it leads to territorial fights."

Today such structures are being replaced by fluid, ambiguous, and deliberately ill-defined tasks and roles.[2] Just because work roles are no longer defined by traditional structures, however, does not mean that differences in skills, authority, and talent disappear.

A barrier-free organization enables a company to bridge individual and organizational differences in culture, function, and goals to find common ground that facilitates information sharing and other forms of cooperative behavior. To be successful, a barrier-free organization must promote shared interests and trust. Eliminating the multiple boundaries that stifle productivity and innovation can enhance the potential of the entire organization.

Let's see how Du Pont's elimination of a key tenet of bureaucracy really paid dividends:

Early in the AIDS era, the New York Blood Bank asked Du Pont's Medical Products division for help in tracking the history of every pint of blood it distributed. A massive database was needed—and within ninety days.

Typically, the medical products unit supplied the blood bank with blood analyzers, not computer software. However, the blood bank was a good customer, and it was desperate to prevent HIV infections. The medical products staff sought assistance from the departmental and corporate information technology staffs, but none could deliver within the ninety-day window.

Following the traditional rules of bureaucracy, the medical products account executive could have considered his job completed; he had followed the hierarchical and divisional lines of authority and could not come up with a solution. Fortunately, however, he was aware of a small, highly skilled, information technology group within Du Pont's huge fibers business, which manufactured fibers for textiles, carpets, and industrial uses like tire cords. The information engineering associates (IEA) had recently been created to exploit computer-aided software engineering (CASE) tools, a technology for writing software faster, and had already solved a problem similar to that posed by the New York Blood Bank: building a database to track the history and quality of every bobbin of Kevlar fibers as they moved through Du Pont's Richmond, Virginia, plant.

Bureaucratic rules would dictate that a staff group from one unit would not do major jobs for other divisions. But since this was an emergency, IEA was assigned the job. The group delivered the blood-tracking database within the ninety-day deadline, and the medical products staff were able to deliver a service that far exceeded their customer's expectations. Breaking the rules of bureaucracy had literally saved lives.

When word of IEA's accomplishments spread, the group became an extremely valued internal vendor. Another project it completed within ninety days was a groundwater database designed to monitor radiation in the groundwater around Du Pont's nuclear materials production site at the Savannah River in South Carolina.

In short, IEA went from being a staff group serving only the fibers group to becoming an intraprise (short for intracorporate enterprise), with clients throughout Du Pont. And while other information technology groups in Du Pont were downsized, IEA grew to 120 employees. Lives were saved, customers were amazed, and serious safety problems were brought under control—all because boundaries were made more permeable.

For barrier-free organizations to work effectively, organizations must raise the level of trust throughout the workplace and develop among their employees the skills and attitudes required to work in a more democratic organization. Barrier-free organizations also require a shift in philosophy from executive development to organizational development, and from investments in high-potential individuals to investments in leveraging the talents of all individuals. Consider, for example, how Oticon uses teams to enhance its competitive position:

Creating a barrier-free organization is not limited to cutting-edge, high-growth industries. The hearing aid industry, for example, is not a high-growth sector. Industry-level sales have been flat for five years, at about $1 billion annually. But one company has bucked that trend; Oticon doubled its revenues in less than five years to $166.5 million. The profits for 1996 increased tenfold over five years, to $18.3 million. Oticon is quick to market too. In that time period, in an otherwise sleepy industry, it launched ten major product innovations, including the world's first digital hearing aid. What drives Oticon's success is that it uses teams to innovate more quickly and efficiently than the competition. Eight years ago it identified organizational structures as being a major impediment to creating a team-oriented culture, so it completely changed the organization.

A quick way to lower functional boundaries is to eliminate physical ones first. Oticon employees work in a renovated soda factory, with hardwood floors, high ceilings, and plenty of open space. There are no offices or cubicles. Instead, each employee is assigned a freewheeling "pod," which contains some desk space, a computer, and little else. When a new project emerges, employees roll their pods together in whatever open space happens to be handy. Marketing types sit next to programmers, who sit next to support personnel, who sit next to researchers. When the project ends, employees roll their pods toward their next assignment.

Oticon is high tech. Bright red cables are plentiful throughout the work area; suspended from the ceiling, each cable contains a dial tone and Internet access. When employees roll their work pod to a new area, they pull down a cord and plug their computer into the network. There are no filing cabinets to slow employees down as they roll toward a new project. To keep employees mobile, the company digitizes its paper flow. Each day every employee walks to the mailroom, picks up his or her mail, then shreds 99 percent of the mail that comes into the building. If a piece of mail seems to be important, the employee scans it electronically into the network, where it is filed, readily accessible when needed. Electronic storage eliminates the need for filing cabinets. Similarly, employees are assigned mobile phones, which they carry with them throughout the building so they can take calls wherever they are.

By focusing on eliminating all physical barriers, Oticon finds it easier to eliminate functional ones as well. Because everyone sits next to everyone else, functional rivalries rarely develop. Employees share information easily, and trust emerges. If you want to know what some other department is working on, you simply lean over and ask. If someone needs your help, you roll your work area over to that person's and plug in. People talk face to face. There are no functional areas, no organization charts—only projects and project leaders. The project is the function. Once a project is completed, it disbands. There's a deliberate deemphasis on project budgets;

Oticon would rather deliver on time but slightly over budget than to deliver late. This mind-set encourages team leaders to seek out any help they need to further a project's progress. Almost everyone works on multiple projects. People don't dissipate resources on frivolous spending because there's no perverse budgetary incentive to spend all of the annual budget allotment. Meeting deadlines matters. Oticon's culture emphasizes working in teams, teaming with each other, and teaming across the company. Most companies want to use employee teams; Oticon's approach is to dismantle not only the functional barriers to teaming, but also the physical, technological, and cultural barriers.[3]

Jeffrey Pfeffer, author of several insightful books, including *The Human Equation*, suggests three primary advantages of teams.[4] First, teams substitute peer-based for hierarchical control of work activities. In essence, employees control themselves, lessening the time and energy management would devote to control. Second, teams frequently develop more creative solutions to problems because they encourage individual team members to share tacit knowledge. Brainstorming, or group problem solving, involves the pooling of ideas and expertise to improve the chances that at least one group member will think of a way to solve problems. Third, by substituting peer for hierarchical control, teams permit the removal of layers of hierarchy and absorption of administrative tasks previously performed by specialists. This avoids the cumbersome costs of having people whose sole job is to watch people who watch other people do the work. To carry the argument one step further, in *Augustine's Laws*, Norman Augustine points out that "if a sufficient number of management layers are superimposed on top of each other, it can be assured that disaster is not left to chance!"

Effective barrier-free organizations must go beyond achieving close integration and coordination with internal constituencies. As GE's Jack Welch notes, they must also create effective links with external stakeholders. Thus, the organization must achieve coordination not only by sharing key information and resources across its internal functions, but also by working closely with other operating units throughout the corporation. Research on the multidivisional type of organization has pointed to the importance of interdivisional coordination and resource sharing.[5] Means to this end include interdivisional task forces and committees, reward and incentive systems that emphasize interdivisional cooperation, and common training programs. In addition, managers in barrier-free organizations must create flexible, porous organizational boundaries and establish communication flows and mutually beneficial relationships with suppliers, customers, and other external constituencies. Chrysler's Neon project provides a recent example:

> Detroit had been unable to develop a small car profitably. In 1990 Lee Iacocca was seeking a partner to build the next-generation subcompact, similar to Ford's joint venture with Mazda to develop the Escort/Tracer. However, Robert P. Marcell, head of Chrysler's small car engineering team, convinced Iacocca that a subcompact could be built and sold at a profit without a partner. Thus began one of the most remarkable development efforts in Detroit's history. Marcell's core group of 150 colleagues mobilized many internal and external stakeholders—600 engineers, 289 suppliers, and many blue-collar workers—in a campaign to deliver the new model in only forty-two months, and for $1.3 billion, a fraction of any other recent small car's cost. (Ford spent $2 billion and five years to develop the money-losing Escort, and GM spent $5 billion and seven years to develop the Saturn.)
>
> From the beginning, Marcell applied the concept of concurrent engineering, which required personnel from diverse functional areas and suppliers to work together to avoid later delays and disagreements or misunderstandings. Thus, Chrysler dissolved traditional barriers and pulled in engineers, marketers, purchasing, finance, labor, suppliers, and consumers—including a group of subcompact owners in San Diego, California—to design its Neon.

To build on the Neon example, consider how Harley-Davidson, the producer of world-class motorcycles, establishes close ongoing relationships with major stakeholder groups:

> First look at the *dealer group*. The demands on its dealers have clearly increased as Harley expanded its goods and services to include collectibles, clothing, financing, and other components of its business. In support of its dealers, Harley has developed a three-day training program with courses as diverse as how to provide top-notch service, how to do a business simulation, and how to plan for ownership succession.
>
> Second, look at its *family of owners.* The Harley Owners Group (HOG) is a fifteen-year-old initiative built to create a life-long relationship between the company and its owners. It's the world's largest factory-sponsored motorcycle club with

325,000 members and 940 chapters. Harley offers HOG seminars—sessions for the club's 7,000 chapter officers to help answer questions on whether and how to incorporate, how to attract new members, and how to organize events.

Third, consider the centerpiece of Harley's unique blend of individuality and teamwork: *its partnership with its two unions*, the International Association of Machinists and Aerospace Workers and the United Paperworkers International. The company and union partners have negotiated a modern operating agreement whereby both sides share a commitment to making Harley a high-performance work organization. At Harley-Davidson, people have the authority and responsibility to do everything the best way they can.

Risks, Challenges, and Potential Downsides

In spite of its potential benefits, many companies are discovering that creating and managing a barrier-free organization is a frustrating experience. For example, Puritan-Bennett Corporation, a Lenexa, Kansas, manufacturer of respiratory equipment, found that its product development time has more than doubled since it adopted team management. Roger J. Dolida, director of R&D, attributes this failure to lack of top management commitment, high turnover among team members, and infrequent meetings. Similarly, efforts at Jerome Goods, a turkey producer in Baron, Wisconsin, to switch to entrepreneurial teams have largely stalled due to a failure to link executive compensation to team performance. Very often, managers trained in rigid hierarchies find it difficult to make the transition to the more democratic, participative style that teamwork requires.

Christopher Barnes, now a consultant with Price Waterhouse in Atlanta, also provides some useful insights on why teams fail.[6] Previously he had worked as an industrial engineer for Challenger Electrical Distribution (a subsidiary of the former Westinghouse), at a plant in Jackson, Mississippi, that produced circuit-breaker boxes. His assignment was to lead a team of workers from the plant's troubled final assembly operation with this mission: "Make things better." Not surprisingly, that vague notion set the team up for failure. After a year of futility, the team was disbanded. In retrospect, and after several successes with teams, Barnes identified several reasons for the debacle in Jackson: (1) limited personal credibility—he was viewed as an "outsider"; (2) a lack of commitment to the team—everyone involved was forced to be on the team; (3) poor communications—nobody was told why the team was important; (4) limited autonomy—line managers refused to give up control over team members; and (5) misaligned incentives—the culture rewarded individual versus team performance.

We believe that Barnes's experience has important implications for all types of teams, whether composed of managerial, professional, clerical, or production personnel.

Making It Work

Although a barrier-free organization is capable of rapid and continual adaptation to environmental changes, its ability to adapt is sometimes hindered by the overwhelming challenges that management faces in guiding an organization toward more democratic processes. To be successful, this type must go well beyond a single product development group or team to permeate the entire organization. The organization's vision, goals, and objectives must be widely shared and well understood. Strategic planning processes should encourage the open sharing of both organizational and individual knowledge and expertise, and emphasize the benefits of internal cooperation among the units within the company.

Barrier-free organizations, as well as other innovative forms, should be complemented by well-designed and effectively implemented information technology systems—the infrastructure that, among other functions, supports the gathering, storage, and sharing of organizational knowledge.[7] Some have argued that information technology must be viewed more as a prime component of an organization's overall strategy rather than simply in terms of its more traditional role as administrative support. The role and multiple applications of technology—and the close relationships that must exist between technology, organization design, and task design—were addressed in Chapter 3.

Two critical success factors can make the difference between average-performing teams and superior teams: (1) relationships among team members and (2) meaningful diversity in the composition of the team.

■ *Relationships among team members.* In a recent speech, David Pottruck, CEO of Charles Schwab, discussed some of the key findings of studies conducted by Frank Carubba, head of Hewlett-Packard's Research Laboratories in the late 1980s and early 1990s.[8] Carubba had compared teams that had failed to meet objectives with teams that attained good results. Then he looked at superior teams: those that consistently exceeded expectations:

He discovered that the factors that made the difference between mediocre teams and good teams were motivation and talent. Clearly, the good teams had better-quality leadership and better-qualified researchers. But the difference between the good teams and the superior teams could not be accounted for by talent and motivation alone. What is really impressive was that he judged the difference between good teams and superior teams to be in the range of 40 percent.

Carruba found that the difference lay in the quality of the relationships among the team members. This 40 percent increment in team performance was accounted for by the way they treated one another—the degree to which they believed in one another and created an atmosphere of encouragement rather than competition. In other words, in this high-tech and competitive industry, vision, talent, and motivation could carry a team only so far. To optimize and expand performance fully, personal values such as caring for their teammates and communicating with integrity and authenticity made the difference between plain success and extraordinary results. Relationships are everything.

What he discovered suggests that talent alone might be insufficient to ensure the best results. It takes a generosity of spirit to bring out the spirit of the collective, and therefore the best results for the team.

■ *Meaningful diversity in team composition.* Recall the old saying: "If two people think exactly alike, why keep both of them on the payroll?" Effective teams, especially those that value creativity and innovation as an outcome, heed this warning. Diversity must be viewed more broadly than along the usual racial, ethnic, and gender lines. Certainly, that can help; Reebok's early success in aerobic shoes was largely credited to the women on Reebok's product development team.[9] However, diversity must also include one's general approach to thinking and problem solving. Consider Jerry Hirshberg's approach at Nissan Design International (NDI), the influential automotive design studio located in La Jolla, California:

Jerry Hirshberg, NDI's founder, has instituted the practice of "hiring in divergent pairs." He argues that when it comes to creativity, the best person is often two people—individuals who see the world in utterly different ways. Claims Hirshberg, "I believe in creative abrasion. And I mean abrasion. We have titans in their fields going at each other: 'I'm sorry, I see the project this way. The way you're approaching it is just absurd.' That friction can produce wonderful sparks." There are about two dozen odd couples creating cars at NDI.

When Tom Semple begins designing a new car, for example, he removes all traces of earlier projects. He loves the freedom of a blank sheet of paper. Although he might glance at some engineering specs or a marketing report, what he's searching for is artistic intuition. To Tom, design means inventing entirely new forms. In contrast, when Allan Flowers starts to design a new car, he worries about nuts and bolts. He undertakes a methodical assessment of potential components and materials, of schedules and priorities. To Flowers, form follows function: design involves understanding how things work.

The approach has worked. Since Hirshberg left GM in 1979 to create Nissan's first studio in the United States, his organization has produced a stream of trend-setting innovations. These include the Pathfinder sport utility vehicle, the Infiniti series, and the Mercury Villager minivan. Over 4 million cars designed by Hirshberg are on the road today, the studio has won numerous awards, and Hirshberg is recognized as a design visionary.

Similarly, at Xerox PARC, a PAIR (PARC Artist in Residence) program has been established to link computer scientists with artists. This enables each to influence the other's perceptions of the world. And, at Interval Research, a California think tank dedicated to multimedia technologies, director David Liddle invites leaders from various disciplines in for short sabbaticals. The objective is to stimulate cross-fertilization of ideas and approaches to solving problems. The resulting exchanges have enabled Interval Research to create and spin off several highly innovative startups.

We summarize the pros and cons of the barrier-free structure in Exhibit 4-2.

The Modular Organization

As Charles Handy, the author of *The Age of Unreason*, has noted:

Organizations have realized that, while it may be convenient to have everyone around all the time, having all of your workforce's time at your command is an extravagant way of

EXHIBIT 4-2.
Pros and cons of the barrier-free structure.

Pros	Cons
■ Leverages talents of all employees ■ Enhances cooperation, coordination, and information-sharing among functions, divisions, strategic business units, and external groups ■ Enables a quicker response to market through a single-goal focus	■ Difficult to overcome political and authority boundaries ■ Lacks strong leadership and common vision which can lead to coordination problems ■ Time-consuming and difficult-to-manage democratic processes ■ Lacks high levels of trust which can impede performance

marshalling the necessary resources. It is cheaper to keep them outside the organization, employed by themselves or by specialist contractors, and to buy their services when you need them.[10]

To capture Handy's vision, the modular organization type outsources nonvital functions, tapping into the knowledge and expertise of best-in-class suppliers of goods and services, but retains full strategic control. Outsiders may be used to manufacture parts, handle logistics, or perform accounting activities. The organization is actually a central hub surrounded by networks of outside suppliers and specialists, and parts can be easily added or taken away. Both manufacturing and service units may be modular.

In the personal computer industry, the shift to the modular structure has been pioneered by relative newcomers like Dell, Gateway, and CompuAdd, as well as by workstation innovators like Sun Microsystems. These companies either buy their products ready-made or purchase all the parts from suppliers and perform only the final assembly. Their large, established competitors—IBM, Hewlett-Packard, and Digital Equipment—produce most of their parts in-house. As a result, the smaller modular companies typically outperform their older rivals in profitability.

Michael Dell, founder and CEO of Dell Computer, points out some of the advantages of the outsourcing strategy that made the company the top performer in the S&P 500 in 1997:

There are fewer things to manage, fewer things to go wrong. You don't have the drag effect of taking 50,000 people with you. Suppose we have two suppliers building monitors for us, and one of them loses its edge. It's a lot easier for us to get more capacity from the remaining supplier than to set up a new manufacturing plant ourselves. If we had to build our own factories for every single component of the system, growing at 57% per year just would not be possible. I would spend 500% of my time interviewing prospective vice presidents because the company would have not 15,000 employees but 80,000.

Indirectly, we employ something like that many people today. There are, for example, 10,000 service technicians in the field who service our products, but only a small number of them work for us. They're contracted with other firms. But ask the customer, "Who was that person who just fixed your computer?" The vast majority think that person works for us, which is just great. That's part of virtual integration.[11]

How much can a company outsource and still remain competitive? The example of Monorail, a successful new entrant in the hotly contested personal computer industry, illustrates how outsourcing virtually all value-producing activities can be a viable competitive strategy:

Sleek, black, and beautiful, Monorail PCs take up only 20 percent of the space needed by most of the other personal computers sold today. Complete with cutting-edge technology, their striking design, low cost, and small footprint have boosted Monorail's sales in three short years from a start-up company to the fourteenth largest PC maker in the world. CEO Douglas Johns wants Monorail to achieve $2 billion in sales by 2003. Monorail's success results from its lean structure; the company outsources everything but management, product design, marketing, and logistics.

Take a typical order. Monorail sells through CompUSA. When an order arrives, FedEx is electronically notified to deliver parts to contract manufacturers, which assemble the final product and ship it to CompUSA, within two to four business days. Meanwhile, the invoice is electronically routed to SunBank's credit and billing department. SunBank then factors Monorail's invoices, quickly remitting cash to the company. Should the customer have a question, a call center in Tampa provides Monorail's 800 customer support.

Letting go of core competencies could be a recipe for disaster, but it works for Monorail. Its secret? Ask Monorail executives what they believe to be their core competencies, and they'll give you a list of just two: management expertise and partnership development. Monorail understands the importance of close ties to suppliers. Its veteran management team has considerable experience in identifying and partnering with suppliers. Monorail develops mutually beneficial relationships with its suppliers and keeps the needs of its partners in mind when it designs its products. Consider shipping. Monorail contracts with FedEx to provide shipping and inventory management, just as most direct mail resellers do. But Monorail partnered early with FedEx, and asked the critical question: What computer design works best for FedEx to handle? The solution? Design the PC to fit into a standard FedEx shipping box, thus driving down handling problems and costs. Designing for logistics rewards Monorail with some of the lowest shipping costs in the business.

Monorail's relationships with other partners work the same way. Here, too, the question is: how can we best leverage the talents of our suppliers? Not surprisingly, Monorail finds no shortage of potential partner prospects. Suppliers understand that the skills and knowledge they learn from partnering with Monorail can be applied to other ventures. Meanwhile Monorail enjoys the flexibility of outsourcing and the benefits of tightly cohesive partner relationships.

Apparel is another industry in which the modular type has been widely adopted. Nike and Reebok have succeeded by concentrating on their strengths: designing and marketing high-tech, fashionable footwear. Nike has very limited production facilities, and Reebok owns no plants. These two companies contract virtually all their footwear production to suppliers in Taiwan, South Korea, and other low-cost-labor countries. Avoiding large investments in fixed assets helps them derive large profits on minor sales increases. By being modular, Nike and Reebok can keep pace with changing tastes in the marketplace because their suppliers have become expert at rapidly retooling for the manufacture of new products.

In a modular company, outsourcing the noncore functions offers three advantages. First, it can decrease overall costs, quicken new product development by hiring suppliers whose talent may be superior to that of in-house personnel, avoid idle capacity, realize inventory savings, and avoid becoming locked into a particular technology. Second, outsourcing enables a company to focus scarce resources on the areas where it holds a competitive advantage. These benefits can translate into more funding for research and development, hiring the best engineers, and providing continual training for sales and service staff. Finally, by enabling an organization to tap into the knowledge and expertise of its specialized supply chain partners, it adds critical skills and accelerates organizational learning.[12]

The modular type enables a company to leverage relatively small amounts of capital and a small management team to achieve seemingly unattainable strategic objectives. Freed from the need to make big investments in fixed assets, the modular company can achieve rapid growth. Certain preconditions must exist or be created, however, before the approach can be successful. First, the company must work closely with suppliers to ensure that the interests of each party are being fulfilled. Companies need to find loyal, reliable vendors that can be trusted with trade secrets. They also need assurances that suppliers will dedicate their financial, physical, and human resources to satisfy strategic objectives such as lowering costs or being first to market. Second, the modular company must make sure that it chooses the right competence to keep in-house. An organization must be wary of outsourcing critical components of its business that may compromise long-term competitive advantages.

Organizations applying the modular concept must develop a strategic plan that identifies core competencies and areas that are important for future development, and then attempt to outsource noncritical functions. For Nike and Reebok, the core competencies are design and marketing, not shoe manufacturing. For Honda, the core competence is engine technology. These companies are unlikely to outsource any activity that involves their core competence.

While adopting the modular form clearly has some advantages, managers must also weigh its disadvantages. For example, mindless outsourcing in the pursuit of temporary cost advantages can lead to firms' becoming "hollow" and losing their competitive advantage.[13] The world leader in the bicycle business for almost a century, Schwinn filed for bankruptcy after it outsourced most of its production in response to a labor strike:

> Schwinn's managers handed over technology and production to Giant Manufacturing Company of Taiwan and China Bicycle Company. These companies now dominate the world bicycle business. Schwinn's demise can be traced to its inability to protect its technology, its failure to establish global brand equity, its lack of innovation, and severe labor-management

EXHIBIT 4-3.
Pros and cons of the modular structure.

Pros	Cons
■ Directs a firm's managerial and technical talent to the most critical activities	■ Inhibits common vision through reliance on outsiders
■ Maintains full strategic control over most critical activities—core competencies	■ Diminishes future competitive advantages if critical technologies are outsourced
■ Increases focus on customers and markets	■ Increases the difficulty of bringing back into the firm activities that now add value due to market shifts
■ Achieves "best in class" performance at each link in the value chain	■ Focuses too narrowly on professional development; opportunities may be missed
■ Leverages core competencies by outsourcing with smaller capital commitment	■ Decreases operational control[15]
■ Encourages information sharing and accelerates organizational learning	
■ Quickens response to environmental shifts	

problems. Instead of addressing these basic problems, Schwinn responded with a poorly devised strategy rooted in its inability to keep high-value activities in-house, failure to invest in core competencies, and preoccupation with short-term cost control instead of viewing outsourcing as a strategic weapon to improve its competitive position.

Exhibit 4-3 summarizes the pros and cons of modular structures.[14]

The Virtual Organization

One of the lessons America's legendary cowboys learned well in the rough and tumble days on the frontier was that paranoia was smart psychology: "Don't trust anyone—they're all out to get you. They'll all steal from you (or worse yet, shoot you!) once your back is turned." Staking an ownership claim to a territory or to a herd was necessary (but not sufficient) to guarantee a piece of the action. Similarly, "self-reliance" was the best-known phrase associated with the influential nineteenth-century New Englander Ralph Waldo Emerson. A century later, another New Englander, Robert Frost, observed, "Good fences make good neighbors."[15]

Traditional management assumptions echo these themes: Good fences make good corporations. After all, if you don't own it, if it hasn't been branded with your mark, you don't control it; and it might hurt you. What you own is "inside" the fence; everything else is "outside" and must be treated as a potential enemy or adversary unless brought under your domination.

Times have certainly changed. Now, the strategic challenge becomes one of doing more with less—looking outward for opportunities and solutions to problems. Leaders must recognize the potential for applying elements of the virtual type of organization as a means of leveraging resources and exploiting opportunities.

The virtual type can be viewed as a continually evolving network of independent companies—suppliers, customers, even competitors—linked together to share skills, costs, and access to one another's markets. The members of a virtual organization, by pooling and sharing the knowledge and expertise of each of the component organizations, simultaneously "knows" more and can "do" more than any one member of the group could do alone. By working closely together in a cooperative effort, each gains in the long run from the resulting individual and organizational learning that takes place. The term *virtual*, meaning "being in effect but not actually so," is commonly used in the computer industry. A computer's ability to appear to have more storage capacity than it really possesses is called virtual memory. Similarly, by assembling resources from a variety of entities, a virtual organization may seem to have more capabilities than it really possesses.

The virtual organization consists of a grouping of units of different organizations that have joined in an alliance to exploit complementary skills in pursuing common strategic objectives. A case in point is Lockheed Martin's use of specialized coalitions between and among three entities—the company, academia, and government—to sharpen competitiveness. According to former CEO Norman Augustine:

> The underlying beauty of this approach is that it forces us to reach outward. No matter what your size, you have to look broadly for new ideas, new approaches, new products. Lockheed Martin used this approach in a surprising manner when it set out during the height of the Cold War to make stealth aircraft and missiles. The technical idea came from research

done at the Institute of Radio Engineering in Moscow in the 1960s that was published, and publicized, quite openly in the academic media.

Despite the great contrasts among government, academia and private business, we have found ways to work together that have produced very positive results, not the least of which is our ability to compete on a global scale.

Virtual organizations need not be permanent. Participating firms may be working in multiple alliances at any one time. Virtual organizations may consist of different organizations performing complementary value activities, or different organizations involved jointly in the same value activities such as production, R&D, advertising, and distribution. The percentage of activities that are jointly performed with alliance partners may vary significantly from alliance to alliance.

Unlike the modular type, in which the focal organization maintains full strategic control, the virtual organization is characterized by participating companies that give up part of their control and accept interdependent destinies. Participating companies pursue a collective strategy that enables them to cope with uncertainty in the environment through cooperative efforts. Just as virtual memory increases storage capacity, virtual organizations increase the capacity or competitive advantage of participating companies. In its purest form, a virtual organization need not have a central office, an organization chart, or a hierarchy. Participating companies unite to exploit specific opportunities or attain specific strategic objectives; when the objective is met, they disband.[16] Apache, a new and successful Internet company, epitomizes the concept of the virtual organization:

> Sometimes organizations unite because the goal appears greater than any individual one can accomplish. In the computer industry, establishing an industry standard nearly always generates long-term profits. For organizations to do so, most follow the strategy made famous by King Gillette almost one hundred years ago: give customers a razor for free, and sell them the blades. Larger companies, such as Netscape and Microsoft, give away their desktop browser software, hoping to establish profitable beachheads in the corporate Internet server market.
>
> While the Microsoft-Netscape battle rages daily in the press, Apache has moved with stealth and acquired almost half of the Internet server market. Its market share exceeds

that of both Microsoft and Netscape. One reason for Apache's success is that it doesn't give away the desktop browser in order to enter the server market; it just gives away the server software for free. No strings attached. So if it is the market leader, why does Apache rarely generate any headlines? One reason is that it doesn't have a transformational CEO captivating the press every day; in fact, it doesn't have a CEO at all—or any employees, advertising, or anything of the like. Apache is, in effect, nothing more than a network of volunteers who provide a cutting-edge technology for anyone who wants to download it. For free.

Where's the business sense to this model? Apache delivers a product its customers desire and provides its volunteers with valuable name recognition. Software companies know the individuals who have generated code for Apache. One visit to its web site explains why: volunteer names are displayed conspicuously on the opening page. Because Apache enjoys a hot reputation for delivering new releases on time, the people who develop the releases are also hot. Their exposure leads to better-paying jobs and bigger projects. For entrepreneurial-oriented volunteers, there's a cottage industry growing up around the Apache software, selling plug-in modules for a fee. Most of the founders of these start-ups have worked or still work for Apache.

Apache has two core competencies: it can assemble programmers who write good code quickly, and it knows how to listen to customers. Customers identify features they need, and those changes are incorporated into the software quickly. Speed is valuable; customers are willing to pay handsomely for desirable add-ons that appear much more quickly than on competing Netscape and Microsoft software. Programmers are free to take what they have learned from customers and build new products as well. Some features go into the Apache software, while others become commercial add-ons. Rather than fragment the market with incompatible versions of Apache, all the software changes remain compatible to the Apache software, enabling programmers to support and expand the large installed user base. Each volunteer understands how important it is to improve the razor so the blades continue to sell. By cooperating to develop a community good, the individual programmers can reap tangible benefits as well.

Each company (or, as the example illustrates, individual) that links up with others to create a virtual organization contributes only what it considers its core competencies. It will mix and match what it does best with the best of other companies by identifying its critical capabilities and the necessary links to other capabilities.[17] For example, consider how some leading-edge venture capital firms are forming networks to add value. At the venture capital firm Kleiner, Perkins, Caufield & Byers, for example, John Doerr has become known as an activist investor who will stitch together collaborative networks among companies and their executives. Doerr and his associates recently joined with others to raise a $100 million venture fund to invest in and create a community of companies that will use Java to spawn products and services for the Internet. Similarly, Ron Fisher of Softbank Holdings is leading the investment of more than $500 million to establish an intricate web of mutually supportive Internet media companies. Softbank, which owns the Comdex computer industry conferences, hosted a conference in 1998 for companies it owned or in which it had an investment. The goal was to facilitate cross-fertilization.

Despite their many advantages, however, alliances often fail to meet expectations. For example, the IBM-Microsoft alliance soured in early 1991 when Microsoft began shipping Windows in direct competition to OS/2, which was jointly developed by the two companies. Windows' runaway success frustrated IBM's ability to set an industry standard. In retaliation, IBM entered into an alliance with Microsoft's archrival, Novell, to develop network software to compete with Microsoft's LAN Manager.

The virtual organization demands a unique set of managerial skills. Managers must build relationships with other companies, negotiate win-win deals for all parties, find the right partners with compatible goals and values, and provide the temporary organization with the right balance of freedom and control. In addition, information systems must be designed and integrated to facilitate communication with current and potential partners.

An ever-changing pattern of alliances that are constantly being formed and dissolved does not necessarily imply mutually exploitative arrangements or lack of long-term relationships. The key is to be clear about the strategic objectives while alliances are being formed. Some objectives are time bound, and those alliances need to be dissolved once the objective is fulfilled. Some alliances may have relatively long-term objectives and will need to be clearly monitored and nurtured to produce mutual commitment and avoid bitter fights for control. The highly dynamic PC industry, for example, is characterized by multiple temporary alliances among hardware, operating systems, and software producers.[18] But alliances in the more stable automobile industry, such as those involving Nissan and Volkswagen as well as Mazda and Ford, have long-term objectives and tend to be relatively stable.

The virtual organization is a logical culmination of joint venture strategies of the past. Shared risks, shared costs, and shared rewards are the facts of life in a virtual organization. When virtual organizations are formed, such as Time Warner's multimedia ventures, they pose tremendous challenges for strategic planning. As with the modular corporation, it is essential to identify the core competencies. However, for virtual structures to be successful, a strategic plan must also determine the effectiveness of combining core competencies. Virtual structures require more analysis than traditional types to determine where the synergies exist. Also, strategic plans must address the issues of diminished operational control and increased need for trust and common vision among the partners. This new structure may be appropriate for companies whose strategies require merging technologies (computing and communication, for example), or for those exploiting shrinking product life cycles that require simultaneous entry into multiple geographical markets. Also, it may be effective for companies that desire to be quick to the market with a new product or service—an example being the recent profusion of alliances among airlines primarily motivated by the need to provide seamless travel demanded by the full-fare-paying business traveler.

Exhibit 4-4 summarizes the advantages and disadvantages of the virtual form.[19]

EXHIBIT 4-4.
Pros and cons of the virtual structure.

Pros	Cons
■ Enables the sharing of costs and skills	■ Harder to determine where one company ends and another begins due to close interdependencies among players
■ Enhances access to global markets	
■ Increases market responsiveness	
■ Creates a "best of everything" organization since each partner brings core competencies to the alliance	■ Leads to potential loss of operational control among partners
	■ Results in loss of strategic control over emerging technology
■ Encourages both individual and organizational knowledge-sharing and accelerates organizational learning	■ Requires new and difficult-to-acquire managerial skills

Moving Toward the Boundaryless Organization

In looking for opportunities to maximize the potential of their human capital resources, managers must simultaneously consider the modular, virtual, and barrier-free approaches to organizational design. Designing an organization that supports the requirements of the organization's strategy, is consistent with the demands of the environment, and can be effectively implemented is a tall order for any manager. Many times, the most effective solution combines different organizational types. That is, a company may outsource many parts of its value chain to reduce costs and increase quality, engage simultaneously in multiple alliances to take advantage of technological developments or penetrate new markets, and break down barriers within the organization to increase flexibility. Next, we will look at how an innovative organization effectively combines both boundarylessness and the virtual form of organization.

The Technical Computer Graphics (TCG) group provides a variety of hardware and software products that facilitate electronic data exchange—products like hand-held bar code readers and scanning software. TCG's business model features about thirteen alliances—small project teams employing 200 employees. Each team is market oriented, geared toward either specific customers or specific products. The alliances share a common overhead infrastructure, but have the authority to seek out business opportunities as they see fit. It becomes difficult to discern where the firm ends and where customers and suppliers begin.

Each alliance draws its boundaries so that they include customers, suppliers, and other alliances. TCG likes to call it a triangulation approach. Suppliers and customers that provide funding are involved at the outset of the project. Projects often emerge from listening to what customers need. The alliances recognize that attaining the initial customer funding is crucial, an understanding that stimulates them to focus on what customers have to say. Sometimes another alliance acts as either the customer or the supplier and provides funding. With an emphasis on speed, new products come to market quickly, providing the organization and its partners with tangible benefits.

Each alliance can act independently, but each is tasked with

seeking out new growth opportunities, for either itself or another alliance. When one is found, an existing project provides
some seed capital, which is used to attract additional external
funding. Equally important, however, is that the alliance seeks
out assistance from the other alliances. The purpose is not
only to acquire some needed expertise for the new project,
but also to share the learning accumulated through work on
the project. There's no benefit to hoarding information; learning gained from one software project might prove especially
valuable to one underway in another alliance. The TCG model
emphasizes sharing this information rapidly and efficiently.
It's a business model of purposeful technological diffusion
with a process geared for fast-cycle markets. TCG's formal
structure is designed to ensure that technical diffusion occurs.
The culture, structured to encourage this as well, attracts both
entrepreneurs and team-oriented people. TCG rewards employees for being able to manage complex partner relationships. Because customer needs are continually changing,
triangulation forces employees to listen to the market and respond quickly. Because the customer matters more than the
functional title, teams lend expertise to each other, in return
for sharing the gains realized from supplying value to the customer.[20]

Often when organizations face external pressures, resource scarcity, and declining performance, they tend to become more internally
focused, rather than directing efforts toward managing and strengthening relationships with existing and potential external stakeholders. We
believe, however, that this may be the most opportune time for managers to analyze their value chain activities and evaluate the potential for
adopting elements of modular, virtual, and barrier-free organizational
types. This examination may help an organization to enhance or establish multiple forms of competitive advantage—differentiation, overall
low cost, quick response—when they are most needed to compete effectively.

Tools and Techniques for Coordination and Integration

Regardless of the form of organization ultimately chosen, achieving the
coordination and integration necessary to maximize the potential of an

organization's human capital involves much more than just creating a new structure. Techniques designed and implemented to ensure the necessary coordination and integration of an organization's key business processes are an important element of structural capital.[21] Teams are key building blocks of the new organizational forms, and teamwork requires new and flexible approaches to coordination and integration.

Often managers trained in rigid hierarchies find it difficult to make the transition to the more democratic, participative style that teamwork requires. As Douglas K. Smith, coauthor of *The Wisdom of Teams,* points out, "Few groups become real teams without taking risks to overcome constraints imposed by individual, functional and hierarchical boundaries. And team members do depend on one another in pursuit of common performance." Within the framework of an appropriate organizational architecture, managers must select a mix and balance of tools and techniques to facilitate the effective coordination and integration of key activities. A number of factors must be considered—for example:

- *Understanding the strategic context.* An appropriate understanding of the strategic context—the organization's environment of customers, suppliers, competitors, regulatory authorities, and alliance partners—and the relationships and interdependencies among these organizations is critical to effective coordination and integration of activities, both within and across organizational boundaries. This understanding must be communicated, understood, and accepted throughout, to facilitate and ensure consistent behavior and interaction among the parties involved, at multiple levels throughout each organization.

- *Clear communication of goals and objectives.* Effective coordination and integration begins at the top. Senior managers must clearly articulate organizational goals, objectives, and values, and employees must identify with and buy in to these goals and objectives. In the traditional approach, objectives and goals are defined in terms of a single organization and broken down into divisional and functional objectives that support the higher-level goals. A broader view is required in implementing the modular, virtual, or barrier-free organizational architectures, as a sense of common purpose must transcend traditional organizational boundaries to include customers, suppliers, alliance partners, and team members, regardless of the structure. Clear and effective communication and the careful avoidance of goal conflicts are essential.

■ *Common culture and shared values.* Shared goals, mutual objectives, and a high degree of trust are essential to the success of boundaryless organizations. It is neither feasible nor desirable to attempt to control suppliers, customers, or alliance partners in the traditional sense. In the fluid and flexible environments of the new organizational architectures, common cultures, shared values, and carefully aligned incentives are usually easier to implement and are often a more effective means of strategic control than rules, boundaries, and formal procedures.

■ *Horizontal organization structures.* Horizontal organization structures, which group similar or related business units under common management control, facilitate sharing resources and infrastructures, exploit synergies among operating units, and help to create a sense of common purpose. Consistency in training and the development of similar structures across business units facilitates job rotation and cross training and clarifies the understanding of common problems and opportunities. Cross-functional teams and interdivisional committees and task groups represent important opportunities to improve understanding and foster cooperation among operating units. Service strategies based on the smallest replicable unit are perhaps the ultimate expression of horizontal structure. These strategies often achieve extraordinary levels of quality, flexibility, and customer service, while maximizing efficiency through shared infrastructures and the leveraging of organizational experience and learning.

■ *Horizontal systems and processes.* Organizational systems, policies, and procedures are the traditional mechanisms for achieving integration among functional units. Too often, however, existing policies and procedures do little more than institutionalize the barriers that exist from years of managing within the framework of the traditional model. The popular concept of business reengineering focuses primarily on these internal processes and procedures. Beginning with an understanding of basic business processes in the context of "a collection of activities that takes one or more kinds of input and creates an output that is of value to the customer," Michael Hammer and James Champy's 1993 best-seller, *Reengineering the Corporation*, outlined a methodology for redesigning internal systems and procedures that has been embraced, in its various forms, by many organizations.[22] Proponents claim that successful reengineering lowers costs, reduces inventories, improves quality, speeds response times, and improves organizational flexibility. Others advocate similar benefits through the reduction of cycle times, total quality management, and the like. GE and others have used benchmarking and adopted best practices from leading companies around the world in their efforts to streamline their internal systems and procedures.

■ *Communications and information technologies.* Improved communications through the effective use of information technologies plays an important role in bridging gaps and breaking down barriers between organizations. E-mail and videoconferencing can improve lateral communications across long distances and multiple time zones and, by short-circuiting vertical structures, tend to circumvent many of the barriers of the traditional model. Information technology can be a powerful ally in the redesign and streamlining of internal business processes and in improving coordination and integration between suppliers and customers. Electronic data interchange (EDI) has eliminated the paperwork of purchase order and invoice documentation in many buyer-supplier relationships, enabling cooperating organizations to reduce inventories, shorten delivery cycles, and reduce operating costs. On the other hand, ineffective implementation that uses technology to automate existing processes but without thoughtful redesign often has the opposite result: increasing cost and reducing flexibility. Regardless of the methodology, the basic principles are the same. The key is in the perspective: looking at business processes as a sequence of activities that add value to the ultimate product or service, and then optimizing those processes without regard to organizational boundaries.

■ *Human resources practices.* Change, in structure, process, or procedure, always has an effect on the human dimension of organizations. Training and education of the workforce must be an important part of any effort to improve organizational coordination and integration. As new architectures are implemented, processes are reengineered, and organizations become increasingly dependent on sophisticated information technologies, the skills of workers and managers alike must be upgraded to realize the full benefits. Both the GE and Chrysler examples testify to the value of close labor-management cooperation in realizing operational efficiencies.

The Cellular Organization

A number of leading companies are experimenting with a new way of organizing: the cellular form, built on the principles of entrepreneurship, self-organization, and member ownership. Cellular forms provide a robust method for incorporating an entrepreneurial spirit throughout a large organization. In the future, cellular organizations are likely to be used extensively in situations requiring continuous learning and innovation.[23]

A New Organizational Form for a New Economic Era

Elements of increasing complexity are visible in a growing number of industries. In computer software, for example, there are few limits on potentially profitable product designs, and a vast array of independent designers move in and around software companies of every size. The choices that companies face at both the input and output ends of their operation are many and constantly changing. Faced with these challenges, we expect many twenty-first-century organizations to rely heavily on clusters of self-organizing components collaboratively investing the enterprise's know-how in product and service innovations for markets that they have helped create and develop. Such organizations can best be described as cellular.

The cellular metaphor suggests a living, adaptive organization. Cells in living organisms possess fundamental functions of life and can act alone to meet a particular need. However, by acting in concert, cells can perform more complex functions. Evolving characteristics, or learning, if shared across all cells, can create a higher-order organism. Similarly, a cellular organization is made up of cells (self-managing teams, autonomous business units, etc.) that can operate alone, but often interact with other cells to produce a more potent and competent business mechanism. It is this combination of independence and interdependence that allows the cellular organization to generate and share the knowledge, expertise, and know-how that produces continuous innovation.

Building Blocks of the Cellular Form

In the future, complete cellular firms will achieve a level of know-how well beyond that of earlier organizational forms by combining entrepreneurship, self-organization, and member ownership in mutually reinforcing ways. Each cell (team, strategic business unit, firm) will have an entrepreneurial responsibility to the larger organization. The customers of a particular cell can be outside clients or other cells in the organization. In either case, the purpose is to spread an entrepreneurial mind-set throughout the organization so that every cell is concerned with improvement and growth. Indeed, giving each cell entrepreneurial responsibility is essential to the full utilization of the company's constantly growing know-how. Each cell must also have the entrepreneurial skills required to generate business for itself and the overall organization.

Each cell must be able to continually reorganize in order to make its expected contribution to the overall organization. Of particular value here are the technical skills needed to perform its function, the collaborative skills necessary to make appropriate linkages with other organizational units and external partner firms, and the governance skills required to manage its own activities. Application of this cellular principle may require the company to strip away most of the bureaucracy in place, replacing it with jointly defined protocols that guide internal and external collaboration.

Each cell must be rewarded for acting entrepreneurially and operating in a business-like manner. If the cellular units are teams or strategic business units instead of complete companies, psychological ownership can be achieved by organizing cells as profit centers, allowing them to participate in company stock purchase plans, for example. However, the ultimate cellular solution is probably actual member ownership of those cell assets and resources that they have created and that they voluntarily invest with the organization in expectation of a joint return.

Acer: A Global Cellular Company

Examples of cellular organizations, in which the individual cellular principles and their interconnectedness are clearly seen, are rather rare. The Acer Group, a rapidly growing personal computer company, is a significant user of cellular principles on a global scale and is one of the largest companies to apply this form of organization. In less than ten years, it has grown from less than $500 million in sales (nearly all in Taiwan) to over $8 billion in 1996 worldwide sales, including a $5 billion share of the U.S. computer market.

> The cellular organization form is evident at the Acer Group, where cofounder Stan Shih has created a vision of a global personal computer company. Shih's design calls for a federation of self-managing companies held together by mutual interest rather than hierarchical control. Shih's driving slogan is "21 in 21": a federation of at least twenty-one independent companies located around the world by the twenty-first century, each operating in what Shih calls a "client-server" mode.

That is, each organization, depending on the type of transaction, is either a client or a server of the other organizations in the federation. Some companies, called regional business units (RBUs), are operated primarily as marketing organizations—advertising, selling, and servicing computers according to particular national or regional needs. Others, called strategic business units (SBUs), are primarily R&D, manufacturing, and distribution units. For the most part, RBUs are clients that receive products from servers, the SBUs. However, RBUs are regularly required to submit short-, medium-, and long-term forecasts of their product needs. In this mode, the SBUs are the clients of the RBUs—depending on each RBU's knowledge of its local market to provide information that will drive product development and manufacturing.

Although each company has a core task to perform, new product concepts can and do originate anywhere in the federation. For example, Acer America (an RBU) wanted a stylish yet affordable PC for the North American market. It contracted with Frog Design, an independent industrial design firm, to assist it in the development of the highly acclaimed Acer Aspire. Manufacturing was performed by an Acer SBU; the marketing campaign was jointly developed by Acer America and Acer International, another RBU based in Singapore. Other Acer units are free to borrow from the Aspire design or to create unique designs suited to their respective markets. Every new product proposal is evaluated as a business venture by the federation's partners. And they are evaluated quickly: Shih's vision of the computer industry employs ten-month product life cycles: three months to develop the product, six months to sell it, and one month to close it out and prepare for the next cycle. For CD-ROM drives, Acer's product life cycle is closer to ten weeks. This short time frame creates a sense of urgency for the RBUs to generate new business. As an example, Acer introduced its own version of an internet box, which gives users internet access without the use of a computer, and has other internet-related products under development.

Shih's vision for the Acer federation appears to go one step beyond that of most other cellular companies by reinforcing both the responsibility of the individual company for its own destiny and the responsibility of all companies for the long-term success of the total organization. At Acer, each company is jointly owned by its own management and home country investors, with a (usually) minority ownership position held by Acer, Inc., the parent. Shih intends that Acer companies around the world will be listed on local stock exchanges and be free to seek capital for their own expansion. He believes that local ownership unleashes the motivation to run each business prudently.

With all Acer companies enjoying the freedom to operate and expand, the value of their membership in the federation is the capacity of the cells to continue to serve one another in an increasingly competitive global marketplace. Acer has developed the competence to produce all its products efficiently for just-in-time assembly and distribution. With minimal inventories, the latest models are available at all times at every sales site. To reduce inventory, Acer maintains thirty distinct manufacturing sites worldwide, allowing them to partner with local firms more easily, reducing the problem of lost sales from stock-outs.

Acer's business model provides the opportunity for each company to draw on federation partners as preferred providers or clients. Currently, Acer's worldwide training programs are being used to translate Shih's global vision into action programs at the local level. Part of their job is to convince their local suppliers they are not in the PC design or manufacturing business, but in the channel and logistics business. Design and manufacturing have to be geared toward reducing the distribution costs.

Adding Value by Using the Cellular Form

A close examination of cellularly structured businesses such as Acer indicates that they also share some of the features of earlier organizational forms. Indeed, each new form incorporates the major value-adding characteristics of the previous forms and adds new capabilities to them. Thus, the cellular form includes the dispersed entrepreneurship of the divisional form, customer responsiveness of the matrix form, and self-organizing knowledge and asset sharing of the network form.

The cellular organizational form, however, offers the potential to add value even beyond asset and know-how sharing. In its fully developed state, it adds value through its unique ability to create and use knowledge. For example, knowledge sharing occurs in networks as a by-product of asset sharing rather than as a specific focus of such activity. Similarly, matrix and divisionalized companies recognize the value that may be added when knowledge is shared across projects or divisions, but they must create special-purpose mechanisms (e.g., task forces) in order to generate and share new knowledge. By contrast, the cellular form lends itself to sharing not only the explicit know-how that cells have accumulated and articulated, but also the tacit know-how that emerges when cells combine to design unique new customer solutions. Such learning focuses not on the output of the innovation process, but on the innovation process itself. It is know-how that can be achieved and shared only by doing.

Beyond knowledge creation and sharing, the cellular form has the potential to add value through its related ability to keep the organization's total knowledge assets more fully invested than do the other organizational forms. Because each cell has entrepreneurial responsibility and is empowered to draw on any of the company's assets for each new business opportunity, high levels of knowledge utilization across cells should be expected. Network organizations aspire to high utilization of know-how and assets, but upstream companies are ultimately dependent on downstream partners to find new product or service uses. In the cellular organization, the product-service innovation process is continual and fully shared. The sharing isn't merely internal but extends beyond the organization boundaries to include partners, collaborators, and suppliers. As an example, Acer's manufacturing strategy involves producing a greater percentage of components than do most of its competitors. With localized assembly in most of its markets, Acer is able to reduce its suppliers' inventory requirements while still maintaining high efficiency. This contrasts with Dell computer, also a highly efficient manufacturer. Dell's extremely low inventory levels result directly from its requirement for suppliers to maintain higher inventory levels. Acer's model lowers the investment and production costs of its suppliers, which lowers its cost of producing goods to the final consumer. It allows its partners to earn a profit and motivates them to act entrepreneurially as well. Everyone wins.

A Checklist:
Designing High Performance Organizations

Concerning the Barrier-Free Organization

☐ Does the organization effectively eliminate cumbersome aspects of bureaucracy?

☐ Are horizontal and vertical boundaries permeable within the organization?

☐ Are boundaries with key external stakeholders (e.g., suppliers, customers, governmental entities) permeable?

☐ Is there a strong sense of shared mission across functions, divisions, and strategic business units?

☐ Are teams used effectively across the organization? Is teamwork encouraged and outputs rewarded?

☐ Is technology used to strengthen collaborative efforts both within the organization as well as with external constituencies?

Concerning the Modular Organization

☐ Are the organization's human and capital resources directed toward its most critical activities?

☐ Are the organization's core competencies effectively leveraged through outsourcing activities, while its capital requirements are lessened?

☐ Is the organization able to focus on strategic threats and opportunities more effectively as a result of its outsourcing activities?

☐ Is the organization constantly aware of the need to avoid the outsourcing of critical technology or other capabilities that might erode its competitiveness?

☐ Is there a healthy disrespect for the NIH ("Not Invented Here") factor?

Concerning the Virtual Organization

☐ Does the participation in networks of organizations enable the company to:
  ■ Share resources (capital, human, physical)?
  ■ Effectively leverage core skills and capabilities?
  ■ React quickly to competitive threats and opportunities?
  ■ Learn new capabilities and core skills?
  ■ Avoid a loss of operational control?
  ■ Strengthen its access to global markets?
  ■ Avoid a loss of control over key technologies?

Concerning Tools and Techniques for Coordination and Integration

☐ Does everyone understand the goals and objectives? Do they buy into them?

☐ Has the company made the best use of horizontal structures?

☐ Do the company's systems, policies, and procedures support its objectives, or do they get in the way and slow its progress?

☐ Does the company's information infrastructure facilitate cross-functional communications?

☐ Are the right skills in place? Has the right training been provided to ensure that the workforce has the skills to do the job?

☐ Are all tools and techniques working together—or are they competing with each other?

Notes

1. K. Otani, "GE: A Strong Company," *Nikkei Business*, February 21, 1994, p. 11. The discussion of organizational forms is based, in part, on G. G. Dess, A. M. A. Rasheed, K. J. McLaughlin, and R. L. Priem, "The New Corporate Architecture," *Academy of Management Executive* 9(3) (1995): 7–20.

2. G. Pinchot, "Creating Organizations With Many Leaders," in F. Hesselbein, M. Goldsmith, and R. Beckhard (eds.), *The Leader of the Future* (San Francisco: Jossey-Bass, 1996), pp. 30–32.

3. The Oticon case is based on a variety of sources, including: R. Patterson, "Hearing Aids Lifted to a Sharper Level by New Technologies; Digital Devices, While Tiny, Have Power Comparable to a Laptop Computer's," *The Wall Street Journal*, May 12, 1997, p. A1; D. Dearlove, "The Man Who Caused Chaos," *The Times*, May 7, 1998, p. F1; H. Miller, "Hitting the Gas on Organizational Change: Companies Must Be Willing to Shed Old Habits to Survive," *San Jose Business Journal*, March 16, 1998, p. 19; and S. Course, "Paperless Pays Off," *Auckland Sunday News*, October 12, 1997, p. 27.

4. J. Pfeffer, *The Human Equation: Building Profits by Putting People First* (Boston: Harvard Business School Press, 1998).

5. See, for example, R. E. Hoskisson, C. W. L. Hill, and H. Kim, "The Multidivisional Structure: Organizational Fossil or Source of Value?" *Journal of Management* 19(2) (1993): 269–298. For a discussion of the need to consider carefully the linkages between an organization's value chain activities and those of its suppliers and customers, refer to B. C. Reimann, "Sustaining Competitive Advantage," *Planning Review* (March–April 1989): 30–39; T. Peters, *Liberation Management* (New York: Knopf, 1992); "Tearing Down Corporate Walls," *Industry Week*, April 18, 1998, pp. 35–39; and J. A. Byrne, "The Horizontal Corporation," *Business Week*, December 20, 1993, pp. 76–81. The examples in this section draw on various sources, including D. Woodruff and K. L. Miller," Chrysler's Neon: Is This the Small Car Detroit Couldn't Build?" *Business Week*, May 3, 1993: 116–126; G. Imperato, "Harley Shifts Gears," *Fast Company* (June–July 1997): 104–113; L. R. Quinn, "Harley-Davidson Integrates Its Distribution," *American Shipper* 34(5) (May 1992): 16; and M. J. Stark, W. Luther, and S. Valvano, "Jaguar Cars Drives Toward Competency-Based Pay," *Compensation and Benefits Review*, November 21, 1996, p. 34.

6. C. Barnes, "A Fatal Case," *Fast Company* (February–March 1998): 173.

7. J. C. Henderson and N. Venkatraman, "Strategic Alignment: Leveraging Information Technology for Transforming Organizations," *IBM Systems Journal* 32 (1993): 4–16.

8. David Pottruck, speech at the Retail Leadership Meeting, San Francisco, January 30, 1997.

9. The examples that follow are based on: "Managing Diversity in the Workplace," *Vision:* 2 (July 1997) (UPS internal company publication); E. Miezkowski, "Opposites Attract," *Fast Company* (December–January 1998): 42, 44; A. Muoio (ed.), "They Have a Better Idea . . . Do You?" *Fast Company* (August–September 1997): 73; and D. Leonard and S. Straus, "Putting Your Company's Whole Brain to Work," *Harvard Business Review* 75(4) (July–August 1997): 110–121.

10. This section draws on C. Handy, *The Age of Unreason* (Boston: Harvard Business School Press, 1989); S. Tully, "The Modular Corporation," *Fortune,* February 8, 1993, p. 196; E. Ramstead, "APC Maker's Low-Tech Formula: Start With the Box," *The Wall Street Journal,* December 29, 1997, p. B1; W. Mussberg, "Thin Screen PCs Are Looking Good but Still Fall Flat," *The Wall Street Journal,* January 2, 1997, p. 9; E. Brown, "Monorail: Low Cost PCs," *Fortune,* July 7, 1997, pp. 106–108; and M. Young, "Ex-Compaq Executives Start New Company," *Computer Reseller News,* November 11, 1996, p. 181.

11. J. Magretta, "The Power of Virtual Integration: An Interview With Dell Computer's Michael Dell," *Harvard Business Review* 76(2) (March–April 1998): 75.

12. Interesting examples of successful outsourcing efforts include G. Anthes, "HUD, Martin Marietta Celebrate Outsourcing Success," *Computerworld,* November 16, 1992, p. 16; T. Guimaraes and S. Wells, "Outsourcing for Novices," *Computerworld,* June 8, 1992, pp. 89–91; and R. Huber, "Continental Outsources Its Crown Jewels," *Harvard Business Review* (January–February 1993): 121–129. Perhaps the seminal contribution to the outsourcing literature is found in J. B. Quinn, *Intelligent Enterprise: A Knowledge and Service Based Paradigm for Industry* (New York: Free Press, 1992).

13. For insightful, recent discussions on the strategic limitations of outsourcing, refer to G. A. Walter and J. Barney, "Management Objectives in Mergers and Acquisitions," *Strategic Management Journal* 11 (1990): 79–86; and R. A. Bettis, S. P. Bradley, and G. Hamel, "Outsourcing and Industrial Decline," *Academy of Management Executive* 6(1) (1992): 7–22. The Schwinn example is based on A. Tanzer, "Bury Thy Teacher," *Forbes,* December 21, 1992, pp. 90–95.

14. See, for example, J. Stuckey and D. White, "When and When Not to Vertically Integrate," *Sloan Management Review* (Spring 1993): 71–81; G. Harrar, "Outsource Tales," *Forbes ASAP,* June 7, 1993, pp. 37–39, 42; E. W. Davis, "Global Outsourcing: Have U.S. Managers Thrown the Baby Out With the Bath Water?" *Business Horizons* (July–August 1992): 58–64; M. Davids, "The Outsourcing Source Book," *Journal of Business Strategy* (May–June 1993): 52–56; R. Venkatesan, "Strategic Sourcing: To Make or Not to Make," *Harvard Business Review* (November–December 1992): 98–107; and Bettis et al., "Outsourcing."

15. The opening three paragraphs draw on R. M. Kanter, "Becoming PALS: Pooling, Allying, and Linking Companies," *Academy of Management Executive* (August 1989): 183. Some authors have used a similar term, *constellational structures,* to refer to organizations that are strongly tied to highly supportive collectives. For an illuminating perspective on how such structures can lead to higher growth and flexibility and lower costs in the Italian textile industry, refer to G. Lorenzoni and O. Ornati, "Constellations of Firms and New Ventures," *Journal of Business Venturing* 3 (1988): 41–57. The quote from N. Augustine is drawn from E. Davis, "Interview: Norman Augustine," *Management Review* (November 1997): 14.

16. See J. Byrne, "The Virtual Corporation," *Business Week,* February 8, 1993, pp. 99–103; and Peters, *Liberation Management,* especially the discussion of McKinsey &

Company (Chapter 10) and network organizations (Chapter 20). The examples that follow are based on several sources, including: J. Sandberg, "Apache's Free Software Gives Bigger Foes Fits," *Austin American Statesman*, March 23, 1998, p. 27; C. Wilde, "Webservers—Apache: Freely Successful—The Net's Web Server Shareware Continues to Gain Popularity," *Information Week*, June 2, 1997, pp. 88–93; M. Moeller, "Fort Apache: Freeware's Spirit Outshines Commercial Products," *PC Week*, June 9, 1997, pp. 1–2; and "Apache Freeware Is the Web Server of Choice," *Government Computer News*, April 14, 1997, p. 52.

17. A. Bartness and K. Cerny, "Building Competitive Advantage Through a Global Network of Capabilities," *California Management Review* (Winter 1993): 78–103. For an insightful historical discussion of the usefulness of alliances in the computer industry, see J. F. Moore, "Predators and Prey: A New Ecology of Competition," *Harvard Business Review* (May–June 1993): 75–86.

18. See P. Lorange and J. Roos, "Why Some Strategic Alliances Succeed and Others Fail," *Journal of Business Strategy* (January–February 1991): 25–30; and G. Slowinski, "The Human Touch in Strategic Alliances," *Mergers and Acquisitions* (July–August 1992): 44–47. A compelling argument for strategic alliances is provided by K. Ohmae, "The Global Logic of Strategic Alliances," *Harvard Business Review* (March–April 1989): 143–154.

19. See R. E. Miles and C. C. Snow, "Organizations: New Concepts for New Forms," *California Management Review* (Spring 1986): 62–73; R. E. Miles and C. C. Snow, "Causes of Failure in Network Organizations," *California Management Review* (Summer 1992): 53–72; and H. Bahrami, "The Emerging Flexible Organization: Perspectives from Silicon Valley," *California Management Review* (Summer 1991): 33–52.

20. See C. Snow, "Twenty-First Century Organizations: Implications for a New Marketing Paradigm," *Journal of the Academy of Marketing Science* (Winter 1997): 72–74, and B. Allred, C. Snow, and R. Miles, "Characteristics of Managerial Careers of the 21st Century," *Academy of Management Executive* (November 1996): 17–27.

21. This section draws on J. C. Picken and G. G. Dess, *Mission Critical: The 7 Strategic Traps That Derail Even the Smartest Companies* (Chicago: Irwin, 1997).

22. Michael Hammer and James Champy. *Reengineering the Corporation: A Manifesto for Business Revolution* (New York, HarperBusiness, 1993).

23. This case study draws on R. Miles, C. Snow, J. Mathews, G. Miles, and H. Coleman, Jr., "Organizing in the Knowledge Age: Anticipating the Cellular Form," *Academy of Management Executive* 11(4) (1997): 7–20 (with permission). Other sources include: A. Tanzer, "Silicon Valley," *Forbes*, June 1, 1998, pp. 122–127; C. Kenji Beer, "Breakthroughs and 'Turnarounds': Habits of an Ex-IBM Executive/Acer President," *Asia Pacific Economic Review*, April 1, 1997, p. B1; and G. Wheelwright, "PC Industry: Race to Cut Costs," *The Financial Times*, October 1, 1997, p. 4.

5

STAYING ON COURSE:
CULTURE, INCENTIVES,
AND BOUNDARIES

Norman R. Augustine, the former chairman of Lockheed Martin and one of America's most respected executives, recently told this interesting—and humorous—story:

> I am reminded of an article I once read in a British newspaper . . . that described a problem with the local bus service between the towns of Bagnall and Greenfields. It seemed that, to the great annoyance of customers, drivers had been passing long queues of would-be passengers with a smile and a wave of the hand. This practice was, however, clarified by a bus company official who explained, "It is impossible for the drivers to keep their timetables if they must stop for passengers."[1]

Augustine's story illustrates the extent to which some organizations will go to stifle employees with rules and boundaries. Here the implicit message is: "Don't worry about anything. Just make the schedule!" Generalizing a bit, phrases that come to mind depicting such a mentality include, "Park your brain at the door!" "We pay you to work, not to think!" And so on. And recall Henry Ford's famous lament: "Why is it that I always get the whole person when what I really want is a pair of hands?"

Culture, incentives, and boundaries (internal controls) are key elements of an organization's structural capital. They are important to leverage because they help align individual goals and organizational objectives, focusing and concentrating human capital resources on the most important tasks and priorities. They also shape employee attitudes and values and influence individual motivation, commitment, and social behavior. An organization that lacks appropriate incentives and controls may fail to concentrate its resources or motivate its employees to share their knowledge and expertise. An overly controlled environment may stifle employees, not permitting them to apply the full range of their capabilities for the benefit of the organization. The challenge for organizations seeking to leverage their human capital resources is to ensure that all of their initiatives and each of the key elements—structures, processes, incentives, controls, and culture—are consistently focused on the same objective, rather than working at cross-purposes. Exhibit 5-1 illustrates the pervasive nature and role of culture, incentives, and boundaries in our framework, which illustrates the opportunities for leveraging human capital resources.

An organization's culture and values can have a significant impact on its ability to attract the kinds of employees it seeks and to retain them over time. A culture that encourages humor and fun, cultivates and reinforces dominant values through storytelling and rituals, and is institutionalized in organizational structures and internalized by

EXHIBIT 5-1.
Leveraging human capital with culture, incentives, and boundaries.

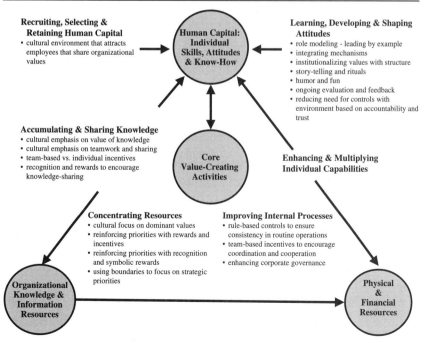

Recruiting, Selecting & Retaining Human Capital
- cultural environment that attracts employees that share organizational values

Human Capital: Individual Skills, Attitudes & Know-How

Learning, Developing & Shaping Attitudes
- role modeling - leading by example
- integrating mechanisms
- institutionalizing values with structure
- story-telling and rituals
- humor and fun
- ongoing evaluation and feedback
- reducing need for controls with environment based on accountability and trust

Accumulating & Sharing Knowledge
- cultural emphasis on value of knowledge
- cultural emphasis on teamwork and sharing
- team-based vs. individual incentives
- recognition and rewards to encourage knowledge-sharing

Core Value-Creating Activities

Enhancing & Multiplying Individual Capabilities

Concentrating Resources
- cultural focus on dominant values
- reinforcing priorities with rewards and incentives
- reinforcing priorities with recognition and symbolic rewards
- using boundaries to focus on strategic priorities

Improving Internal Processes
- rule-based controls to ensure consistency in routine operations
- team-based incentives to encourage coordination and cooperation
- enhancing corporate governance

Organizational Knowledge & Information Resources

Physical & Financial Resources

employees can be a powerful tool for motivating and leveraging human capital resources. Leaders can have a significant influence on this culture through role modeling and in the design and implementation of structures, incentives, and control mechanisms that reinforce the core values and basic objectives of the organization.

Collectively, culture, incentives, and controls that are working in concert can powerfully support management's initiatives: focusing resources on top organizational priorities, improving the efficiency and effectiveness of internal processes, and encouraging the widespread sharing and dissemination of individual and organizational knowledge. On the other hand, these elements of structural capital may also represent significant barriers to the successful implementation of leverage initiatives.

Organizations wanting to leverage human capital must go far beyond the days of the 1950s and 1960s (and earlier) when machine-like bureaucracies were the norm.[2] Then, managers exercised control by telling people how to do their jobs and closely monitoring them to ensure compliance. The goal was to minimize idiosyncratic behavior. After all, unintended consequences were anathema to the efficient functioning of organizations. However, stringent controls may lead to unanticipated, and often dysfunctional, outcomes. An overemphasis on task specialization, standardization, and rigid controls tended to stifle creativity, minimize organizational flexibility, and breed resentment. After all, affected employees would think, "If I am told exactly what to do, why try to improve things, work harder than I have to, or worry about the customers?" Further, legions of middle managers and direct supervisors were required to implement a system geared toward monitoring and control.

One of us recalls how dense the red tape was while he was working as an entry-level engineer at a large telecommunications company. Changing the schedule of reimbursement for his M.B.A. tuition expenses required three levels of management and thirteen separate sign-offs as the paperwork made its way up and down the engineering and administration hierarchies. The amount in question: about $50!

Most contemporary organizations can no longer afford such overhead costs and resultant inflexibility. Today's global competitive environment is far more unpredictable, complex, and interconnected and requires different approaches to control. As indicated in Exhibit 5-2, effective strategic control requires using and balancing three separate but highly interdependent elements: culture, rewards, and boundaries.

In this chapter, we urge leaders to keep in mind two guiding prin-

EXHIBIT 5-2.
Three interdependent elements of control.

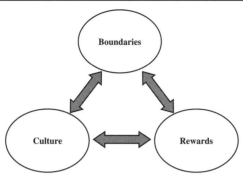

ciples. The first is to maintain a balance among the three elements. If there are inconsistencies, the elements work at cross-purposes. For example, companies will be unable to foster a culture of innovation and risk taking if tangible rewards are absent and red tape, in the form of rules and regulations, constrains behavior. Second, most successful organizations minimize the need for explicit (and cumbersome) rules, regulations, and other boundaries by internalizing the organization's goals and objectives in employees at all levels, developing sound cultures, and designing effective reward systems. However, boundaries can't be ignored; they do have their place.

Using Culture to Leverage Human Capital

Organization culture has a pervasive influence on what goes on inside organizations and how they perform. Culture can best be defined as the system of shared values (what is important) and beliefs (how things work) that shape a company's people, organizational structures, and control systems to produce behavioral norms (the way we do things around here). Culture's influence is directed largely toward the values, beliefs, and attitudes of the individual employee and on establishing norms for work ethic and social behavior. Effective leaders recognize its importance and constantly work to shape and use it as perhaps their most important lever of strategic control. As the CEO of a consumer products company told us, "CEO means Chief Evangelical Officer!" And over the past several years, numerous books about the importance of organizational culture have become best-sellers, among them *Theory Z, Corporate Cultures, In Search of Excellence, A Passion for Excellence,* and *Built to Last.*

Built to Last highlights the importance of culture to organizational success. Eighteen star performers, all founded prior to 1950, were compared to a control group of eighteen similar companies that had not done as well (e.g., Procter & Gamble versus Colgate, Citibank versus Chase Manhattan). Between 1926 and 1990, the stock value of the eighteen top performers increased fifteen times more than the general market. The stocks of the control companies improved only twice as much as the general market. Although the authors identified eight factors to explain the differences (promotion of insiders, predisposition to experimentation, etc.), the key factor was culture.

The authors concluded that cultlike cultures serve to create an environment where all employees share such a strong vision that they know in their hearts what is best for the company. Examples include Hewlett-Packard whose employees "know" that changes in the company's culture, operating practices, and business practices will not mean losing the spirit of what has been dubbed the "HP Way." And although Johnson & Johnson continually questions its structure and changes its processes, it preserves its credo. As Ralph S. Larsen, CEO, explains, "The core values embodied in our credo might be a competitive advantage, but that's not why we have them. We have them because they define what we stand for, and we would hold on to them even if they became a competitive disadvantage."[3]

Culture, as a key element of structural capital, can facilitate or impede efforts to leverage an organization's human capital resources. Culture works most effectively to influence the "soft side" of the employee's bundle of skills and capabilities—his or her social skills, values, beliefs, and attitudes (see Exhibit 1-3 in Chapter 1)—and to focus efforts on the organization's top priorities. The influence is pervasive, because values, beliefs, and attitudes affect everything an employee thinks, says, and does. Culture also plays an important role in motivating employees to share their knowledge and to use skills and capabilities fully in the performance of the assigned tasks. An open culture—one that trusts employees and values them as individuals, encourages the widespread sharing of information, cultivates teamwork, and promotes a strong and positive commitment to the goals and values of the organization—will contribute positively. A culture that rewards individualism rather than collective accomplishment, focuses on the numbers more than on people, and relies more on controls than on trust will, in most environments, work at cross purposes to the organization's efforts to leverage its human capital resources.

Successful leaders instill distinctive cultures that pervade their organization. In practice, the basic set of values a company develops is influenced by a variety of factors, including its products, the nature of its competition, the kinds of customers it seeks, and the technology it employs. Most successful organizations are strongly oriented toward a single dominant value that becomes, in a sense, the root of their competitive advantage—for example:[4]

■ FedEx's commitment is to customer service, reinforced by two straightforward and ambitious quality goals: 100 percent customer satisfaction after every interaction and 100 percent service performance on every package handled.

■ 3M's quest is for innovation, reinforced by policies designed to help the company regularly achieve its corporate-wide "30 percent" rule. This rule requires each division to produce 30 percent of its sales from products developed within the most recent four-year period. (Incidentally, this figure is far more aggressive than the earlier "25 percent/ five year" criterion.) And for 1998, a new criterion was introduced: 10 percent of sales for the year must be from products developed in the current year.

■ Wal-Mart seeks to dominate the mass merchandise industry by emphasizing efficiency. Central to this strategy are its highly successful cross-docking strategy and its emphasis on logistics and information systems that have redefined the nature of competition in its segment of the retail industry.

For most leaders, understanding their company's culture is at best an imperfect science. Actually inculcating and sustaining meaningful core values throughout the organization becomes even more of an art. There are no simple prescriptions. We believe, however, that two components underlie the broad concept of organization culture: *sociability,* an indicator of sincere friendliness among members of the organization, and *solidarity,* a measure of the organization's ability to pursue shared objectives quickly and effectively, regardless of personal relationships.[5] (Goffee and Jones point out some potential dysfunctions of each component of culture taken to an extreme. For example, excessive sociability may lead to a lack of "objective" criteria for personnel and other company decisions, the overreliance on informal networks, and dominance of personal agendas. Too much solidarity, on the other hand, may result in less cooperation and sharing of ideas as well as a minimization of the exchange of creativity.)

These two components provide useful benchmarks that managers can consider in assessing their culture. Taken together, they underlie the extent of social processes that serve to, among other things, facilitate interactions; promote give and take; lower the need for rules, regulations, and other governance mechanisms; promote sharing of information; enhance flexibility; and "pull" (versus "push") all organizational members toward common goals and objectives.

Six mechanisms can serve to strengthen both the sociability and solidarity of an organization's culture: (1) role modeling, (2) integrating mechanisms, (3) structural elements, (4) storytelling and rituals, (5) humor and fun, and (6) ongoing evaluation and feedback. The effects of these elements can be multiplicative; the strengthening of culture can be multiplied by stronger friendliness and sharing of common goals through the effective use of the mechanisms. For example, serving on Southwest Airlines Culture Committee or attending Unilever's international training center should not only promote social ties, attraction, and friendliness but also develop a shared understanding and reinforcement of common goals and objectives.

Developing and nurturing a culture is clearly not akin to tending a plant nursery.[6] There, one prepares the soil, plants the seeds, occasionally adds water, and watches Mother Nature work her magic with the flora. Leaders work with no superior entity—no Mother Nature. Successful cultures must be continually nurtured, evaluated, and reinforced, not left to chance. Nike's motto applies: "There is no finish line."

Role Modeling

Successful leaders "walk the talk" and provide a role model for the rest of the organization.[7] Few articulate this better than Percy Barnevik, one of the world's most admired global leaders. He is now head of Investor, a holding company that includes in its portfolio Asea Brown Boveri (where he was recently chairman and CEO):

> There are many different ways we can do that. I would say that the most important thing of all, overshadowing everything else, is to live that way yourself. If you say people development is important, and then don't develop your own people, you lose credibility. If you talk about speed in action and you procrastinate on certain difficult decisions, you are

not believable. So I think that I and the members of the executive committee, and further down, must "walk the talk." That's the single most important thing. We must always check that we are living up to what we say.

John Correnti, recently named CEO of Nucor, also fosters the esprit de corps and openness of his company's culture through his actions. To combat the evils of bureaucracy and insulated and distant top-level managers, he insists on visiting every plant at least twice a year to "shake everyone's hand and shoot the breeze. I want them to know if they have a problem, they can pick up the phone or write a letter and communicate with someone who is not a nameless, faceless stranger who's pulling the strings."

We can attest to Nucor's accessibility, having called Nucor's home office four times over the past few years and spoken directly with the CEO on each occasion—three times with Ken Iverson and, most recently, with John Correnti. Nucor's management has also "walked the talk" on the core value of egalitarianism. In addition to spartan facilities and virtually no executive perks, management more than "shares the pain" during the difficult times inherent in the cyclical steel industry. In 1982, for example, Nucor survived a severe downturn without laying off a single employee. According to former CEO Iverson, "In a downturn, hourly workers may earn 20 to 25 percent less than in good times. Department heads earn 30 to 45 percent less, while compensation to corporate officers may drop as much as 60 to 70 percent. I think in 1980 I earned $430,000. In 1982, I earned $108,000."

Similarly, during a recent interview, Vince Prothro, CEO of Dallas Semiconductor, mentioned several symbolic and substantive measures taken to drive home his company's focus on frugality, cost control, and "profit culture." These measures include just three secretaries for the entire corporation (he has only one-third of one's time), no car phones, and a "corporate obesity checklist." He also asked us how much we thought the company spent for decoration of the new 55,000-square-foot headquarters facility. The answer: $1,000, consisting mostly of prints that were inexpensively framed by a local company. Symbolic gestures are also inherent in how the CEO of a large construction company told us he builds esprit de corps: "Once a month I put on jeans and do the dirtiest job on the construction project."

Core values of openness and egalitarianism are vital in organizations where teamwork, a strong work ethic, productivity, and the sharing of ideas are vital to success. Not only do such values contribute to personal relationships and trust, but they also inculcate the sharing and acceptance of organization-wide goals.

Andy Grove, Intel's chairman, also sets the tone for his organization's culture. Like all other top executives, Grove has a cubicle, not a private office. And when they travel, Intel executives fly coach class and rent what are jokingly referred to as "Intel limousines": Ford Escorts.

The role of top executives as role models becomes even more vital during periods of organizational transformations. David Kearns, CEO of Xerox, consistently "walked the talk" as he made quality the new dominant value of his company during its remarkable turnaround in the 1980s. His consistency in words, actions, and strategies during the implementation of "Leadership Through Quality" sent a steady message to every employee.

Top executives also set the tone for diligence, long hours, and hard work. Consider Bill Gates, CEO of Microsoft, and America's richest citizen, with an astonishing estimated net worth of $70 billion in late 1998. He claims he doesn't work as hard as he used to; still, "Most days I don't work more than 12 hours. On weekends I rarely work more than 8 hours. There are weekends I take off and I take vacations."

Finally, consider the leader's role in providing straightforward and honest communication with employees. Lew Platt, CEO of Hewlett-Packard, observes:

> It's obvious that a lot of [employees] haven't been communicated with very frankly. They haven't been told the real story; somebody has sugar-coated the bad news or somebody has fed them a line of b.s. because they didn't think employees could understand or accept the truth. Our people really want us to be truthful with them, and I think truth in communications is something we need to emphasize.

Integrating Mechanisms

Integrating mechanisms are processes designed to foster collaboration, share ideas, promote empathy, and facilitate communication across and up and down organizational levels. They come in an almost infinite range of shapes and sizes. We have already described the role of integrating mechanisms in ensuring effective coordination and control across organizational boundaries. Integrating mechanisms also play an important role in keeping all employees on the same page of the playbook and focused on the same goals. An example at the small, informal end is the "All-Hands Meetings" that take place each Tuesday at Mirimba, a forty-person software start-up founded in 1996 in the Silicon Valley. There are no real protocols; everybody can speak up, and Kim Polese, the founder, typically provides a status report and addresses staffing, a vital issue given the company's rapid growth. The overarching goal is to keep employees focused on the goal of outpacing the pack of push technology competitors. Cleverly, the meeting starts at 11 a.m. so everyone can get together at lunch and address issues that were cut off during "All Hands."[8]

At the other end of the continuum are more sophisticated (and expensive) processes at large, global competitors. Unilever, for example, goes to great lengths to ensure its values of cooperation and consensus. At Four Acres, the company's international training center outside London, hundreds of executives a year participate in activities rich in social rituals, including multicourse dinners, group photographs, sports on the lawn, and a bar that never closes. According to chairman Floris Maljers, "This shared experience creates an informal network of equals who know one another well and continue to meet and exchange perspectives." Additionally, social ties are reinforced through annual conferences attended by the company's top five hundred managers. Young managers are transferred frequently—across borders, products, and divisions—to broaden their perspective and develop a strong network of colleagues.

Structural Elements

Here, the focus is on the formation of committees, task forces, and integrators to amplify and transmit the culture of the organization. Southwest Airlines' Culture Committee—now with a local committee in all fifty cities the airline serves—is a unique vehicle whose purpose is to perpetuate the company's noteworthy culture. Congratulations to all committee members as well as the committees' objectives were included in a recent internal company publication, *Luv Lines*:

> Congratulations to the Southwest "family" members who were chosen to serve on this year's 1997 Culture Committee. They have committed to reach out to their Fellow Coworkers; our mutual, valued Customers; and our Company at large and spread our undying Southwest Spirit coast-to-

coast. There is now a local Culture Committee in every Southwest city, so keep your eyes open while you're in the air and on the ground for the special touches they may be adding to your Station/Location. The Culture Committee is here to support you!

The Culture Committee's Mission Statement is, "to help create the SOUTHWEST SPIRIT and Culture where needed; to enrich it and make it better where it already exists; and to liven it up in places where it might be "floundering." In short, this group's goal is to do "WHATEVER IT TAKES" to create, enhance, and enrich the special SOUTHWEST SPIRIT and Culture that has made this such a wonderful Company/ Family.[9]

Tandem Computers (recently acquired by Compaq Computer) has a special group of employees responsible for overseeing the corporate culture. Called the Philosophy Group, they report directly to the vice president of human resources. The group works with employee focus groups to help ascertain the values of the company, as well as to solicit suggestions regarding employee perspectives on company values.

In addition to groups of employees involved in perpetuating a culture, individuals may have official job titles and responsibilities designed to achieve the same end. Courtney Dickinson is the "culture team leader" for Sapient Corporation, a fast-growing $44 million systems integrator based in Cambridge, Massachusetts. She contends that the team is focused on helping newly hired employees succeed faster through an understanding of the company's core values. These values are illustrated with a compass: client-focused delivery is at the center; client relationships are the North Star; and pioneering, growth, and openness are on the East, West, and South, respectively. Regarding her biggest challenge, she says, "People think they have all the answers and that 'culture' is ridiculous. The challenge is to get them to try something new." Another innovative job title is that of Mona Cabler, "Director of Fun" for Sprint Paranet, a Houston-based network services company. In addition to helping employees achieve their personal goals, her challenge is to instill loyalty and create a supportive culture in an organization where at any one time 90 percent of the employees are off-site with clients. She believes that having a Director of Fun is a great recruiting tool for her rapidly growing company.

Storytelling and Rituals

In his seminal book, *Leadership is an Art*, CEO Max DePree (now retired) of Herman Miller, Inc., the office furniture maker based in Zeeland, Michigan, articulated some of the warning signs of a company in decline. Among them are not taking enough time for rituals such as retirement and holiday parties and people failing to tell or to understand historic company anecdotes—what he called "tribal stories." Such mechanisms serve to bond people to the organization, infuse commitment and enthusiasm, and, most important, reinforce core values.

Annual reports, company publications, and speeches by top executives provide a means to relate incidents in the company's past that dramatically illustrate the dedication of employees to the company's core values.[10] For example, Roadway Express includes letters from customers that exemplify outstanding customer service in its quarterly inhouse publication, *Spotlight Magazine*. Such information not only serves to role-model excellent behavior but also drives home the company's commitment to service excellence. Consider a few typical letters published in the Third Quarter 1997 issue:

> My company needed a shipment expedited to one of our latest customers. Greg Brown, terminal operations manager, Nashville, Tenn., reacted quickly and professionally and made the delivery happen. It's not just the fact that the delivery was made, but Greg's effort and responsiveness was above and beyond what I expected. *Dublin, Ohio*

> While unloading my shipment Mike Lowry, combination driver, Ft. Collins, Colorado, realized there was a discrepancy with the weight on the freight bill. Mike took charge of an investigation that resulted in a $300.00 reduction of our charge. With the help of Ron Quass, terminal manager, and Bart Glateher, dispatcher, my company received reimbursement. I greatly appreciate their attention to my company's plight. *Ft. Collins, Colorado*

Next, consider an excerpt from a recent speech by William Coyne, 3M's senior vice president for research and development. Here he powerfully illustrates the value of 3M's "15 percent rule": all technical employees can devote 15 percent of their time to a project of their own invention:

> We want to institutionalize a bit of rebellion in our labs. We can't have all our people off totally on their own . . . we do

believe in discipline . . . but at the same time 3M management encourages a healthy disrespect for 3M management. This is not the sort of thing we publicize in our annual report, but the stories we tell—with relish—are frequently about 3Mers who have circumvented their supervisors and succeeded.

One of the boldest of these incidents concerns a young researcher named Lew Lehr. Lehr was a key developer of 3M's first surgical drapes, and he remained convinced of their potential even when they faltered initially in the marketplace. And he remained convinced even after his superiors told him that they were tired of losing money on the product and wanted to drop it. Lehr agreed to kill the project just as soon as the inventory was used up. But in the spirit of Dick Drew (an earlier 3M innovator), he neglected to tell the factory until he'd built up a substantial inventory. And while that inventory was being used up, he finagled a contract from the U.S. military—a key account that 3M wanted to keep happy. The company didn't want to renege on the contract, so production started up again.

Eventually, the product took hold and became both a solid performer and the first in a long line of health care products—a $2 billion business for 3M today. And Lew Lehr was not punished for his persistence. To the contrary, he worked his way up through the ranks and eventually became Chairman of the Board.

James Ericson, CEO of Northwestern Mutual Life Insurance, uses stories effectively to illustrate his company's traditions, emphasis on communication and education, and thriftiness. Consider this excerpt from a recent speech:

Most companies reward agents by whisking them away to far-flung resorts. To say we don't is an understatement. For more than a hundred years, we've held our annual meeting each summer in Milwaukee. Agents bring their families, and even pay their own way. That's right. I said they pay their own way to Milwaukee, Wisconsin! More than 9,000 agents and family members attended the meeting last July. They enjoyed a number of social events, but education and communication was the main focus of the meeting, as it always is. We call it unique and it is. But our industry colleagues probably just call us cheap. I remember talking to a woman at an industry meeting. She was telling me where her company takes their agents, at company expense: Spain, Italy, the Bahamas. An acquaintance of mine overheard and said "Jim, tell her where you take Northwestern agents." So I said, "The Milwaukee Zoo" because that's where we hold our opening party. As she stood there speechless I added, "but we only make them pay for half of their food and drink." I don't think I made a convert to our values and traditions.

Humor aside, whose agents would you guess are the highest paid in the industry and which company has led the industry every year in *Fortune*'s annual "Most Admired" surveys?

Rituals can also play a key role in reinforcing a company's culture by inculcating shared values, goals, and objectives as well as by encouraging friendliness and sociability among all employees. In a way, rituals may be viewed as social bonding activities. Rallies or pep talks by top executives can also be very effective. Recall the late Sam Walton, who was well known for his pep rallies at local Wal-Mart stores. Similarly, four times a year, the founders of Home Depot, CEO Bernard Marcus and President Arthur Blank, don their orange aprons and stage "Breakfast with Bernie and Arthur," a 6:30 A.M. pep rally broadcast live over the company's closed-circuit TV network to most of its 45,000 employees.

Humor and Fun

Levity and humor can contribute to social relationships and help relieve stress for companies competing in hotly contested industries. CEO Scott McNealy has been effective in building a corporate culture based on his motto, "Kick butt and have fun," at Sun Microsystems' Mountain View, California, headquarters. Sun has become equally famous for its juvenile antics around its headquarters as well as its aggressive marketing. Each April Fool's Day, scores of photographers arrive to record the elaborate pranks Sun engineers play on executives, including McNealy. Once they built a golf course hole in McNealy's office, complete with green and water hazard. McNealy also gets directly involved in the high jinks. He has, for example, played general in an intramural squirt gun war. Such humor has an important effect. According to Thomas J. Meredith, a former Sun treasurer, "His humor and ability to raise a crowd to its feet is in many respects exactly what you need in CEOs and leaders of today's industry." And Carol A. Bartz, CEO of Autodesk Inc. (and a former Sun sales vice president), feels that McNealy's special gift is his ability to energize his workforce: "Energy comes right out of his pores."

Humor also makes it over to the other coast. At Cognex, a Boston software company, former MIT professor and CEO Robert Shillman does a Three Stooges routine to welcome new employees. Dr. Bob, as he is known, has used dozens of stunts to motivate his troops. For example, he leads his employees, known as "Cognoids," in a corporate anthem accompanied by an employee rock band. Few could argue that his antics aren't working. Starting from $100,000 of his life savings sixteen years ago, Cognex has $131 million in sales and ranked Number 52 in a recent *Fortune* survey of America's fastest-growing companies. Clearly, fun has its place in leading-edge organizations. In the words of Virgin's Group founder and CEO, Richard Branson:

> I think fun should be a motivator for all businesses. I think the reason we've been successful is that we've had this great bunch of people around. We've done things differently and that's made life more fun and enjoyable than if we'd taken a slightly more conservative approach. I've been determined to have a good time.

Ongoing Evaluation and Feedback

In addition to informal evaluations of company culture by executives through MBWA (management by walking around), on-site visits of facilities, genuine two-way communication across as well as up and down the hierarchy, many leading-edge companies conduct formal evaluations. Without such mechanisms, top management may fall into the trap of attending to highly filtered information, seeing only what they want to see and hearing only what they want to hear, and attending to harder, more quantifiable issues than soft values. Two companies that regularly and explicitly evaluate their underlying values are Washington Mutual Savings and AES:

> Washington Mutual Savings, headquartered in Seattle, Washington, strives to maintain a strong bond with its employees

through a caring workplace with solid values and open communication. In addition to routine visits by executives to the various regions and direct solicitation of input, the CEO uses an electronic system the company developed, called a Voting Booth. Each month, employees are asked a series of questions on topics including employee morale, customer service, communications, and stock ownership. All responses are anonymous.

Typically, about 1,500 people respond to the Voting Booth surveys through personal computers. Not only do top executives receive honest, unbiased feedback, but also the electronic system provides instantaneous feedback, and the results are reported in the employee newsletter.

One of the most comprehensive company evaluations of core values is that of AES, an independent producer of electric power headquartered in Arlington, Virginia:

Each year, AES conducts an employee survey to assess how well the company has adhered to its core values. Dennis Bakke, cofounder and current CEO, claims that "our values are the only thing that is centrally managed in the company." The survey is both exhaustive—generating 7,500 individual comments in 1996—and down to earth. Employees are asked how well various descriptors—"friendly," "arrogant," "is growing too fast," "is taking on too much risk"—reflect the realities of life at AES. Further, the survey asks employees to what extent they agree or disagree with certain provocative statements such as, "We work because the work is fun, fulfilling, and exciting and when it stops being that way we will change what and how we do things," and, "we do not try to get the most out of a deal at the cost of being unfair to a customer, supplier, or related party."

In using the survey as a management tool, the results determine a portion of the salary increase and bonus for top executives. Furthermore, plant-by-plant results are considered a leading (as opposed to lagging) indicator of performance.[11]

The recent performance of AES has been superb. Between 1990 and 1996, annual revenues and profits grew from $200 million to $835 million and from less than $16 million to $125 million, respectively. And its market capitalization soared from $750 million when the company went public in 1991 to around $6 billion by early 1998. Clearly, culture can play a key role in motivating employees throughout the organization and aligning individual, group, and organizational objectives. However, people also demand a "return" for their investment in the organization. There are ways that financial and nonfinancial incentives and rewards can help companies attract and retain their most mobile of assets, human capital.

Leveraging Human Capital With Rewards and Incentives

Reward and incentive systems represent a powerful means of influencing an organization's culture, focusing efforts on high-priority tasks, and motivating high levels of individual and collective task performance.[12] Since much of culture deals with influencing beliefs, behaviors, and attitudes of people within the organization, the reward system—by specifying who gets rewarded and why—is an effective motivator and control mechanism. As a construction executive noted during our interview, "Loyalty is a two-way street; the only way the employee can believe in the dream is to share in the dream."

Generally people in organizations act rationally, each motivated by his or her personal best interest. However, the collective sum of individual behaviors of an organization's employees does not always necessarily result in what's best for the organization. That is, individual rationality does not always guarantee organizational rationality.

As corporations grow and evolve, they usually consist of many different businesses with multiple reward systems. Although they share some fundamental philosophies and values, they may differ based on industry contexts, business situations, stage of product life cycles, and so on. Thus, subcultures within the organization may reflect differences among an organization's functional areas, products, services, and divisions.

The Potential Downside

Problems arise when countercultures emerge that have shared values in direct opposition to the patterns of the dominant culture.[13] To the extent that reward systems reinforce such behavioral norms, attitudes, and belief systems, organizational solidarity is compromised; important information is hoarded rather than shared, individuals begin working at cross purposes, and they lose sight of overarching goals and objectives.

We're all aware of such conflicts. Sales and marketing personnel promise unrealistically quick delivery times to bring in business, much to the dismay of operations and logistics; "overengineering" by R&D creates headaches for manufacturing; and so on. Conflicts also arise across divisions when divisional profits become a key compensation criterion. Among other things, the shifting of expense and capital items becomes a game with no real winners. As ill will and rancor escalate, sociability and solidarity decline.

Lantech, a small manufacturer of packaging material in Louisville, Kentucky, provides an instructive and colorful example:

> Lantech is a privately owned company with 325 employees and revenues of approximately $65 million. In a bid to spur productivity, each of the company's five manufacturing divisions was given a bonus, based on its profits, which could amount to up to 10 percent of each worker's pay. Problems arose because the divisions were so highly interdependent that it was difficult to sort out what division was entitled to what profits. For example, the division that built standard machines and the one that added custom features to those machines depended on each other for parts, engineering expertise, and so on. Inevitably the groups clashed, and each tried to assign costs to the other as well as claim credit for revenues.
>
> According to Pat Lancaster, the chairman, "By the early nineties, I was spending 95 percent of my time on conflict resolution instead of on how to serve our customers." His son, Jim, CEO, added that the incentive system led "to so much secrecy, politicking, and sucking noise that you wouldn't believe it." Things got so bad that some employees argued over who would be charged for the toilet paper in the common rest room. This motivated one aspiring bean counter to suggest that toilet paper costs should reflect the sexual makeup of the division, based on the shaky theory that one gender uses more than the other!
>
> Not surprisingly, the divisional performance pay program was scrapped, and now Lantech uses a profit-sharing system in which all employees receive a bonus based on salary. Furious passions have subsided; performance is up. Concludes Pat Lancaster: "Incentive pay is toxic because it is so open to favoritism and manipulation."

Creating Effective Reward and Incentive Programs

Perhaps the Lantech example overstates the case, but it serves to illustrate the potential downside of incentive systems. To be effective, incentive and reward systems need to reinforce basic core values and enhance cohesion and commitment to goals and objectives that are not at odds with the organization's overall mission and purpose.[14] Consider the obsession that John Chambers, CEO of Cisco Systems, has with customer service:

> He ordered the phrase "Dedication to Customer Success" attached to each employee's ID badge. He half-jokingly asserts, "If I find someone who looks at the customer as a burden or problem, I'll strangle them. That's unacceptable." Importantly, every manager's compensation is tied directly to customer satisfaction. Cisco surveys its clients extensively each year, polling them on approximately sixty performance criteria, from product functionality to service quality. Says Chambers, "If a manager improves his scores, he can get a fair amount. But if the scores go down, we'll take money out of the manager's pocket." Such tactics have increased the number of completely satisfied end users from 81 percent in 1995 to 85 percent in 1996.

Logical consistency is also vital: reward systems must be consistent with regard to time (the short, intermediate, and long term) as well as hierarchical level and function (team, department functional area, division, and so on).

Let's look at how Nucor uses four incentive compensation programs that correspond to the levels of management:

1. *Production incentive program.* Groups of twenty to forty people are put in groups and paid a weekly bonus based on either anticipated product time or tonnage produced. Each shift and production line is in a separate bonus group.

2. *Department managers.* Bonuses are based on divisional performance, primarily measured by return on assets.

3. *Employees not directly involved in production.* These include engineers, accountants, secretaries, receptionists, and others. Bonuses are based on two factors: divisional and corporate return on assets.

4. *Senior incentive program.* Salaries are lower than comparable companies, but a significant portion of total compensation is based on return on stockholder equity. A portion of pretax earnings is placed in

a pool and divided among officers as bonuses that are part cash and part stock.

Since incentive compensation can account for more than half of their paycheck, employees become nearly obsessed with productivity and apply a lot of pressure to each other. Ken Iverson, a former CEO, recalled an instance in which one employee arrived at work in sunglasses instead of safety glasses, preventing the team from doing any work. Furious, the other workers chased him around the plant with a piece of angle iron.

Nucor's reward system also leads to greater innovation. Since the incentive program encourages employees to stick together and find ways to increase productivity, more new ideas are generated. According to Gene Harris, a shift supervisor at Vulcraft Indiana:

> If they come up with an idea, unless it's a tremendous amount of money, we'll try it. If it doesn't work, we'll go back to something else. But even if the original idea doesn't work, it gets a lot of other people thinking. When you have 25 guys thinking about something, somebody usually comes up with something that is really helpful.

At General Mills, the reward system truly leverages human capital through the potential for financial leverage. Half of a manager's annual bonus is linked to business unit results and half to individual performance. For example, if a manager simply matches a rival manufacturer's performance, his or her salary is roughly 5 percent lower. But if the manager's product ranks in the industry's top 10 percent in earnings growth and return on capital, the manager's total compensation can rise to nearly 30 percent beyond the industry norm.

Successful incentive systems address not only team (or larger organizational unit) incentives but also individual accountability. Without individual assessments or strong cultural norms, shirking may become evident, and if it is not controlled, it can permeate the entire organization. One approach to enhance teamwork and individual contribution—while still remaining focused on the organization's bottom line—is the novel way that Hull Trading Company allocates its bonus pool:

> Hull Trading Company, one of America's largest independent trading companies, has experienced dramatic growth. Started by Blair Hull in 1985 with four people and $1 million, it has

grown to one hundred people with $80 million of capital. Hull generates its profits by using sophisticated technology and mathematical modeling to place bets on complex securities such as options on the S&P 500 stock index, futures contracts on those index options, and options on individual stocks. On a typical day, Hull's traders generate 7 percent of the options traded in the United States, 3 percent of the equity options, and 1 percent of the total number of shares traded on the New York Stock Exchange.

Hull stresses teamwork as a core value. For example, to respond quickly to market turbulence, the company has created the Fast Market Team that kicks into gear when markets dramatically change. Employees normally close to headquarters—programmers, accountants, lawyers—rush to the pits to help clear trades. To stay operationally fit, the team even conducts "fire drills." To keep everyone pulling in the same direction, the company distributes its multimillion dollar bonus pool through an electoral process involving the entire company. Clearly, it's business democracy at work—the more votes you get, the bigger your bonus—with an important dose of meritocracy built in. "It's easy to determine who has the most credibility around here," claims Hull. "They are the people with the most votes."

Using Equity as a Reward

In today's economy, companies of all sizes are using stock ownership as a means of aligning individual efforts and commitments with organizational goals.[15] More and more, companies like General Electric, PepsiCo, Home Depot, and countless others are making stock ownership a reward vehicle for employees throughout their ranks. Starbucks, the fast-growing Seattle-based chain of coffee houses, goes even a step further. It provides stock ownership for part-time workers through its innovative "Beanstock" program, a clever play on the endearing children's story. This has improved morale and commitment, as well as dramatically reduced employee and manager turnover in an industry traditionally beset by a revolving-door mentality.

For science and technology professionals, stock ownership can provide a tremendous financial incentive to help a young company grow and prosper. Recently, for example, Gordon Gould, a 27-year-old "information architect," left a comfortable job at Sony Corporation for a new start-up called Thinking Pictures, Inc. Before he made his move, he negotiated a major equity stake. His rationale is shared by many of today's high-in-demand technology professionals: "I'm young but I'm not dumb. I know I'm a prime producer and I want my compensation to reflect that. If I'm going to spend 16 hours a day in an office, I want to be rewarded for the upside my work generates. I want to feel that the company is partly my baby."

Beyond managers and talented knowledge professionals, equity ownership can be a powerful motivating force for employees in the more mundane positions. According to Cisco Systems' CEO, John Chambers, 42 percent of Cisco's stock options are held by rank-and-file employees. These outstanding options carry an average gain of $100,000. Thirty-five-year-old Jennifer A. Overstreet, employee No. 35 at Oracle, worked for more than twelve years as personal assistant to CEO Lawrence Ellison. Since her hiring, Oracle has grown from 35 employees to 24,000 and from $5 million in revenues to $5 billion. Her stock options originally granted fourteen years ago at $5 per share became worth at least $2,000 each, thanks to thirty-six stock splits. She recently quit her job, plans to get married, and spends time decorating her 8,000-square-foot home in San Francisco's exclusive Pacific Heights.

Despite the potential benefits that stock ownership and stock options can have on aligning the efforts of employees at all levels with the interests of the shareholders of the corporation, it is no panacea. Without strong core values, shirking may likely become a norm as many employees realistically come to realize how little their individual efforts can materially affect the company's bottom line. Further, executives may become too bottom-line, short-term oriented and become consumed more with financial engineering (e.g., stock splits, capitalizing expenses, trade loading) to meet the immediate and pressing expectations of institutional investors and Wall Street. Clearly, the owners and managers of a publicly held company are responsible not only for the short-term performance of its stock but also for "creating an entity of value," in the words of Paul Meger, an executive pay consultant in New York City. That is, they must create and sustain a pile of tangible and intangible assets and a business of lasting and sustainable worth.

The Changing Nature of Reward and Incentive Systems

Successful companies realize that in today's complex and rapidly changing competitive environment, nothing is cast in concrete. This, of course, applies to how companies go about rewarding their employees at all levels.[16]

At times, a minor change may be needed to spur effort and commitment. For example, to boost morale for nonexecutive employees, David House, CEO of Bay Networks, recently reset the price of Bay's stock options down to $19.50, well below the elevated level that many were stuck with before Bay's stock slid. He recognized that the drop in stock value could largely be attributed to the fears of an Asia-led industry slowdown in late 1997.

The perception that a plan is fair and equitable is critically important, as is the flexibility to respond to changing requirements as an organization's direction and objectives change. Many companies have begun to place more emphasis on growth, and their organizations have become so "lean and mean" that only marginal returns are available from further cost cutting. Emerson Electric is one company shifting its emphasis, and the compensation program is one of the key levers of strategic control. Planning sessions now focus exclusively on sales, new product development, overseas expansion, and the like, and discussions about profits are handled separately. This approach leads to a culture that encourages risk taking. To ensure that the change takes hold, the management compensation formula has moved from a focus largely on the bottom line to one that emphasizes growth, new products, acquisitions, and international expansion.

Sometimes wholesale change is needed. Leaders need to recognize telltale signs that the system is simply not working and opt for radical surgery. At times, such major changes require great courage because the changes that are made fly in the face of industry norms and conventional wisdom. This was the case at Marshall Industries:

> Marshall Industries is a billion-dollar electronics distributor headquartered outside Los Angeles. The company moves boxes from 150 powerful suppliers such as Hitachi and Texas Instruments to more than 30,000 demanding customers such as Bay Networks and WebTV. It sells parts—170,000 different items from semiconductors and capacitors to liquid crystal displays and programmatic logic devices. The company operates huge sales and distribution facilities and has overhauled its global operating system, creating 700 new computer programs to process more than 700,000 transactions per day.
>
> Soon after he became CEO in 1992, Rod Rodin recognized many symptoms of an incentive and reward system out of control. Among them: (1) more than 20 percent of each month's total sales were shipped in the last three days, stretching the warehouse to the breaking point; (2) divisions

would hide customer returns or open bad credit accounts just to make monthly targets; (3) if a product became scarce, one division would hide its inventory from another division—and send it out on a UPS truck so that it could truthfully say there was no supply on hand; and (4) there was constant bickering, for example, over how to split commissions from a customer who did design in Boston but purchasing in Texas.

The underlying problem was a compensation program with a wide array of incentives that led to myopic behavior. Given the reward system, people behaved rationally. People were ranked and reviewed based on individual or small group performance—the credit department on days' receivables outstanding, division managers on P&L, the sales staff on gross profit dollars. This all resulted in intense internal competition—while customers clamored for unprecedented demands for quality and suppliers expected new standards of service.

Rodin's draconian solution was to scrap the compensation system Marshall used to pay every one of its employees, including its 600 salespeople. He declared there would be no more commissions, contests, or prizes and abolished bonuses for individual victories. Everyone at Marshall would be paid the same way and share in the company-wide bonus pool.

Rodin was hammered when he unveiled the plan in an open letter to the industry. After all, contests and commissions—internal competition—were a way of life in the industry. One competitor accused him of "kissing Deming's ring" and another labeled the system "communistic." The industry bible, *Electronic Buyers News*, published a biting editorial. And when he told his wife he was taking salespeople off commissions, she screamed, "Are you crazy?"

Perhaps the crazier thing is that it worked. In 1991, the year before Rodin made the changes, sales stood at $582 million with a stock price of $9. Four years later, the corresponding numbers were $1.2 billion and $37. All this was accomplished with 250 fewer people; sales per person have doubled, and profits have tripled.

Why did the new system work? In essence, it focused people on the whole company as well as the long term—not just the "proverbial fast buck." According to Dan Kates, for example, a salesperson in the Silicon Valley, it encourages salespeople to invest months, even years, in prying companies away from distributors and turning them into Marshall customers. According to Kates, "the new system is an advantage to me. I can invest time with a new customer without worrying about paying my gas bill." CEO Rodin adds, "People who were skeptical about the new system would ask, 'What about my upside?' I'd ask back 'What about your downside?' Do you really want a career where your success depends on the short-term health of five or six accounts? Wouldn't you rather be part of an organization where what matters is how effectively you contribute to the work of 1,400 people?"

Beyond Compensation: Recognition and Symbolic Rewards

Although compensation programs and performance measures are generally highly visible in most companies, intangibles may not often be given sufficient consideration.[17] Awards, certificates, forms of recognition, and modest cash and noncash incentives can have a dramatic effect on employee commitment and motivation. Consider Mary Kay's awards (in many cases not so modest) of jewelry, furs, and use of luxury automobiles for star salespeople, all of whom are independent beauty consultants. Also, many organizations such as communications giant Gannett provide numerous awards for excellence. A partial listing of Gannett's television award categories includes Spot News, Big Story Coverage, Investigative/In-Depth Reporting, Series/Extra, General News, Photography, Graphic Journalism, and Public Service.

Recognition can be a powerful motivator when it is prompt and directly linked to performance that is "above and beyond." At FedEx, a separate system, based primarily on recognition, targets the intangibles of customer service and extraordinary effort. Two different programs are involved:

■ The Bravo Zulu program (the Navy signal for "well done") uses modest cash awards and gift certificates to reward employees on the spot for outstanding efforts and achievement.

■ The Golden Falcon award, which includes ten shares of stock and a congratulatory phone call or visit from a top executive, is triggered directly by a letter or telephone call from a customer praising an employee's performance.

GE Medical Systems has a similar program. Called "Quick Thanks!" it allows employees to nominate a colleague to receive a $25 gift certificate, redeemable at certain stores and restaurants, in appreciation for a job well done. In a recent year, over 10,000 Quick Thanks! awards were presented, often by the coworker who placed the nomination. Typically, the acknowledgment is more valuable than the $25.

Recognition can be a powerful motivator even when there is no direct financial reward. At 3M, the Carlson Society honors members who are chosen in recognition of their outstanding and original technical contributions. Similarly, Illinois Tool Works (ITW) has rewarded its top inventors with induction into the company's Hall of Fame. Only nine of the more than 200 members of the ITW Patent Society—employees who are responsible for many of the more than 4,450 patents that the company holds—have received this honor.

Focusing Resources With Boundaries and Constraints

In an ideal world, a strong culture and effective rewards should be sufficient to ensure that all individuals and subunits work toward the common goals and objectives of the total organization. However, whether the counterproductive behavior can be attributed to motivated self-interest, lack of a clear understanding of goals and objectives, or outright malfeasance, such is not usually the case. Boundaries and constraints, when used properly, can serve many useful purposes for the organizations, including minimizing improper and unethical conduct, focusing individual efforts on organizational priorities, improving efficiency and effectiveness, and enhancing corporate governance.

Minimizing Improper and Unethical Conduct

Guidelines can be useful in specifying proper relationships with a company's customers and suppliers. For example, many companies have explicit rules regarding commercial practices, including the prohibition of any form of payment, commission, fee, or rebate that could be construed as a bribe, payoff, or kickback.[18] Cadbury Schweppes has followed a rather simple but effective step in controlling the use of bribes by specifying that all payments, no matter how unusual, are recorded on the company's books. Sir Adrian Cadbury, chairman, contends that such a practice causes managers to pause and consider whether a payment is a necessary and standard cost of doing business or simply a bribe. And consulting companies typically have strong rules and regulations directed at protecting client confidentiality and conflicts of interests.

With regard to rules and regulations concerning suppliers, Levi Strauss & Co. recently developed a set of global sourcing guidelines that is enforced through on-site audits of each of its 700 contractors worldwide. And Chemical Bank, in an effort to ensure fair and equitable treatment of its suppliers, forbids any review that determines whether suppliers are Chemical customers before the bank awards contracts. Regulations backed up with strong sanctions can also help an organization to avoid conducting business in an improper and unethical manner. Tenet Healthcare, the nation's second largest hospital chain with 1997 revenues of $9 billion, wants to avoid Columbia HCA's legal woes. The CEO has initiated a plan whereby executives can lose up to 20 percent of their bonus if they are found approving incorrect Medicare codes that exaggerate the severity of a patient's illness.

Focusing Efforts on Strategic Priorities

Boundaries and constraints play a valuable role in focusing a company's strategic priorities. Perhaps, the best-known strategic boundary in U.S. industry is Jack Welch's (GE's CEO) demand that all businesses in the corporate portfolio be ranked first or second in their industry. In a similar vein, Eli Lilly has reduced its research efforts to five broad disease areas, down from eight or nine a decade ago.[19] This concentration provides it with greater strategic focus and the potential for stronger competitive advantage in the remaining areas. Norman Augustine, Lockheed Martin's former chairman, provided four criteria for selecting candidates for diversification into "closely related" businesses: (1) they must be high tech, (2) they must be systems oriented, (3) they typically must deal with large customers (either corporations or government) as opposed to consumers, and (4) they must be in growing markets. He says, "We have found that if we can meet most of those standards, then we can move into adjacent markets and grow. Today, only about 50 percent of Lockheed Martin's business is with the U.S. Department of Defense (down from about 75 percent five years ago). The other part is growing very rapidly."

Boundaries also have a place in the nonprofit sector. For example, a British relief organization uses a system to monitor strategic boundaries by maintaining a gray list of companies whose contributions it will neither solicit nor accept. Such boundaries clearly go beyond simply taking the moral high road. Rather, it is essential for maintaining legitimacy with existing and potential benefactors.

Improving Operational Efficiency and Effectiveness

Rule-based controls are appropriate and vital in organizations with the following characteristics:

- Environments are stable and predictable.
- Employees are largely unskilled and interchangeable.
- Consistency in product and service is critical.
- The risk of malfeasance is extremely high (as in banking or casino operations), and controls must be implemented to guard against improper conduct.[20]

For example, McDonald's has extensive rules and regulations that regulate the operation of its franchises. Its policy manual states that "cooks must turn, never flip, hamburgers. If they haven't been purchased, Big Macs must be discarded in ten minutes after being cooked and French fries in seven minutes. Cashiers must make eye contact with and smile at every customer."

Guidelines can also be effective in setting spending limits and the range of discretion for employees and managers, such as the $2,500 limit that hotelier Ritz Carlton uses to empower employees to placate dissatisfied customers. Also, regulations can be initiated to improve the use of employees' time at work. Consider Computer Associates' (perhaps controversial) restrictions on the use of e-mail during the hours of 10 a.m. to noon and 2 p.m. to 4 p.m. each day. According to CEO Charles Wang, "I felt that if you restricted it, people would begin to use e-mail in a smarter and more efficient way. And that they would begin to do other things, little things like visiting clients, writing a little software, things like that." A little sarcasm never hurts!

Enhancing Corporate Governance

As we all know, members of a corporation's board of directors have a fiduciary responsibility to act independently of management and in the best interests of the owners: the shareholders. Clearly, that is not always the case.[21] One of the best (or worst, depending on one's perspective) examples of corporate governance failure is found in the recent demise of Morrison Knudsen under the inept leadership of its CEO, Bill Agee. Among the sins were these:

- No outside directors had ever run or managed an industrial business.
- Most directors were either business affiliates or personal friends of CEO William Agee or his wife, Mary Cunningham Agee.
- No board meetings were held at corporate headquarters for more than a year.
- Excessive attention was given to executive compensation; thirty-

eight of the forty-three pages in the 1993 proxy dealt with the compensation programs for top officials.

Here are some more recent governance snafus:

■ Occidental Petroleum continued its tradition of shareholder disrespect established by former CEO Armand Hammer by buying out CEO Ray Irani's seven-year employment contract for an astonishing $95 million and then giving him another contract worth at least $1.2 million a year.

■ Reader's Digest (with an average annual five-year return to investors of −32 percent) has a seriously flawed governance setup: 71 percent of the voting shares are held by two charitable trusts. Who chairs them? CEO George Grune.

■ When AMD's stock price has fallen below the options strike price over the last fourteen years, the board has repeatedly lowered that price, netting CEO Jerry Sanders tens of millions. Message to Sanders: *Don't worry: you'll clean up, regardless.* Message to shareholders: *You're betting on somebody who'll clean up regardless of whether you do or not.*

Cronyism and indifferent or ineffective board members have been one of the chief culprits of the competitive decline of many highly visible, large corporations over the past several years in corporate America. Chief among their ills has been a reluctance to remove poorly performing CEOs. A very brief list would include Bob Allen at AT&T, Bob Stempel at General Motors, John Akers at IBM, Paul Lego at Westinghouse, and Kay Whitmore at Eastman Kodak. In contrasting the effective and ineffective board practices at Campbell Soup and Heinz, respectively, a recent *Business Week* article has suggested some useful boundaries for corporate governance:

■ Have a majority of outside directors
■ Ban insiders from the nominating committee
■ Ban former executives from the board
■ Set a mandatory retirement age
■ Allow the outside directors to meet without the CEO
■ Appoint a "lead director"
■ Establish a governance committee
■ Conduct periodic self-evaluations of board effectiveness
■ Do not provide pensions for directors
■ Require directors to own company shares

Perhaps members of a company's board of directors should heed the straightforward advice of GE's CEO, Jack Welch:

Look, I think the board's job is to hire a chairman and CEO in charge of the whole company and to hold him to a high standard; and, if that person isn't delivering, to remove him. It's probably the board's biggest responsibility. Know where the company's going. Pick the person. Then get out of the way. And if he doesn't deliver, call him in and say, "Go home—go to the beach."

Evolving From Boundaries to Rewards and Culture

Boundaries and constraints have their place. However, in most competitive environments, organizations need to establish a system of rewards and incentives, coupled with a culture strong enough that boundaries become internalized in each employee. If this effort is successful, sociability and solidarity will be enhanced, trust will be increased, information sharing will be encouraged, the organization will become more adaptable and flexible, and the costly dysfunctions of rules and regulations will be minimized.

Semco, Inc.: Reducing the Need for Boundaries

We close with the example of a Brazilian company, Semco, Inc.[22] It is a unique success story that dramatically drives home how a strong culture and effective reward systems help to focus employee attention on organizational priorities, motivate their best efforts, and lessen the need for boundaries:

Evolving from a simple manufacturer of pump machinery equipment to a diversified company in several lines of business, Semco S/A's sales have grown over 900 percent in the past ten years. Originally a sleepy, Brazilian family–owned business, it has become the fourth largest business in its industry. Semco S/A has done so, despite a near-crippling South American recession, by encouraging its employees to blur the boundaries of the company. It has policies that sound offbeat, unworkable, or—worse yet—utopian to many North American managers. Underlying the company's policies, however, is an insightful understanding of how the blend of rewards and culture can eliminate the need for controls based on extensive policies and procedures.

The company has cultivated a culture based on the twin pillars of accountability, which stems from market-based controls, readily available to all employees, and a culture of trust, carefully nurtured by CEO Ricardo Semler. He believes that if employees are given sufficient information to make informed decisions, they will in fact do so. In essence, Semler's approach removes the manager as buffer between the employees and the market. What makes the Semler way work is not a reliance on internal control mechanisms, but instead the ability to internalize market controls. In effect, the market becomes the company's boundaries in its strategy, compensation, organizational structure, and culture.

This isn't feel-good management, just good management all around. Semler insists the bottom line is the ultimate measuring stick for the company, "My point is that it is financial solidarity that gets rid of what I call boarding school issues. But if the financial solidarity isn't there, then all we have is a kind of Woodstock association of cooperatives for peace, and I don't believe in that."

Semler's goal is not a worker's paradise where profits don't matter. Rather, it is a good place to work where enthusiastic employees generate good profits for the company. Although he claims to eschew having a corporate culture, in fact he stresses a culture based on respect and accountability. He describes the culture by saying, "Another way of looking at Semco is to say we treat our employees as responsible adults. We never assume that they will take advantage of us, or our rules, or our lack of them. We always assume they will do their level best to achieve results beneficial to the company, the customer, their colleagues, and themselves." Sounds good, but what happens when someone abuses that trust? "We've had a few employees take advantage of our open stockrooms and trusting atmosphere, but we were lucky enough to find and prosecute them without putting into place a lot of insulting watchdog procedures for the nine out of ten who are honest." Such a policy means resisting the urge to insert controls as an answer to observed problems. Semler refuses to manage to what he calls the "lowest common denominator." Such a policy is not easy to administer. It's often easier to implement administrative controls that affect the honest and dishonest alike; it's tougher to maintain trust and punish personally those who abuse the trust.

This rigor extends to other policies as well. As an example, Semco permits titles on employees' business cards outside the company, but the business cards and titles remain outside the plant. Employees work without titles; they are expected to familiarize themselves with the plant's business to the extent that they know what to expect from nearly everyone. Semco expects its employees to know whom they need to talk to, whom to coordinate with, who performs what duties. It's a policy that discourages "Not Invented Here," because "Here" involves the entire plant, not just isolated functional areas. Semler insists it sharpens an employee's focus: "Everyone knows what they are doing there, why they are there, and how they are contributing to the final results."

Similarly, the company successfully avoids the fractious divisions that can occur at salary determination time. Most employees determine their own salary; the company helps them do so. Semco publishes a semiannual report outlining the prevailing wage rates for similar external positions, as well as internal wage rates for all employees. Employees are encouraged to calculate their value to the company and price their salary accordingly. Anyone wanting a large pay increase can sign up for one, provided he or she is willing to produce output worthy of the pay raise. Semler asserts this is the logical approach: "Why debate salary? We all want to make as much as possible." So what keeps employees from setting their salaries too high? "When establishing pay rates," he adds, "employees know that six months later a department may no longer want to buy their work if they have priced their services too high." Rather than put management at risk for trying to match output and wages—and getting it wrong—Semler gives employees the information to do it themselves. In a culture where employees are trusted and given the information to act responsibly, they do so.

Semler is paving the way for a new cooperation between workers and management, something he calls a satellite system. Most North American companies outsource employees to save costs, not to generate revenues. Support personnel (information systems, security, janitorial, etc.) are often struck from the payroll and then contracted back (albeit often with fewer benefits). Semler also outsources large numbers of employees; the ones he often lets go are the moneymakers for the company—employees in the operations area. It's hard to distinguish them from other employees; they remain in the building, continue to use Semco's equipment and furnishings, and continue to do Semco S/A work. But they are also encouraged to prospect for additional work. Profits from the additional work they find belong to them. Employee gains are limited only by the size of their own drive. Why encourage potential competitors? Semler explains that the satellites "have obvious advantages to Semco. We have reduced our payroll and cut costs, yet enjoy the advantage of sub-contractors who know our business and the idiosyncrasies of our company and our customers." The company also enjoys extremely loyal subcontractors who recognize how beneficial this type of partnership can be. As an example, a key group of Semler's administrators moved from roles as Semco S/A support personnel to becoming their own profit center and business. Last May the group, Semco, Cushman and Wakefield (a joint venture), entered the Argentine market, providing outsourcing advice and support to multinationals that employ third-party vendors. Having developed expertise with managing the coordination of the satellites, they recognized that other businesses would benefit from their expertise. This group of executives took an overhead function at Semco and turned it into a profitable business. When they pitched this idea to Semler, he didn't understand it but agreed to allow them to try it.

It's not surprising Semler didn't initially understand the concept behind the Semco, Cushman and Wakefield joint venture; he's not often there! He visits the plant a few days a week to lobby—not dictate—for ideas he thinks might work and to listen to others' ideas as well. Because employees elect managers, Semler finds it easier to stay out of their way. Although he has many ideas on how to improve things, he makes a point of not dictating changes, relying more on the merits of his ideas than the power that comes from his owning the company. Sometimes employees implement his ideas, but equally often they reject his plans. He enjoyed giving plant tours to journalists, but employees found them distracting, so they were cancelled. So how does he feel about lobbying for change and not simply dictating it? "Does it make me feel I have given up power and governance? You bet it does. But I probably sleep better at night than the manufacturer who runs his business every night with an iron fist and whose employees leave their troubles in his lap every night."

It's an approach that acknowledges a truth suggested over sixty years ago by Fritz Roethlisberger, director of the famous Hawthorne studies conducted in Chicago. Roethlisberger contended that organizations have both formal and informal structures, and that if there is a disparity between the two, the informal structure eventually predominates. Rather than opposing the informal structure, companies succeed by gently shaping the informal structure through a strong culture, then ensuring that the formal structure remains in alignment with the informal. When the two are in alignment, formal boundaries and controls become less necessary. But the more companies need to rely on formal controls, the more rules they find they have to enforce, and the less time they have for more important managerial duties.

Giving up control provides a personal upside for Ricardo Semler as well. Although he is CEO and owner, he shares the CEO responsibilities with employees who rotate into the position. This arrangement frees him to pursue other interests. He has found time to write two best-selling books, develop a consulting and speechmaking business, and pursue a childhood dream of being a playwright. His first play, *Checkmate*, recently opened in Sao Paulo; he has hopes for it to make its way to the New York and London stages eventually. He has created a powerful corporate culture, premised on accountability and trust. It may be informal, but it frees him from having to implement a myriad of formal rules; better yet, it frees him from having to monitor and enforce them. In short, by giving up formal controls and relying on informal ones, he has provided himself with the time to pursue other activities of greater interest.

A Checklist: Culture, Rewards and Boundaries

Using Culture to Leverage Human Resources

☐ Is the organization strongly oriented toward a single dominant value (e.g., customer service) that is the primary source of competitive value?

☐ Does the organization effectively use these five mechanisms to strengthen its culture:
- Role modeling?
- Integrating mechanisms (e.g., meetings, training activities)?
- Structural elements (e.g., committees, task forces)?
- Storytelling and rituals?
- Ongoing evaluation and assessment?

Leveraging Human Capital Through the Use of Rewards and Incentives

☐ Does the reward system effectively align individual and organizational interests as well as reinforce core organizational values?

☐ Are the downsides of the reward systems (e.g., zero-sum thinking) minimized?

☐ Is the reward system consistent with regard to:
  - Time (i.e., short, medium, long term)?
  - Hierarchical levels?
  - Functional areas?
  - Geographic levels?
  - Business units?

☐ Does the reward system encourage innovation and productivity?

☐ Does the reward system foster both individual excellence and effective teamwork?

☐ Is the reward system continually evaluated to be consistent with changes within the company and in the competitive environment?

☐ Does the organization make effective use of recognition and symbolic rewards?

Effectively Using Boundaries and Constraints

☐ Are rules, regulations, and guidelines effectively used to:
  - Minimize improper and unethical conduct?
  - Ensure consistent strategic initiatives?
  - Improve efficiency and effectiveness?
  - Enhance corporate governance?

☐ Are there proper enforcement mechanisms to ensure fairness and effective implementation of rules, regulations, and guidelines?

General

☐ Is more emphasis placed on culture and rewards (than on boundaries and constraints) as the primary means of enhancing control?

Notes

1. Norman R. Augustine, address at the Crummer Business School, Winter Park, Florida, October 20, 1989.
2. R. Simons, "Control in an Age of Empowerment," *Harvard Business Review* 73 (March–April 1995): 80–88. For a classic discussion of the dysfunctions of bureaucracy, refer to J. G. March and H. A. Simon, *Organizations* (New York: Wiley, 1958), pp. 36–47.
3. "Core Ideology: In the Midst of Change, What Remains the Same?" *Vision: A Newsletter for UPS Leadership* (January 1997): 1.
4. The examples in this section were derived from *Blueprints for Service Quality*, 2d ed. (New York: American Management Association, 1994), p. 48, and based on

personal communications with Katherine Hagmeier, program manager, external communications, 3M Corporation, March 26, 1998.

5. R. Goffee and G. Jones, "What Holds the Modern Company Together?" *Harvard Business Review* 74 (November–December 1996): 133–148.

6. Adapted from Abraham Zaleznik's discussion of the managerial mystique in "The Leadership Gap," *Academy of Management Executive* 4(1) (1990): 11.

7. The examples in this section are drawn from a number of sources, including: M. F. R. Kets de Vries, "Charisma in Action: The Transformational Abilities of Virgin's Richard Branson and ABB's Percy Barnevik," *Organizational Dynamics* 26 (Winter 1998): 7–21; J. L. Rodengen, *The Legend of Nucor Corporation* (Fort Lauderdale, FL: Write Stuff Enterprises, 1997), p. vii; B. Gates, "Watching His Windows," *Forbes ASAP*, December 1, 1997, p. 162; and "Quoteworthy," *Measure* (May–June 1993): 31 (an internal HP publication).

8. The examples in this section were drawn from M. Goldberg, "How Mirimba Keeps in Step," *Fast Company* (June–July 1997): 34; and Goffee and Jones, "What Holds the Modern Company Together?"

9. The examples in this section were based on the following sources: "Keepin' the Spirit Alive in 50 Cities" *Luvlines* (May–June 1997): 14 (an internal company publication of Southwest Airlines); D. Filipowski, "The Tao of Tandem," *Personnel Journal* (October 1991): 72–78; K. Kane, "Job Titles of the Future," *Fast Company* (June–July 1997): 34; and L. Chadderson, "Job Titles of the Future," *Fast Company* (December–January 1998): 74.

10. The examples in this section draw on the following sources: William E. Coyne, "Building on a Tradition of Innovation" (speech at the Fifth UK Innovation lecture, March 5, 1996); James D. Ericson, speech at the *Fortune Magazine* Corporate Communications Seminar, March 13, 1993; P. Sellers, "Companies That Serve You Best," *Fortune*, May 31, 1993, 88; R. D. Hof, K. Rebello, and P. Burrows, "Scott McNealy's Rising Sun," *Business Week*, January 26, 1996, pp. 66–73; "Smart Managing: Best Practices, Careers, and Ideas," *Fortune*, March 31, 1997, p. 113; Kets de Vries, "Charisma in Action."

11. These examples are drawn from the following sources: Washington Mutual Savings, 1993 Annual Report, pp. 14–15; A. Markels, "Power to the People," *Fast Company* (February–March 1998): 155–165; and A. B. Graham and V. G. Pozzo, "A Question of Balance: Case Studies in Strategic Knowledge Management," *European Management Journal* 14(4) (August 1996): 338–346.

12. J. Kerr and J. W. Slocum, Jr., "Managing Corporate Culture Through Reward Systems," *Academy of Management Executive* 1 (May 1987): 99–107.

13. See L. G. Hrebiniak and W. F. Joyce, "The Strategic Importance of Managing Myopia," *Sloan Management Review* (1986): 28: 5–14, for an insightful perspective on goal conflict in organizations. The Lantech example is based on P. Nulty, "Incentive Pay Can Be Crippling," *Fortune*, November 13, 1995, p. 235; and "The Downside of Division-Focused Incentive Pay Plans," *Pay for Performance Report* (February 1997): 4.

14. The examples in this section are drawn from: G. Baum, "Cisco's CEO: John Chambers" *Forbes ASAP*, February 23, 1998, p. 52, 80; P. Nakache, "Cisco's Recruiting Edge," *Fortune*, September 29, 1997, pp. 275–276; J. L. Rodengen, *The Legend of Nucor Corporation* (Fort Lauderdale, FL: Write Stuff Enterprises, 1997); S. Tully, "Your Paycheck Gets Exciting," *Fortune*, November 13, 1993, p. 89; A. Sterge, "By the Numbers: Trading Vast Volumes, Stock Company Consults Only Its 'Black Box,' " *The Wall Street*

Journal, December 16, 1997, p. A1; S. Wolfe, "Hull Trading Wins Specialist Allocation for AME's Standard and Poor's," *PR Newswire*, January 9, 1992; and K. Kane, "Risky Business, Sound Thinking," *Fast Company* (December–January 1997): 85–90.

15. The examples in this section are drawn from: E. Matson, "How to Get a Piece of the Action," *Fast Company* (October–November 1996): 92; L. Himelstein, "Even Receptionists Are Millionaires," *Business Week*, August 25, 1997, p. 130, and T. A. Stewart, "CEO Pay: Mom Wouldn't Approve," *Fortune*, March 31, 1997, pp. 119–120.

16. The examples in this section are drawn from: A. Reinhardt, "Mr. House Finds His Fixer-Upper," *Business Week*, February 2, 1998, pp. 66–68; W. Zellner, R. D. Hof, R. Brandt, S. Baker, and D. Greising, "Go-Go Goliaths," *Business Week*, February 13, 1995, pp. 66–67; S. Lubov, "It Ain't Broke but Fix It Anyway," *Forbes*, August 1, 1994, pp. 56–60; C. Hartman, "Sales Force," *Fast Company* (June–July 1997): 134–146; and S. E. Wisnia, "Time Is of the Essence: Marshall Industries," *Industrial Distribution* 86(4) (April 1997): 115.

17. The examples in this section are based on: A. Farnham, "Mary Kay's Lessons in Leadership," *Fortune*, September 20, 1993, pp. 68–77; *Blueprints for Service Quality*, 2d ed. (New York: American Management Association, 1994), pp. 30–31; S. Kerr, "Risky Business: The New Pay Game," *Fortune*, July 22, 1996, p. 95; and D. Young, "Illinois Tool Still Fastened to Keep-It-Simple Formula," *Chicago Tribune*, April 26, 1993, 4:1.

18. The examples in this section are based on the following sources: S. A. Cadbury, "Ethical Managers Make Their Own Rules," *Harvard Business Review* 65 (1987): 69–73; R. D. Haas, "Ethics—A Global Business Challenge," *Vital Speeches of the Day*, June 1, 1994, pp. 506–509; "Corporate Ethics: A Prime Asset," *Business Roundtable* (February 1988); and G. Lau, "Mr. Nice Guy, Inc.," *Forbes*, February 9, 1998, pp. 54–55.

19. These examples draw on R. Simons, "Control in an Age of Empowerment," *Harvard Business Review* 73 (March–April 1995): 80–88; J. C. Picken and G. Dess, *Mission Critical: The 7 Strategic Traps That Derail Even the Smartest Companies*, (Chicago: Irwin, 1997); and E. Davis, "Interview: Norman Augustine," *Management Review* (November 1997): 11.

20. The examples in this section are drawn from: A. A. Thompson, Jr., and A. J. Strickland III, *Strategic Management: Concepts and Cases*, 10th ed. (New York: McGraw-Hill, 1998), p. 313; C. Wang, "Turning Point," *Forbes ASAP*, December 1, 1997, p. 147; and R. Teitelbaum, "Tough Guys Finish First," *Fortune*, July 21, 1997, pp. 82–84.

21. The examples in this section are drawn from: R. W. Lear and B. Yavitz, "The Best and Worst Boards of 1995: Evaluating the Boardroom," *Chief Executive* (November 1995); G. Colvin, "The 1998 Don't Get It All-Stars," *Fortune*, March 30, 1998, pp. 169–170; J. A. Byrne, "The CEO and the Board," *Business Week*, September 15, 1997, p. 110; and "GE: Just Your Average Everyday $60 Billion Family Grocery Store," *Industry Week*, May 2, 1994, pp. 13–18.

22. Sources for the Semco example include: J. Fierman, "Winning Ideas from Maverick Managers," *Fortune*, February 6, 1995, pp. 70, 73; R. Semler, "Managing Without Managers," *Harvard Business Review* 67(September–October 1989): 76–84; J. Wheatley, "It's Still Rock 'N' Roll to Me: Semco's Chief Has Applied Some of the Lessons He Learned from Playing in a Band to Running His Own Business," *Financial Times* (London ed.), May 15, 1977, p. 18; R. Donkin, "Welcome Breath of Laissez Faire," *Financial Times* (London ed.), October 30, 1996, p. 11; "Semco Enters Argentinean Market," *Gazetta Mercantil Online*, November 1, 1996; and Institute of Personnel and Development, "Empowering Employees—Maverick Style," *M2 Presswire*, May 15, 1997.

6

MAKING IT HAPPEN:
LEADERSHIP AND
ORGANIZATIONAL LEARNING

Thus far, we have described a number of different approaches for leveraging human capital resources, focusing primarily on the elements of structural capital: the organization's operating systems, processes, procedures, and task designs; information and communications infrastructure; resource acquisition, development, and allocation systems; decision processes and information flows; and incentives, controls, culture, and performance measurement systems. As we looked at each of these elements, we examined the ways organizations could develop, strengthen, and leverage the knowledge, experience, and task-specific skills of the individual. Although we addressed organizational culture in terms of its value as a lever of strategic control, we did not discuss how it could be managed or changed.

As a consequence, we did not examine the roles of leadership and learning in effecting the changes in business practices, structures, systems, internal processes, and culture usually necessary to leverage an organization's human capital resources. In this chapter, our focus shifts to implementation, and the essential roles of leadership and organizational learning in making these changes. Exhibit 6-1 places these activities in context within the framework developed in Chapter 1.

Leaders play an important, often pivotal, role in the development and implementation of strategies for leveraging human capital resources. By setting the direction for the organization, and designing structures, incentives, controls, and coordinating mechanisms, top managers can concentrate resources on the most important organizational objectives. By challenging the status quo and empowering employees at all levels, leaders can energize organizations, overcome

FIGURE 6-1.

Leveraging human capital: Leadership and organizational learning.

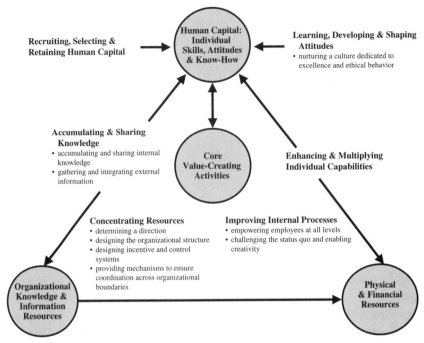

resistance to change, and engage the resources and talents of all employees in achieving organizational goals. By nurturing a culture dedicated to excellence and ethical behavior, the leader can shape values
and motivate each individual to make the fullest contribution to the
accomplishment of the objectives of the company.

A culture that reinforces organizational learning and the uninhib-
ited sharing of information is pivotal to success in rapidly changing
environments. Leaders must play a key role in setting the tone, breaking down the barriers of inertia and resistance, and enabling the development of the processes and mechanisms required to create a learning
organization.

Understanding Leadership

Leadership is a complex topic that is often oversimplified and frequently misunderstood.[1] To paraphrase an old saw, definitions of leadership are like noses—everybody has one, and no two seem to be

exactly alike. Perhaps that is one reason that there is so little consensus on what leadership is all about. Manfred Kets de Vries, a noted authority on leadership, observes:

> When we plunge into the organizational literature on leadership we quickly become lost in a labyrinth: there are endless definitions, countless articles and never-ending polemics. As far as leadership studies go, it seems that more and more has been studied about less and less, to end up ironically with a group of researchers studying everything about nothing.

Many would heartily agree with this perspective. However, two alternate perspectives seem to capture much of the thinking and writing on leadership: the *romantic* and the *external control* views. The romantic perspective is usually found in articles in the popular business press: *Fortune, Business Week,* and *Forbes.* Here, leaders are either lionized for their companies' spectacular successes or blamed for their organizations' colossal failures. After all, how often do we see pictures of committees on the covers of such magazines?

The external control perspective is diametrically opposite. It holds that leaders really can't have much of an effect on their organization. After all, constraints such as limited resources, industry and broad economic conditions, and institutional investors put the leaders in a straightjacket from which there is little mobility or freedom to maneuver.

Both perspectives have some merit. Few would argue that leaders such as Arthur Martinez, Lou Gerstner, and Jack Welch, respectively, have not had a major impact on Sears', IBM's, and GE's recent successes. And successful leaders do not operate in a vacuum; they must constantly be aware of economic and noneconomic trends and events both within and outside their organization's increasingly fuzzy boundaries. Effective leaders, however, don't permit constraints to be an overriding focus. Instead, they apply their skills and knowledge through the development of creative solutions.

This chapter provides insights into how organizations can manage change and cope with increased environmental complexity and uncertainty more effectively. We introduce what are considered to be the three most important leadership activities and then provide a framework for how leaders can help their companies learn and adapt in the face of accelerating change in the competitive landscape. Central to this idea is the concept of empowerment: that employees and managers truly come to have a sense of self-determination, meaning, competence, and impact. We will also address the other key activities in the learning organization: accumulating and sharing internal knowledge, gathering and integrating external information, and challenging the status quo and enabling creativity.

The Importance of Leadership

What is leadership? Is it enough merely to keep the organization afloat, or is it essential to make steady progress toward some more or less well-defined objective? We believe that custodial management is not leadership. Rather, leadership is proactive, goal oriented, and focused on the creation and implementation of a creative vision. Succinctly: *Leadership is about the process of transforming organizations from what they are to what the leader would have them become.* This definition implies quite a bit: dissatisfaction with the status quo, a vision of what should be, and a process for bringing about change.

An insurance company executive recently shared the following insight on leadership: "I lead by the Noah Principle: It's all right to know when it's going to rain, but, by God, you had better build the ark." Warren Bennis, one of today's foremost authorities on leadership, makes an important distinction between leadership and management:

> Leaders are people who do the right things. Managers are people who do things right. There's a profound difference. When you think about doing the right things, your mind immediately goes toward thinking about the future, thinking about dreams, missions, visions, strategic intent, purpose. But when you think about doing things right, you think about control mechanisms. You think about how-to. Leaders ask the what and why question, not the how question.[2]

Doing the "right thing" is becoming increasingly important in today's competitive environment. After all, many industries are declining; the global village is becoming increasingly complex, interconnected, and unpredictable; and product and market life cycles are becoming increasingly compressed. Recently, when one of us asked the CEO of a supplier of computer components to describe the life cycle of his company's products, he replied: "Seven months from cradle to grave—and that includes three months to design the product and get it into production!" Richard D'Aveni, author of *Hypercompetition,* goes even further.

He argues that in a world where all dimensions of competition appear to be compressed in time and heightened in complexity, sustainable competitive advantages are no longer possible.

Three Interdependent Leadership Activities

We define the role of a leader in terms of three interdependent activities, as illustrated in Exhibit 6-2:

- Determining a direction
- Designing the organization
- Nurturing a culture dedicated to excellence and ethical behavior[3]

The interdependent nature of these three activities is evident. Consider an organization with a great mission and a wonderful organization structure and design, but a culture that implicitly encourages shirking and unethical behavior. Or, a superb culture and organization design but little direction and vision—in caricature, a highly ethical and efficient buggy whip manufacturer. Or, one with a sound direction and strong culture, but counterproductive teams and a zero-sum reward system. In our view, many organizations fall short of their potential because their leaders do not give equal consideration to each of these three activities. The imagery of a three-legged stool is instructive; it will collapse if one leg is missing or broken.

Determining a Direction

Leaders need a holistic understanding of their organization's stakeholders, including customers, suppliers, and shareholders. This means they

EXHIBIT 6-2.
Three interdependent activities of leadership.

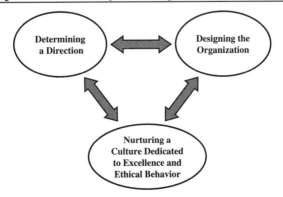

must be able to scan the environment to develop a knowledge of all of the stakeholders and other salient environmental trends and events and integrate this knowledge into a vision of what the organization could become. It requires the capacity to solve increasingly complex problems, become proactive in approach, and develop viable strategic options. A strategic vision provides many benefits: a clear future direction, a framework for their organization's mission and goals, and improved employee communication, participation, and commitment.

At times, the creative process involves what the CEO of Yokogawa, GE's Japanese partner in the medical systems business, calls "bullet train" thinking. That is, if you want to increase the speed by 10 mph, you look for incremental advances; however, if you want to double the speed, you've got to think out of the box, considering, for example, widening the track or changing the overall suspension system. Leaders typically don't just need to keep the same train with a few minor tweaks, but rather come up with more revolutionary visions.

Consider how Enron's CEO, Kenneth Lay, completely changed his company's (and its industry's) mental model of the natural gas pipeline industry:

> In 1986, after Enron was formed by the merger of two natural gas pipeline giants, Lay determined that it was time to change the entire way his company did business. According to Lay, "I was trained as an economist, love free markets, and was convinced that government regulation was causing most of the problems in the industry."
>
> By pushing for deregulation, Lay felt that Enron could use all of those natural gas lines as a network to buy gas where it was cheap and sell it where it was needed. (Regulation required a gas pipeline to run from a specific field to a particular utility company, with few shifts or diversions.) Although other gas utilities pressed for continued regulation, Enron hired aggressive, well-paid traders and almost single-handedly began creating spot markets in gas. Enron found that its new approach and structure could reduce the cost of gas for some utilities by 30 percent to 50 percent. "We changed the concept of how the natural gas industry was run—new products, new services, new kinds of contracts, new ways of pricing," says Lay. Texas senator Phil Gramm had this to say about Kenneth Lay: "He has the ability to step back from an issue and see the big picture, something that I don't see in a lot of people in business."

> Enron's financial results have been impressive. Sales soared 52 percent to $20.2 billion in 1997, and the average annual total return to investors over the past decade has been 19.7 percent.

Visionary thinking is not restricted to a company's top executive. Back in 1994, during the early stages of Sears' dramatic transformation, the company's top 120 executives were grouped into task forces on teams that examined customers, employees, and financial performance. Working together, they arrived at a vision for the business: a "compelling place to shop, work, and invest." Fourteen of the proposed measurements were eventually reduced to six to build Sears' performance index: one measure for compelling place to work, two for compelling place to shop, and three for compelling place to invest. Then a consulting company was hired to develop a quantitative model that goes beyond simple correlation and permits management to make inferences about cause and effect with a rather high level of predictability. For example, according to Anthony Ricci, chief administrative officer:

> Now we know that if a store increases its employee satisfaction score by five measuring units this quarter, the following quarter its customer-satisfaction scores will go up by two units. And if a store increases its customer satisfaction by two units this quarter, its revenue growth the following quarter will beat our stores' national average by 0.5 percent. It's not guesswork or theory anymore. We have built an empirical model that says unless you have a trained, literate, motivated, competent work force, and give them decision-making authority, you don't get satisfied customers no matter how good the merchandise is.

This example illustrates the importance of incorporating a vision into the design of the organization's structure, evaluation, and control system, which leads us to the next activity.

Designing the Organization

Leaders must be actively involved in building structures, teams, systems, and organizational processes that facilitate the implementation of their strategic vision. Poor organizational design can result in a myriad of problems, including these:

- Inadequate understanding of responsibility and accountability among managers and employees
- Reward systems that fail to motivate individuals toward objectives
- Poor or inappropriate budgeting and control systems
- Inappropriate or insufficient mechanisms to integrate and coordinate activities across the company.

Sears thus converted its vision into a quantitative means of evaluation and control. Bill Parzybok, CEO of Fluke Manufacturing, based in Everett, Washington, both created and implemented his vision for the company through the effective use of teams.[4] Each team typically consisted of six people: two each from marketing, finance, and engineering.

When Parzybok became CEO in 1991, he declared the company's mission to be the market leader in portable electronic testing tools for professionals. A team-based approach was designed to turn that mission into a reality.

Four principles underlay the innovative team-based approach. First, team members should "live with customers" instead of studying them at a distance. Rather than interviewing technicians, team members were required to walk around with the people actually doing the job.

Second, the teams valued curiosity over expertise. Believing that experts are often less creative than novices, team members were selected for their lack of knowledge of the markets they were researching.

Third, the team members had absolute focus; each team member made a full-time commitment to its assignment. Team members even stationed themselves in "war rooms" to avoid distractions.

Fourth is the principle of independence. For example, just as one Fluke team began to understand the opportunities in network maintenance, another company, Forte Networks, showed the team its own hand-held product. The Fluke team began discussing an alliance in which Fluke would own exclusive marketing rights and let Forte manufacture the device. The alliance was already underway by the time the team presented the business plan to top executives.

Fluke's team concept has paid off. The company now introduces twelve new products each year, up from three per year in the late 1980s. And over a recent three-year period, the stock has more than doubled.

The Fluke example shows how a vision was implemented through a change in the organization's basic design—the move toward a team-based approach. Also, implicit in the new design was a strong cultural element: the autonomy, cohesiveness, independence, and empowerment that team members enjoyed.

Nurturing a Culture Dedicated to Excellence and Ethical Behavior

In Chapter 5 we discussed how organization culture can be an effective and positive means of organizational control. Leaders play a key role in developing and sustaining—as well as changing, when necessary—an organization's culture.[5] Consider how Ray Gilmartin has transformed Merck's "turf-conscious culture" since becoming CEO on June 9, 1994:

> As an outsider to both Merck and the pharmaceutical industry, Gilmartin initially met with Merck's top forty or so executives and humbly admitted he had a lot to learn. He began by posing questions such as, "What do you think are the major issues we need to resolve?" and "If you had my job, what would you focus on?" During the interviews he demonstrated a key element of his leadership style: he likes to air problems and debate without regard for hierarchy. He says, "Where you want the contest is not among people but among ideas. It's very important for people to be able to challenge, to be very open."
>
> Gilmartin also makes symbolic gestures to strengthen Merck's culture. For example, he disdains many of the trappings of his office. And it was not only for symbolic reasons that he unlocked the doors to the executive suite at the Whitehouse Station, New Jersey, headquarters. Further, he has regular breakfast meetings with staffers, partly to improve morale.
>
> He has also won the loyalty of his top executives by granting high levels of autonomy. For example, the highly respected CFO, Judy Lewent, is pleased that Gilmartin has asked her to oversee Merck's ventures with Du Pont, Johnson & Johnson, and Astra. And research chief Dr. Edward M. Scolnick, earlier a rival for the CEO post, says he doesn't regret being passed over: "The company is far better off having him as CEO and me as head of research." Part of the reason for Scolnick's magnanimity is that nonscientist Gilmartin, unlike former CEO Roy Vagelos, is "completely dependent" on Scol-

nick's judgment on lab matters. Scolnick claims, "He's delegated to me . . . and my responsibility is to make sure that I come through for him."

The financial results have been impressive. Sales and profits are way up. And since he took over in June 1994, Merck's stock has zoomed from 30¾ to nearly 130 by the end of March 1998, an impressive gain even for the recently soaring drug stocks.

Guiding the ethical values of an organization is also a central leadership activity. Clearly, the leader is a role model, and deeds speak louder than words. Consider how CEO Robert Haas of Levi Strauss, a company long admired for its ethical values, applied its global sourcing guidelines and corporate values to solve an ethical dilemma:

In 1991, we developed a set of Global Sourcing Guidelines. Drafting these guidelines was difficult. Applying them has proven even more challenging. When we were rolling out our guidelines—which included extensive on-site audits of each of our 700 contractors worldwide—we discovered that two of our manufacturing contractors in Bangladesh and one in Turkey employed under-age workers. This was a clear violation of our guidelines, which prohibit the use of child labor. At the outset, it appeared that we had two options:

■ Instruct our contractors to fire these children, knowing that many are the sole wage earners for their families and that if they lost their jobs, their families would face extreme hardships . . . or we could . . .

■ Continue to employ under-age children, ignoring our stance against the use of child labor.

By referencing our ethical guidelines for decision making we came up with a different approach and one that we believe helped to minimize adverse ethical consequences. The contractors agreed to pay the underage children their salaries and benefits while they go to school full-time. We agreed to pay for books, tuition and uniforms. When the children reach legal working age, they will be offered jobs in the plant. Due to these efforts, 35 children have attended school in Bangladesh, while another six are currently in school in Turkey.

And how did we benefit from this situation? We were able to retain quality contractors that play an important role in our worldwide sourcing strategy. At the same time, we were able to honor our values and protect our brands.

People throughout organizations must become involved in leadership processes and play greater roles in both the formulation and implementation of an organization's strategies and tactics. Put another way, to learn and adapt, companies need "eyes, ears, and brains" throughout the organization. One person or a small group of individuals can no longer think and learn for the entire entity.

Creating the Learning Organization

Charles Handy, author of *The Age of Unreason* and *The Age of Paradox* and one of today's most respected business visionaries, recently told this amusing story:

> The other day, a courier could not find my family's remote cottage. He called his base on his radio, and the base called us to ask directions. He was just around the corner, but his base managed to omit a vital part of the directions. So he called them again, and they called us again. Then the courier repeated the cycle a third time to ask whether we had a dangerous dog. When he eventually arrived, we asked whether it would not have been simpler and less aggravating to everyone if he had called us directly from the roadside telephone booth where he had been parked. "I can't do that," he said, "because they won't refund any money I spend." "But it's only pennies!" I exclaimed. "I know," he said, "but that only shows how little they trust us!"[6]

At first glance, it would appear that the story simply epitomizes the lack of empowerment—and trust—granted to the hapless courier: "Don't ask questions. Do as you're told!" However, implicit in this scenario is also the message that learning, information sharing, adaptation, decision making, and so on are not shared throughout the organization. Although this is admittedly a rather extreme case, leading-edge organizations recognize the importance of having everyone involved in the process of actively learning and adapting.[7] As noted by today's leading expert on learning organizations, MIT's Peter Senge, the days when Henry Ford, Alfred Sloan, and Tom Watson "learned for the organization are gone":

> In an increasingly dynamic, interdependent, and unpredictable world, it is simply no longer possible for anyone to "figure it all out at the top." The old model, "the top thinks and the local acts," must now give way to integrating thinking and acting at all levels. While the challenge is great, so is the potential payoff. "The person who figures out how to harness the collective genius of the people in his or her organization," according to former Citibank CEO Walter Wriston, "is going to blow the competition away."

John Browne, CEO of British Petroleum, the most profitable of the major oil companies, shares a similar perspective:

> Learning is at the heart of a company's ability to adapt to a rapidly changing environment. It is the key to being able both to identify opportunities that others might not see and to exploit those opportunities rapidly and fully. This means that in order to generate extraordinary value for shareholders, a company has to learn better than its competitors and apply that knowledge throughout its businesses faster and more widely than they do. The way we see it, anyone in the organization who is not directly accountable for making a profit should be involved in creating and distributing knowledge that the company can use to make a profit.

Learning and change typically require the ongoing questioning of an organization's status quo or modus operandi. Individuals throughout the organization—not just at the top—must reflect on these processes. In fact, organizations, especially successful ones, are so caught up in carrying out their day-to-day work that they rarely, if ever, stop to think objectively about themselves and their businesses. They often fail to ask the probing questions that might lead them to call into question their basic assumptions, refresh their strategies, or reengineer their work processes. According to Michael Hammer and Steven Stanton, the pioneer consultants who touched off the reengineering movement:

Reflection entails awareness of self, of competitors, of customers. It means thinking without preconception. It means questioning cherished assumptions and replacing them with new approaches. It is the only way in which a winning company can maintain its leadership position, by which a company with great assets can ensure that they continue to be well deployed.

Reflection also requires "double-loop" as opposed to "single-loop" learning throughout the organization, an important distinction noted by Chris Argyris of Harvard University. In single-loop learning, the focus of most traditional (and outdated) control systems, actual performance is simply compared to a predetermined goal. This is fine for companies that compete in simple and unchanging competitive environments, but there are not too many of them left! In double-loop learning, the organization's assumptions, premises, goals, and strategies are continually monitored, tested, and reviewed. Consider the metaphor used by Steven Covey, author of the best-selling book, *The Seven Habits of Highly Effective People*. He says that one level of learning, well suited to management, is like climbing a ladder, whereas a higher level of learning, one that requires leadership, requires questioning whether the ladder is leaning against the right wall. Consider what would happen if an organization attempts to use Covey's ladder during a crisis, say, in response to a flood. One response would be to climb the ladder to a higher level as the water rises and wait for rescue. This is an adaptive solution that Covey would equate to management. An alternative solution would be to take the ladder down and use it as a frame for building a raft that can be poled to safety. This requires a generative solution in the creation of something that is entirely different from what was previously available for the organization to draw on.

Josh Weston, formerly CEO of ADP Corporation, captures the importance of double-loop learning for all employees in an organization:

At ADP, 39 plus 1 adds up to more than 40 plus zero. The 40-plus zero employee is the harried worker who at 40 hours a week just tries to keep up with what's in the "in" basket. He tries to do whatever he thinks he's supposed to do. Because he works his full 40 hours with his head down, he takes zero hours to think about what he's doing, why he's doing it, and how he's doing it. Where does the work go after he does it? Does he need to do it in the first place? On the other hand, a 39-plus-1 employee takes at least one of those 40 hours to think about what he's doing and why he's doing it. That's why the other 39 hours are far more productive.

Implicit in Weston's perspective is the active involvement of all employees in the questioning of their mental models and the organization's status quo. Mental models are mental pictures of how the world works and have a significant influence on how we perceive problems and opportunities, identify courses of action, and make choices. One of us always puts up a slide with the discussion of Weston's $39 + 1 > 40$ proposition in seminars on strategic thinking and leadership. It never fails to get frequently mentioned by participants—from such diverse backgrounds as medicine, education, volunteering, and business—as one of their major learning points.

Successful learning organizations create a proactive, creative approach to the unknown, solicit the involvement of employees at all levels, and enable everyone to use their intelligence and apply their imagination. Higher-level skills are required of everyone, not just those at the top. A learning environment involves organization-wide commitment to change, an action orientation, and applicable tools and methods. It must be viewed by everyone as a guiding philosophy and not simply as another change program, often derisively labeled the new "flavor of the month."

A critical requirement of all learning organizations is that everyone supports a compelling purpose. In the words of William O'Brien, CEO of Hanover Insurance, "Before there can be meaningful participation, people must share certain values and pictures about where we are trying to go. We discovered that people have a real need to feel that they're part of an ennobling mission." Similarly, consider how Percy Barnevik, CEO of the Swedish-Swiss holding company that includes Asea Brown Boveri, nurtures pride and the creative spirit in his organization:

> It is important that people in an organization have something to be proud of. It is important that our people can feel pride in something beyond the numbers. For example, if you look at our company now, we have been pioneering investments in Eastern Europe, spearheading East-West integration. Many of our people are proud of participating in that proc-

ess. The same can be said about our work in the environmental field. I would like to create and develop an image of us as helping to improve the world environment. For example, transferring sustainable technology to China or India, where they have a tremendous need to clean up their coal-fired power plants.

Our employees can look at work like that and see that we contribute something beyond mere shareholder value. Internally, we can pride ourselves on certain environmental improvements without being too bombastic or boastful about them. This is particularly relevant for attracting young people to the company. They are by and large not happy just to work for a big company with high profits; they also like to see a purpose that goes beyond numbers. It is important that a company can be perceived as changing the world in a positive way.*

Inspiring and motivating people with a mission or purpose is a necessary but not a sufficient condition for developing an organization that can learn and adapt to a rapidly changing, complex, and interconnected environment. In the next four sections, we'll address four other critical ongoing processes of learning organizations:

- Empowering employees at all levels
- Accumulating and sharing internal knowledge
- Gathering and integrating external information
- Challenging the status quo and enabling creativity.

We will close the chapter with a discussion of Chaparral Steel's commitment to a learning organization.

Empowering Employees at All Levels

"The great leader is a great servant," asserts Ken Melrose, CEO of Toro Company and author of *Making the Grass Greener on Your Side*. A manager's role becomes creating an environment where employees can achieve their potential as they help move the organization toward its goals. Instead of viewing themselves as resource controllers and as power brokers, leaders must truly envision themselves as flexible re-

---

*M. F. R. Kets de Vries, "Charisma in Action." Reprinted by permission of the publisher, from ORGANIZATIONAL DYNAMICS WINTER 1998 (c) 1998 American Management Association, New York, http:www.amanet.org. All rights reserved.

sources willing to assume numerous (perhaps unaccustomed) roles—coaches, information providers, teachers, decision makers, facilitators, supporters, or listeners—depending on their employees' needs.

The central key to empowerment is effective leadership. Empowerment can't occur in a leadership vacuum. According to Melrose, "I came to understand that you best lead by serving the needs of your people. You don't do their jobs for them; you enable them to learn and progress on the job." In a recent article in *Organizational Dynamics*, Robert Quinn and Gretchen Spreitzer made an interesting point regarding what may be viewed as two diametrically opposite perspectives on empowerment.[8] In the top-down perspective, empowerment is about delegation and accountability; senior management has developed a clear vision and has communicated specific plans to the rest of the organization. This strategy for empowerment becomes:

- Start at the top.
- Clarify the organization's mission, vision, and values.
- Clearly specify the tasks, roles, and rewards for employees.
- Delegate responsibility.
- Hold people accountable for results.

By contrast, the bottom-up view looks at empowerment as concerned with risk taking, growth, and change. It involves trusting people to "do the right thing" and having a tolerance for failure. They'd act with a sense of ownership and typically "ask for forgiveness rather than permission." Here are the salient elements of empowerment:

- Start at the bottom by understanding the needs of employees.
- Model empowered behavior for the employees.
- Build teams to encourage cooperative behavior.
- Encourage intelligent risk taking.
- Trust people to perform.

Clearly these two perspectives draw a sharp contrast in assumptions that people make about trust and control. Interestingly, when Quinn and Spreitzer shared these contrasting views of empowerment with a senior management team, someone from the first group, after an initial heavy silence, voiced a concern about the second group's perspective: "We can't afford loose cannons around here." A person in the second group retorted, "When was the last time you saw a cannon of any kind around here."

Many leading-edge organizations are moving in the direction of the second perspective: recognizing the need for trust, cultural control, and expertise at all levels versus the extensive and cumbersome rules and regulations inherent in hierarchical control.[9] Some have argued that too often organizations fall prey to the "heroes-and-drones syndrome," wherein the value of those in powerful positions is exalted and of those who fail to achieve top rank is diminished. Such an attitude is implicit in phrases such as, "Lead, follow, or get out of the way," or, even less appealing, "Unless you're the lead horse, the view never changes." The fact is, of course, that few will ever reach the top hierarchical positions in organizations, but in the information economy, strong organizations are those that effectively use the talents of all team players.

Consider Chris Turner's perspective. She's an executive called the "Learning Person" for Xerox Business Services (XBS), a $1 billion organization growing at 40 percent a year. Largely through her efforts, XBS has created an environment that not only produces business results but also supports personal growth:

> My job is to disturb the system. I give people new ways to think. It's more a matter of offering people different perspectives and influencing their thinking than trying to drive them. It sounds strangely indirect. Why not adopt a more top-down approach? . . . It turns out you can't "empower" anyone. This is not the freeing of the slaves.

Turner makes the insightful point about empowerment's requiring more than the sprinkling of fairy dust. At first glance, it may appear that this overstates or trivializes the case, but it is critical that organizations look at empowerment as involving more than just "giving more power" to people throughout the organization. It's the "I've given it to you—now run with it" mentality.

Effective organizations must also redistribute information, knowledge (skills to act on the information), and rewards.[10] For example, a company may give front-line employees the power to act as "customer advocates," doing whatever is necessary to satisfy the customers. However, employees would also need to have the appropriate training to act in this manner. The company would need to disseminate information by sharing customer expectations and feedback, as well as financial information. The employees would need to know about the business's goals and objectives, as well as how key value-creating activities in the organization are related to each other. Finally, organizations should allocate rewards on the basis of how effectively employees use information, knowledge, and power to improve customer service quality and the company's financial performance.

Accumulating and Sharing Internal Knowledge

Jack Stack is president and CEO of Springfield ReManufacturing Corporation, in Springfield, Missouri, and author of *The Great Game of Business*.[11] He is generally considered the pioneer of open book management, an innovative way to gather and disseminate internal information. Implementing this system involves three core activities. First, numbers are generated daily for each of the company's employees, reflecting their work performance and production costs. Second, this information, aggregated once a week, is shared with all of the company's employees, from secretaries to top management. Third, extensive training is offered about how to use and interpret the numbers—how to understand balance sheets as well as cash flows and income statements.

In explaining why SRC embraces open book management, Stack provides an insightful counterperspective to the old adage, "Knowledge is power":

> We are building a company in which everyone tells the truth every day—not because everyone is honest but because everyone has access to the same information: operating metrics, financial data, valuation estimates. The more people understand what's really going on in their company, the more eager they are to help solve its problems. Information isn't power. It's a burden. Share information, and you share the burdens of leadership as well.

Similarly, Robert Frey, chairman of Cin-Made Corporation, a manufacturer of mailing tubes, argues, "Owners typically believe information is power. And they want to hold on to that power." However, in the five years since Frey opened the company books, profitability at Cin-Made has grown fivefold. Not only is productivity up 30 percent, but union grievances and employee turnover have virtually disappeared.

These perspectives help to point out both the motivational and utilitarian uses of sharing company information. It can apply to organizations of all sizes. Let's look at a very small company, Leonhardt Plating Company, a $1.5 million company that makes steel plating.

> CEO Daniel Leonhardt became an accidental progressive, so to speak. Recently, instead of trying to replace his polishing foreman, he resorted to a desperate, if cutting-edge, strategy. He decided to let the polishing department rule itself by committee.
>
> The results? Revenues have risen 25 percent in the past year. After employees had access to company information such as material prices, their decisions began paying off for the whole company. Says Leonhardt, "The workers are showing more interest in the company as a whole." Not surprisingly, he plans to introduce committee rule to other departments.

Additional benefits of management's sharing of company information can be gleaned from a look at Whole Foods Market, the largest natural foods grocer in the United States—with forty-three stores in ten states—that is on track to become a $1.4 billion company in 1998. Here, there's a strong emphasis on teamwork; the company's gain-sharing program ties bonuses directly to team performance, and team members vote on who gets hired. What makes the system work is a dedication to sharing virtually all company information with all employees, which CEO John Mackey calls a "no-secrets" management philosophy.

> The curious team member at any level of the company has access to nearly as much operating and financial data as anyone in the Austin, Texas, headquarters. In Ron Megahan's Bread and Circus store, for example, a sheet posted next to the time clock lists the previous day's sales broken down by team. Another sheet lists the sales numbers for the same day last year. Once a week, Megahan's store posts a fax that lists the sales of every store in the New England region broken down by team, with comparisons to the same week last year, as well as year-to-date totals. Another weekly fax gives sales information for every store in the organization, although it doesn't break down sales by team.
>
> Once a month, stores get detailed information on profitability. The report analyzes sales, product costs, wages and salaries, and operating profits for all forty-three stores. Because the data are so sensitive, the list is not posted publicly,

but it is freely available to anyone who wants to see it, and store managers routinely review it with their team leaders. Since individual teams make decisions about labor spending, ordering, and pricing—the factors that determine profitability—the reports are indispensable.

An important additional benefit of the sharing of internal information at Whole Foods becomes the active process of internal benchmarking. Competition is intense at Whole Foods. Teams compete against their own goals for sales, growth, and productivity; they compete against different teams in their stores; and they compete against similar teams at different stores and regions. Similarly, there is an elaborate system of peer reviews through which teams benchmark each other. The "Store Tour" is the most intense. On a periodic schedule, each Whole Foods store is toured by a group of as many as forty visitors from another region. The tour is a mix of social interaction, reviews, performance audits, and structured feedback sessions. Lateral learning—discovering what your colleagues are doing right and carrying those practices into your organization—has become a driving force at Whole Foods. John Mackey puts it bluntly: "If you don't cross-pollinate, you become a hick."

In his address at GE's 1997 annual meeting, CEO Jack Welch emphasized the importance of sharing ideas in his company's "Learning Culture." He views GE as a "bubbling cauldron of ideas and learning—with tens of thousands of people playing alternate roles of teacher and student":

Let me share a small sample of how our businesses learn from each other and how they use that learning. Our Medical Systems business, for instance, is a world leader in remote diagnostics, which means an installed GE CT scanner can be remotely monitored by our service people as it operates in a hospital. They can detect and repair an impending malfunction, sometimes on-line, sometimes before the customer even perceives there is a problem. Medical Systems has shared this technology with our jet engine business, with locomotives, with Motors and Industrial Systems, and with Power Systems, enabling them to monitor the performance of jet engines in flight, of locomotives pulling freight, of running paper mills, and of turbines in operation in customer power plants. This is one of the capabilities that gives us the opportunity to create a multi-billion dollar service business by upgrading the installed GE equipment operating around the world.

In addition to broader sharing of company information, both up and down as well as across the organization, leaders have to develop means to tap into some of the more informal sources of internal information. In a recent survey of presidents, CEOs, board members, and top executives in a variety of nonprofit organizations, respondents were asked what differentiated successful candidates for promotion. The consensus: The executive is a person who listens. According to Peter Meyer, the author of the study:

> The value of listening is clear: You cannot succeed in running a company if you do not hear what your people, customers, and suppliers are telling you. Poor listeners do not survive. Listening and understanding well are key to making good decisions.

Effective leaders must beware the errors of poor listening and misinterpretation. For example, an associate once told movie producer Sam Goldwyn that audiences would not respond to the script he wanted to produce—it was too *caustic*: Goldwyn's reply: "Too *costly*? To hell with the cost. If it's a good picture, we'll make it." Did he miss the point?

How do some executives glean key information, especially from the more informal sources? A well-known, and often effective, technique is MBWA—management by walking around. The term was coined about thirty years ago by Hewlett-Packard's John Doyle, formerly director of corporate development, personnel, and R&D, and it is still practiced by many leading-edge organizations, including Hewlett-Packard. In a recent company publication, CEO Lew Platt shared his insights on the use of MBWA:

> As the CEO of the 16th-largest U.S.-based corporation, my schedule is as demanding as anyone's in Hewlett-Packard. So I make a point of ensuring that MBWA is a part of my everyday life. For example:
>
> ■ I occasionally go to an employee's work area when a phone call or e-mail message would suffice. That gets me away from my desk for a brief time and I usually have three or four other interactions along the way

■ I eat in the HP cafeteria most days, typically with nonexecutives

■ I stop by HP sales offices and manufacturing sites when I'm traveling for other reasons. For instance, the President's Quality Award, which we instituted in 1994, is significant in that it includes 1-1/2 to 2 hours of informal time with employees. It's a time for celebration, and employees are very open to chatting.

MBWA is critically important for two reasons: it shows people that you care about them as individuals, not just as employees, and it's a wonderful opportunity to hear what's on people's minds. It's a great way for managers to motivate employees and to learn from them at the same time. Exhibit 6-3 sets out MBWA tips.

John Chambers, president and CEO of Cisco Systems, the $6 billion networking giant, developed an effective vehicle for getting candid feedback from employees and discovering potential problems. Every year during their birthday month, employees at Cisco's corporate headquarters in San Jose receive an e-mail invitation to a "birthday breakfast" with Chambers. Each month, several dozen of the employees who show up fire some pretty tough questions, including bruising queries

EXHIBIT 6-3.
Ten tips from the pros on management by walking around.

1. Wander frequently.
2. Wander aimlessly without an agenda.
3. Be inconsistent. Be spontaneous. Schedule time for this spontaneity if necessary.
4. Be a good listener. Don't try to steer the conversation. Let the other person do most of the talking.
5. Be open and don't argue. The goal is to provide an open environment of trust.
6. Talk about noncompany matters to really get to know your employees.
7. Wander about even if you're an introvert; it gets easier with time and practice.
8. Remember, this is not a waste of time. Personal involvement is essential to good management.
9. Ask open-ended questions: "Are you happy here?" "Do you like your job?" "What would make it more meaningful and productive?" "How is your family?" "How was the vacation?"
10. Talk with all your employees, not just the ones who are easy to talk with or who have similar interests.

about partnering strategy and stark assessments of perceived management failings. Any question is fair game, and directors and vice presidents are strongly discouraged from attending. Although these sessions are not always pleasant, Chambers believes it is an indispensable hour of unmediated interaction. At times, he finds there's an inconsistency between what his executives say they are doing and what's actually happening. For example, at a recent quarterly meeting with 500 managers, Chambers asked how many managers required job applicants to have five interviews. When all raised their hands, he retorted, "I have a problem, because at the past three birthday breakfasts, I asked the new hires how many had interviewed that way, and only half raised their hands. You've got to fix it." His take on the birthday breakfasts is this: "I'm not there for the cake."

Technology can also play a vital role in creating and disseminating information across an organization. Perhaps a role model in this regard would be PeopleSoft, with over a $5 billion market capitalization and a powerful position in one of technology's hottest sectors: enterprise resource planning (ERP) software.

> To illustrate, each newly hired employee at PeopleSoft receives the same laptop: a top-of-the-line model with a CD-ROM drive, a high-speed modem, and lots of performance enhancements. One purpose in giving everyone the same computer is to underscore the company's aversion to hierarchy. A more important purpose is to support its all-important global network. At PeopleSoft, a laptop isn't just a personal productivity device. It's the point of entry into a massive information infrastructure that spans continents and time zones. "You can take your laptop to any of our offices anywhere in the world, plug it in, and the network recognizes you as if you were in your home office," CIO Steve Zarate says with obvious pride.
>
> CEO Dave Duffield is explicit about the kind of company he's building at PeopleSoft: "The objective is to have all 4,500 people know what matters. If people don't have total access to information, they have to guess what they should be doing." Both e-mail and 400 Lotus Notes databases are powerful forces for open access. These databases store marketing presentations, intelligence on competitors, and status reports on projects. Claims Duffield, "Anyone can get to anyone else or to any piece of information."

Employee training and development also provide an opportunity to gather and disseminate internal information throughout the organization. Although we will not reiterate the points from Chapter 2, we close this section with a brief discussion of the Bank of Montreal's new $50 million residential facility for its Institute for Learning (IFL).

> In part, the design of the physical facility was made to facilitate a dynamic environment for continual learning. Vast hallways are punctuated with windowed alcoves, purposely designed for serendipitous meetings and informal conversations. Additionally, eight role-play rooms with video-playback technology stand ready, and the central hall features an "affinity wall" on which clients engage in dialogue.
>
> According to Diane Blair, manager of meta-learnings at IFL, "Our goal is not as much about teaching a specific skill as developing a person's capacity for learning. That's very different from: Tell me what I need to be."
>
> Ironically, the best class is not a class at all. Open forums are the "penultimate water cooler," says Blair. For example, IFL's Productivity Forum '95 brought together 150 employees from all levels with no planned agenda or presentations. Instead, participants created their own agenda, convened their own sessions, and generated a book of proceedings.[12]

Gathering and Integrating External Information

Recognizing the opportunities—and the threats—in the external environment is vital to a company's success. The organization must become *externally aware* and sensitive to all that is going on around it. Focusing exclusively on the efficiency of internal operations may result in a company's becoming, in effect, the world's most efficient producer of typewriters or leisure suits—hardly an enviable position. As organizations *and* environments become more complex and evolve rapidly, it is far more critical for employees and managers to understand environmental events and trends—and to gather and interpret current intelligence about the company's competitors and customers. How effectively an organization gathers, interprets and integrates relevant external information into its internal decision-making processes has a lot to do with its performance in the competitive environment.

Organizational strategies and competitive responses are frequently based more on management's collective assumptions, premises, and beliefs than on an empirical understanding of the environment.

Hamel and Prahalad, in *Competing for the Future*, maintain that "every manager carries around in his or her head a set of biases, assumptions and presuppositions about the structure of the relevant 'industry,' about how one makes money in the industry, about who the competition is and isn't, about who the customers are and aren't, about which technologies are viable and which aren't, and so on." Peter Drucker calls this interrelated set of assumptions the "theory of the business."[13]

Strategies frequently go awry when management's internal frame of reference is out touch with the realities of the business situation, when one or more of management's assumptions, premises, or beliefs are incorrect, or when internal inconsistencies among them render the overall theory of the business no longer valid. Arthur Martinez, chairman of Sears, Roebuck & Co., puts it this way: "Today's peacock is tomorrow's feather duster."

In the business world, many peacocks have become feather dusters over the past several years (or at least had their plumage dulled). Consider Novell and Silicon Graphics in the high-tech sector; both have hit hard times. Novell, unfortunately, went head to head with Microsoft, and Silicon Graphics ignored the PC market and mistakenly focused on high-end machines (a much smaller market), including its purchase of troubled Cray Research. And McDonald's insular management culture has cost it more than a few feathers in recent years. In addition to an eroding market share, its recent two-year total return was 3 percent. Compare this to the benchmark performance of some of the world's top brands: Coca-Cola (71 percent), Gillette (101 percent), Sony (49 percent), and Walt Disney (49 percent).

On the plus side, recall Andy Grove's legendary "bet-the-company" strategic move in 1985, when Intel walked away from the business that launched the company two decades earlier: memory chips. Sales and profits for 1997 soared to $25.1 billion and $6.9 billion, respectively, and the company enjoys a near-monopoly in microprocessors.

Most readers are probably less familiar with Paul Orfalea's dramatic success story. While most students were whining about the high cost of the University of California at Santa Barbara's library's ten-cent per page charge for copy services, Paul sensed opportunity. With a $5,000 bank loan, he opened his first "copy center" in 1970—a rented former hamburger stand near campus. He went by the name "Kinko" because of his curly red hair; his huge chain now has over 860 stores, expected to grow to 2,000 locations by the year 2000. In January 1997, the New York investment company of Clayton, Dublilier & Rice, Inc.

acquired a one-third interest in Kinko's for $219 million to help spur the organization's growth and expansion.

Two totally different industries, semiconductors and reproduction services, but in both cases, a dramatic success began with the perception of an opportunity that no one else recognized. So how does the learning organization go about ensuring that it is in touch with its environment? We believe the process begins by creating a *culture of environmental awareness.*

Creating a Culture of External Awareness

In small entrepreneurial organizations, one externally-aware visionary who is alert to the potential opportunity or sees the first signs of impending danger may be enough. In larger organizations, however, the CEO can't do it all. He can, however, create and reinforce a culture that is sensitive to and aware of its environment, curious about its surroundings, and responsive to the early signals of change. Hundreds of pairs of eyes and ears will clearly be more effective than one or two in detecting the early signals of environmental change. We believe that five key elements must be addressed in creating a culture of external awareness:

- Priority
- Involvement
- Focus
- Process
- Motivation

Priority. Gathering and sharing relevant external information must become an organizational priority—part of the culture. Its importance and urgency must be demonstrated and communicated by timely and relevant examples of the successful use of current intelligence and the adverse consequences of not having timely and relevant information.

Involvement. Everyone must be involved. Front line customer contact personnel: salesmen, service technicians, purchasing agents, clerks and receptionists, are in constant contact with customers, suppliers and competitors and their committed involvement is essential.

Focus. The effort must be focused. No organization needs to know everything that is going on in its environment—but some things are vital. People need to know what to look for—what kinds of information are relevant and important to the success of the organization—and what can be safely ignored.

Process. Internal processes must be implemented to ensure that relevant information is quickly and accurately communicated within the organization, properly interpreted, and delivered to those who have the authority and responsibility to take appropriate action.

Motivation. Employees must be motivated to participate and contribute. Formal incentives, rewards and recognition have their place, but frequently, positive feedback and an understanding of how an individual contribution helped the organization are sufficient motivation.

Tools and Techniques

While most managers will acknowledge the need for a better understanding of their competitive environments, most organizations are unwilling to invest the organizational resources necessary to implement a formal program of competitor intelligence. More often than not, managers take advantage of a variety of less formal—but not necessarily less effective—means to "keep in touch" with their environments. Some of the most interesting approaches include:

- Using the Internet as a resource
- Networking
- Benchmarking
- Sharing information with customers and suppliers

To illustrate these points, we will provide a few selected examples:

Using the Internet as a resource. The Internet has dramatically accelerated the speed with which anyone can track down useful information, or locate people who might have useful information. Prior to the Net, locating someone who used to work at a company—always a good source of information—was quite a challenge. Today people post their resumes on the Web; they participate in discussion groups and say where they work. It's pretty straightforward.

Once Leonard Fuld, founder of Fuld and Company and creator of many well-accepted research techniques in the area of competitor intelligence, was retained to determine the size, strength, and technical capabilities of a privately held company. At first it was difficult to obtain detailed information. Then, one of his analysts used Deja News (http://www.dejanews.com), a search engine that tracks on-line discussion groups. The company being researched had posted fourteen job openings to one Usenet newsgroup. In essence, the posting was like a road map of its development strategy.

Another use of the Internet is provided by Marc Friedman, manager of market research at Andrew Corporation, a fast-growing manufacturer of wireless communications with annual revenues just under $1 billion. One site that he likes to visit is Corptech (http://www.corpnews.com), which provides information on 45,000 high-tech companies and more than 170,000 executives. One of his company's product lines consisted of antennas for air-traffic control systems. He got a request to provide a country-by-country breakdown of upgrade plans for various airports. Although he knew nothing about air traffic control at the time, he found a site on the net for the International Civil Aviation Organization. It had lots of useful data, including several research companies that had done reports.

Using conventional sources. When everyone is involved, even traditional sources for the acquisition of external information become more powerful. Much can be learned from trade and professional journals, books, and the typical business magazines such as *Forbes, Business Week, Fortune, Fast Company,* and so on, but no one individual has time to read them all. If, however, everyone in the organization is involved in gathering external information, it is more likely that a broader range of sources will be covered. For example, some professional journals can have an extremely narrow focus, but can be very useful.

Networking. Networking among colleagues both inside and outside of one's industry is also a very useful means. Intel's Andy Grove, for example, picks the brains of people like DreamWorks SKG's Steven Spielberg and Tele-Communications Inc.'s John Malone. He believes that such interaction helps to provide insights into how to make PCs more entertaining and better at communicating. Internally, he spends time with the young propeller-heads who run Intel Architecture labs, an Oregon-based skunk-works that Grove hopes will become the de facto R&D lab for the entire PC industry.

Benchmarking. Benchmarking is often a useful source of external information. Here, managers seek out the best examples of a particular practice as part of an ongoing effort to improve the corresponding practice in their own organization.[14] There are two primary types of benchmarking: *competitive benchmarking,* which restricts the search for best practices to competitors, and *functional benchmarking,* which endeavors to determine best practices regardless of industry. Industry-specific standards (such as response times required to repair power outages in the electric utility industry) are typically best handled through competitive benchmarking; more generic processes (such as answering toll-free calls) lend themselves to functional benchmarking because the function is essentially the same in any industry.

When Xerox wanted to improve its order fulfillment operations, it went to L. L. Bean, the Freeport, Maine, mail order house. Although the products of the two companies had little in common, the order-filling processes were very similar. Both involve picking items that vary so much in size and shape that they have to be picked manually. L. L. Bean was able to pick orders three times as fast as Xerox, and through benchmarking and thoroughly studying Bean's process, Xerox was able to cut its warehousing costs by 10 percent. The methods L. L. Bean used were hardly exotic—for example, stocking high-volume items close to the packing stations and having workers periodically plot flowcharts that traced their movements. In line with the theme of this chapter, after Chrysler observed the operation, the carmaker decided that it should rely more on "problem solving at the local level."

Ford Motor Company also benefited from benchmarking by studying Mazda's accounts payable operations. The initial goal of a 20 percent cut in its 500-employee accounts payable staff was ratcheted up to 75 percent—and met. Ford's benchmarkers found that staff spent most of their time trying to match often-conflicting data in a mass of paper, including purchase orders, invoices, and receipts. Following Mazda's example, Ford created an "invoiceless system" in which invoices no longer trigger payments to suppliers. The receipt does the job.

Frank P. Doyle, GE's executive vice president and corporate executive officer, provides some useful insights on the need for modeling best practices:

In the 1980s, we started our process of benchmarking our activities with the outside world—seeking the world-class best way of doing everything we were trying to do. It is extremely valuable—*but it is not a very happy experience.* It seems there is always someone, somewhere, who has figured out how to do it better. The good news is how open people are about what they do and seem happy if you choose to copy them.

Don't go only to the predictable places—we, of course, have spent time with Wal-Mart on distribution and Motorola on quality. But we also found that the best job on continuing training of career employees was being done by the U.S. Army. A side benefit—but a very important one—is that it is amazing how quickly a "humbled" organization can learn to change.

Sharing information with customers and suppliers. Many organizations learn a great deal by regularly sharing information with their customers and suppliers. William McKnight, head of 3M's Chicago sales office, required that sales reps of abrasives products talk directly to the workers in the shop to find out what they needed—instead of calling only on front-office executives. This was quite innovative at the time in 1909 and is still a good practice, illustrating the need to get to a product or service's end user. (McKnight went on to become 3M's president from 1929 to 1949 and chairman from 1949 to 1969.)

More recently, Fred Taylor, senior vice president for global marketing at Gateway 2000, discussed the value of customer input in reducing response time, a critical success factor in the PC industry:

> We talk to 100,000 people a day—people calling to order a computer, shopping around, looking for tech support. Our Web site gets 1.1 million hits per day. The time it takes for an idea to enter this organization, get processed, and then go to customers for feedback is down to minutes. We've designed the company around speed and feedback.

Challenging the Status Quo and Enabling Creativity

Here is Edward Bear, coming downstairs now, bump, bump, bump, on the back of his head, behind Christopher Robin. It is, as far as he knows, the only way of coming downstairs, but sometimes he feels that there really is another way, if only he could stop bumping for a moment and think of it.

A. A. Milne, Winnie-the-Pooh

Unlike Edward Bear, organizations and people do have a choice. So why is there often such resistance to change? There are, of course, many reasons why organizations are prone to inertia, slow to learn, adapt, and change and, in essence, just keep "bumping along." Researchers have identified numerous barriers to organizational change. Some of the most common include:

- Commitment to the status quo
- Structural barriers
- Behavioral barriers
- Political barriers
- Time constraints

Commitment to the status quo. Many people have vested interests in the status quo. There is a broad stream of organizational behavior literature on the subject of "escalation," whereby individuals (in both controlled laboratory and actual management practice) continue to throw "good money at bad decisions" despite negative performance feedback.[15] Management has a vested interest in the status quo and does not want to admit a bad decision or defeat. After all, careers may be on the line.

Structural barriers. Structural barriers—the design of the organization's structure, information processing, reporting relationships, and other elements often impede the proper flow and evaluation of information. A bureaucratic structure with multiple layers, onerous requirements for documentation, and rigid rules and procedures will often inoculate the organization against change.

Behavioral barriers. Individuals often tend to look at issues from a biased or limited perspective. This can be attributed to their education, training, work experiences, and other factors. Consider, for example, an incident shared by David Lieberman, marketing director at GVO, a Palo Alto innovation consulting company:

> A company's creative type had come up with a great idea for a new product. Nearly everybody loved it. However, it was shot down by a high ranking manufacturing executive who exploded: "A new color? Do you have any idea of the spare-parts problem that it will create?"
>
> This was not a dimwit exasperated at having to build a few new storage racks at the warehouse. He'd been hearing for years about cost cutting, lean inventories, and "focus!" Says Lieberman, "Good concepts, but not always good for innovation."

Political barriers. Political barriers refer to conflicts arising from power relationships. This can be the outcome of a myriad of symptoms, such as vested interests (such as the aforementioned escalation problems), refusal to share information, conflicts over resources, conflicts between departments and divisions, and petty interpersonal differences.

Time constraints. The implementation of meaningful change requires a commitment of time and effort. The problem of "not having enough time to drain the swamp when you are up to your neck in alligators" illustrates this point. In effect, Gresham's law of planning states that operational decisions will drive out the time necessary for strategic thinking and reflection. This tendency is accentuated in organizations experiencing severe price competition or retrenchment when managers and employees are spread rather thin.

Overcoming the Barriers

How can organizations overcome these barriers to change and enable and foster the creativity required to take full advantage of organizational learning? Although there are no panaceas, we believe that the following guidelines should promote the challenging of the status quo and help a company to become a learning organization:

- Create a sense of urgency.
- Encourage constructive dissent.
- Encourage experimentation and risk taking.
- Get everyone involved.

Create a sense of urgency. Perhaps the primary means to challenge the status quo directly is for the leader to create a sense of urgency. For example, Tom Kasten, vice president of Levi Strauss, has a very direct approach to initiating change. He is currently charged with leading the campaign to transform the company for the twenty-first century:

> You create a compelling picture of the risks of not changing. We let our people hear directly from customers. We video-taped interviews with customers and played excerpts. One big customer said, "We trust many of your competitors implicitly. We sample their deliveries. We open all Levi's deliveries." Another said, "Your lead times are the worst. If you weren't Levi's, you'd be gone." It was powerful. I wish we had done more of it.

Such initiatives, if sincere and credible, establish a shared mission and emphasize the need for major transformations. If effective, they can channel energies to bring about both change and creative endeavors.

Encourage constructive dissent. Encouraging constructive dissent can be another effective means of questioning the status quo, as well as a spur toward creativity. Here, norms are established whereby dissenters can openly question a superior's perspective without fear of retaliation or retribution. After all, most would agree with Enron's president, Jeffrey Skilling, that a good idea is a fragile thing "that can be blown out by the cold winds of frigid management." In a similar vein, consider the perspective of Steven Ballmer, Microsoft's President:

> Bill [Gates] brings to the company the idea that conflict can be a good thing. . . . Bill knows it's important to avoid that gentle civility that keeps you from getting to the heart of an issue quickly. He likes it when anyone, even a junior employee, challenges him, and you know he respects you when he starts shouting back.

Motorola has gone a step further and institutionalized a culture of dissent. By filing a "minority report," an employee can go above his or her immediate supervisor's head and officially lodge a different point of view on a business decision. In fact, Motorola's recent technology gamble, a multi-billion-dollar satellite project called Iridium, was begun as a minority report. According to former CEO George Fisher, "I'd call it a healthy spirit of discontent and a freedom by and large to express your discontent around here or to disagree with whoever it is in the company, me or anybody else."

The management of Levi Strauss believes people need to be allowed to challenge ideas, no matter where they originate. Dissent is openly encouraged by hanging white boards in the hall for employees to record their observations and criticisms anonymously.

Encourage experimentation and risk-taking. Closely related to the culture of dissent is the fostering of a culture that encourages risk taking. "If you're not making mistakes, you're not taking risks, and that means you're not going anywhere," claims John Holt, coauthor of *Celebrate Your Mistakes*. "The key is to make errors faster than the competition, so you have more chances to learn and win." Minneapolis-based 3M's culture is filled with lore and storytelling of how risk taking and failure led to success. Perhaps one of the best known (other than Post-it Notes) is the story of how inventor Francis G. Okie came up with the idea of a sandpaper product in 1922 to sell to men as a replacement for razor blades. Obviously, that idea didn't fly. However, the technology led to 3M's first blockbuster product: a waterproof sandpaper that became a staple of the automobile industry. A well-known motto at 3M and some other leading-edge companies is, "It's better to ask forgiveness than to request permission."

Companies that cultivate cultures of experimentation and curiosity make sure that *failure* is not a four-letter word. People who stretch the envelope and ruffle feathers are protected. More important, they encourage mistakes as a key part of their competitive advantage. Wood Dickinson, CEO of the Kansas City–based Dickinson movie theater chain, tells his property managers that he wants to see them committing "intelligent failures in the pursuit of service excellence." Such a philosophy is shared by Stan Shih, CEO of the Taiwan-based computer company, Acer. If a manager at Acer takes an intelligent risk and makes a mistake, even a costly one, Shih writes the loss off as tuition payment for the manager's education. Such a culture must permeate the entire organization. As a high-tech executive told us during an interview, "Every person has a freedom to fail."

Along with tolerating—in fact, often encouraging—failure, such organizations exercise patience. They implicitly appreciate Francis Bacon's insight: "As the births of all living creatures are, at first, misshapen, so are all innovations," from his essay "On Innovation" written in 1625.

Get everyone involved. Companies can also benefit from maximizing the number of sources, throughout their organizations, drawn upon for innovative ideas. Concrete mechanisms should be used to supplement management philosophy and cultural norms. For example, executives at the Walt Disney Company sponsor a "Gong Show" in which everyone in the company—including secretaries, janitors, and mailroom staff—gets the opportunity to pitch ideas to the top executives. Jeffrey Bair, a former vice president at Lotus (now CEO of Instinctive Technology), drives the point even harder: "You have to put your corporation's destiny into the hands of someone you wouldn't want your daughter dating."

Ideas can be encouraged throughout the organization by well-designed and -supported suggestion systems. A pacesetter in this area is Dana Corporation, the auto parts maker. As CEO Woody Morcott claims, "It's part of our value system." Also driving the system is a well-understood vital need for the program throughout the organization. Dana competes in a mature industry, and useful suggestions come down to the issue of survival. Steve Moore, a plant manager, says, "We drill into our people that they are responsible for keeping the plant competitive." In addition, instructors at Dana University offer classes on how to come up with better ideas, and awards and luncheons are used to recognize and reward the best idea generators. The result of all of these mechanisms to spur suggestions is that in 1996, each of Dana's 45,500 employees submitted 1.22 ideas per month, for a total of 666,120 suggestions. Astonishingly, 70 percent of ideas are used.

One of us also observed a suggestion system that was quite innovative in its implementation. Kurta Corporation, a Japanese-owned manufacturer of digitizers, installed a huge four-foot-square by ten-foot-tall Plexiglas box in the company cafeteria to reinforce the importance and visibility of its suggestion program. A white Ping-Pong ball was added for each submitted suggestion, and a gold Ping-Pong ball was dropped in for each suggestion that was adopted, which also meant a financial reward.

Chaparral Steel: Learning at Work

Chaparral Steel, located in Midlothian, Texas, owns and operates a technologically advanced steel mill that produces bar and structural steel products by recycling scrap steel.[16] Chaparral's production—which includes beams, reinforcing bars, channels, and merchant quality rounds—increased from 228,000 tons in 1976 to 1.6 million tons in 1995. Labor per ton is an industry-leading 1.2 work-hours. With 1997 sales of roughly $600 million, it earned $61 million before taxes, impressive in a commodity industry characterized by flat prices over the past five years. Its CEO likes to call the company a learning organization. "We talk about 'mentofacturing' here— using our minds, as opposed to manufacturing—just using our hands," says Gordon Forward, the company's president and CEO. This is a company that invests heavily (and profitably) in knowledge. Like other companies we discuss in this book, there are no utopians here; these are bottom-line-driven management teams that recognize the bottom-line value of developing their intellectual capital. Profits matter to this group. So how do they build value from their intellectual capital? Let's look at how Chaparral Steel exemplifies the four key elements of the learning organization.

Empowering Employees at All Levels

Chaparral stresses the importance of employee ownership— not just of the company's equity, but of its knowledge as well. Chaparral features all the attributes of involved employees: 90 percent own stock; everyone is salaried, wears the same white hard hats, drinks the same free coffee, and so forth. Chaparral focuses its employees' attention on the customer. Rather than employing managers as buffers between customers and the factory, Chaparral routes customer concerns directly to the line workers. If an original equipment manufacturer (OEM) rejects a bent bar, the production employees who produced that bar will visit the OEM to understand the effect of the mistake. "Everyone here is part of the sales department," Forward says. "They carry their own business cards. If they visit a customer, we want them to come back and look at their own process differently. Rather than seeing a simple round, they will see [the final product], a sucker rod." This isn't meant as punishment, as Forward notes; senior managers just want everyone to view the business from the customer's perspective. "If a melt-shop crew understands why a customer needs a particular grade of steel, it will make sure the customer gets that exact grade," Forward states. Such an approach encourages employees to think beyond traditional functional boundaries and to integrate the customer's perspective into their efforts. This encourages employees to think of ways to improve the organization that involve decisions beyond the traditional functional areas.

Accumulating and Sharing Internal Knowledge

Chaparral invests heavily in its employees. "Expertise must be in the hands of the people who make the product," says CEO Gordon Forward. To create knowledge, the organization offers on-site courses on more than ninety topics, including Spanish, credit management, and computer software. Employees hired after 1987 enroll as a condition of employment; it's optional for the more senior employees. The courses that workers take depend on their experience and education. More than 85 percent of Chaparral's workforce currently take classes. There's a direct payoff for employees too. "The more you know, the more responsibility you can handle and the more money you can make," says Billy Simmons, Chaparral's manager of meltshop operations. "A lot of people take pride in their work, too. They want to know how things work in their area." Chaparral encourages production employees to learn all the tasks in their area by training in the classroom and on the job. Workers increase their salary by learning more jobs.

Learning is geared toward improving production quality and lowering costs. At the same time, Chaparral continues to explore different methods for squeezing costs from the process. Forward estimates labor costs are less than 9 percent of sales, one-fourth of what traditional steelmakers endure. Concerned about diminishing returns to investment in reducing labor costs further, Chaparral now focuses on reducing energy costs and reducing handling and recycling costs. One outcome of the new efforts is that the company has reduced energy costs by lowering the weight of its beams. The lighter-weight beams have created additional markets for their products: manufactured homes and offices, as well residential construction. While traditionally a lumber-based market, the 30 percent increase in lumber prices in the 1990s has made light-weight steel a viable material substitute; forecasts for residential growth show tremendous promise for Chaparral. Such ideas rarely occur inside functional boundaries; they involve too many functional groups. By cross-training its employees and exposing them to all aspects of the company's operations, Chaparral finds that its employees possess the tools and motivation to create such integrated breakthroughs.

Gathering and Integrating External Information

Learning organizations like Chaparral display an inherent willingness to look outside the company for new ideas. Its most lucrative product, thin slab castings, was developed by German manufacturers and adapted by Chaparral. It applied the thin slab casting process to structural stock and found a lucrative niche. As a steelmaker that relies on scrap cars for raw material, Chaparral faces a challenge: finding environmentally friendly means of disposing of the waste it produces, as well as the waste from scrap cars that it doesn't use. It already sells off the slag by-product to cement makers. Chaparral has also improved the process for separating scrap metal from vehicles. Teaming with a small Belgian company in October 1997, it launched the world's first totally integrated automobile residue shredder. This facility separates not only ferrous and nonferrous metals, but also nonchlorinated plastics. The separation process reduces landfill and transportation requirements—good news to environmentalists—and also provides Chaparral with marketable energy products. As Libor Rostock, vice president of technology and development explains, "By doing this, we will end up with a very valuable stockpile which could be used as a fuel of high-BTU volume. It is as good as or better than the best coal."

It addition, Chaparral can expect to lower its steelmaking costs by over a dollar a ton, significant savings in a commodity business. Selling the separated nonferrous metals will pay for the plant in less than one year, and the sale of clean plastics will generate revenues of up to $500,000 per year. Next, company officials plan to market this new technology world-wide to other steel mills throughout North and South America. Chaparral purchased a 20 percent equity stake in its Belgium partner and assisted the partner in setting up operations near the plant. They're also working with Midlothian economic developers to attract other industries that can use the separated materials Chaparral is now producing at its mill.

Challenging the Status Quo and Enabling Creativity

Chaparral's culture is based on experimentation. This is a company that seeks to try new ideas quickly and then keep the ones that work. As an example, the company wanted to make steel splash guards to place along the way of the rolling mill. This is a high-impact process: a poor design can result in significant worker injury. Rather than call in design consultants or attempt to develop elaborate models, their mockups were simply very wet plywood. The heat and the process quickly consumed the plywood, but plywood models are extremely quick and cheap to make. Before the models were burned, Chaparral identified a suitable design and had its product up to speed faster than its competitors did.

This willingness to experiment carries over into the organizational practices as well. Rather than base bonuses on profits, workers split a pot based on an 8.5 percent return on assets (ROA). Production bonuses, Forward fears, tempt workers to ignore quality, whereas ROA encourages employees to find ways to increase output without adding additional capacity. As a result, a foundry with an initial capacity of 500,000 annual tons now produces double that amount.

In addition, all employees report to one of three customer-based divisions: bar products, structural products, and recycled products. This allows each unit to concentrate more on its customers, Forward asserts. The recycled products group focuses on the recycling and processing of scrap and on melt-shop operations. Dennis Beach, Chaparral's vice president of operations claims: "In a traditionally organized steel company, there is a disconnection between production and the customer. There's one executive in charge for sales, one for marketing, one for production, and one for research. With the reorganization, we want everyone in that unit to focus on one thing, the customer—rather than having production focus on how much it can produce, regardless of the market."

Rather than outsource support sources, Chaparral attempts

EXHIBIT 6-4.

The four key elements of learning organizations at Chaparral Steel.

Learning Parameter	How It Works	Management Mind-Set	Structural Supports
Empowering employees at all levels	Focusing employees on the customer	Everyone is treated the same	Rewards based on company-wide ROA
Creating and synthesizing internal knowledge	K-90 continuing education program	Knowledge is shared among everyone	Investment in every employee's knowledge
Creating and integrating external information	Studying best practices of other companies and industries	Open-minded approach	Heavy involvement in alliances and research and cooperative agreements
Challenging the status quo and encouraging creativity	Experimentation; quick, low-cost projects	Try something, anything, now	Organizational structures focused on customers

to identify new ways of adding value to support positions. Recognizing that security personnel were necessary but often idle, the company trained personnel to run administrative tasks at night, so information would await first-shift employees as they arrive in the morning. The security guards enter quality data into information systems and print out reports, as well as fill fire extinguishers, and related tasks. Rather than accept the overhead burden of necessary support positions, the company seeks to add value at each step of the process.

Exhibit 6-4 summarizes how Chaparral epitomizes the four elements of learning organizations.

A Checklist: Leadership and Organization Learning

Developing Sound Leadership

☐ Do leaders throughout the organization have a holistic understanding of key stakeholders (e.g., customers, suppliers, and employees)?

☐ Is there a compelling strategic vision? Does it provide a framework for: mission, goals, employee commitment, participation, and communication?

☐ Is the vision incorporated into:
- The organization's structure?
- Reward system?
- Control and evaluation systems?

☐ Are leaders actively involved in building structures, teams, systems, and processes that implement the organization's strategic vision?

☐ Does the organization's culture (i.e., shared values, beliefs, and behavioral norms) strengthen commitment to excellence and ethical behavior?

Creating the Learning Organization

☐ Do leaders at all organizational levels take time to reflect and question important goals, strategies, tactics, and underlying assumptions? Is there double-loop learning?

☐ Do all employees feel and support a compelling purpose for the organization (beyond shareholder returns)?

☐ Does the organization support and encourage bottom-up empowerment?

☐ Is the gathering and disseminating of internal information a widely accepted practice? Is it performed effectively and efficiently?

☐ Do managers at all levels have strong listening skills?

☐ Do managers at all levels practice management by walking around and use other techniques to tap informal sources of information?

☐ Is the creation and sharing of external information a widely accepted practice? Is it performed effectively and efficiently?

☐ Do managers throughout the organization have a sound awareness of emerging trends and events in the industry as well as the general environment?

☐ Are managers' internal frames of reference in sync with the realities of the business situation?

☐ Does the organization make effective use of technology to generate and distribute internal and external information?

☐ Do employees throughout the organization actively question the status quo?

☐ Is there a strong culture of dissent and a freedom to fail mentality?

☐ Are ideas encouraged throughout all levels of the organization?

☐ Does the organization have structural mechanisms and a culture that foster creativity?

Notes

1. This introductory section draws on the following sources: M. G. R. Kets de Vries, "The Leadership Mystique," *Academy of Management Executive* 8(3) (August 1994): 73; J. R. Meindl and S. B. Ehrlich, "The Romance of Leadership and the Evaluation of Organizational Performance," *Academy of Management Journal* 30 (1987): 92–109; and R. E. Quinn and G. M. Spreitzer, "The Road to Empowerment: Seven Questions Every Leader Should Consider," *Organizational Dynamics* (Autumn 1997): 37–49.

2. M. Loeb, "Where Leaders Come From," *Fortune*, September 19, 1994, p. 241. For a fuller discussion of some of these ideas, see our earlier work: J. C. Picken and G. G. Dess, *Mission Critical: The Seven Strategic Traps That Derail Even the Smartest Companies* (Burr Ridge. IL: Irwin, 1997).

3. These three activities are frequently addressed in both the strategic management and leadership literatures, such as H. E. R. Uyterhoeven, R. W. Ackerman, and J. W. Rosenblum, *Strategy and Organization: Text and Cases in General Management*, rev. ed. (Homewood, IL: Irwin, 1972); and K. R. Andrews, *The Concept of Corporate Strategy*, 2d ed. (Homewood, IL: Irwin, 1980). These three activities and our discussion draw from J. P. Kotter, "What Leaders Really Do," *Harvard Business Review* 68(3) (1990): 103–111; A. E. Pearson, "Six Basics for General Managers," *Harvard Business Review* 67(4) (1990): 94–101; and S. R. Covey, "Three Roles of the Leader in the New Paradigm," in F. Hesselbein, M. Goldsmith, and R. Beckhard (eds.), *The Leader of the Future* (San Francisco: Jossey-Bass, 1996), pp. 149–160. Some of the discussion of each of the three leadership activity concepts draws on G. G. Dess and A. Miller, *Strategic Management* (New York: McGraw-Hill, 1993), pp. 320–325. Other sources for this section include C. Day, Jr., and P. LaBarre, "GE: Just Your Average Everyday $60 Billion Family Grocery Store," *Industry Week*, May 2, 1994, pp. 13–18; B. O'Reilly, "The Secrets of America's Most Admired Corporations: New Ideas and New Products," *Fortune*, March 3, 1997. 60–64; "Ken Unplugged," *Chief Executive* (October 1997): 40–44; G. McWilliams, "The Quiet Man Who's Jolting Utilities," *Business Week*, June 9, 1997, 84–88; and S. Sherman, "Bringing Sears Into the New World," *Fortune*, October 13, 1997, pp. 183–184.

4. E. Matson, "Here, Innovation Is No Fluke," *Fast Company* (August–September 1997): 42–44; B. Saporito, "John Fluke Mfg.: How to Revive a Fading Firm," *Fortune*, March 22, 1993, p. 8; and A. R. Elliott, "Fluke Survived Cuts in Defense to Lead Portable Test Market," *Investor's Business Daily*, July 24, 1997, p. B14.

5. The Merck and Levi Strauss examples are drawn from: J. Weber, "Mr. Nice Guy With a Mission," *Business Week*, November 25, 1996, pp. 132–142; and Robert D. Haas, speech delivered before the Conference Board, New York City, May 4, 1994.

6. C. Handy, "Trust and the Virtual Organization," *Harvard Business Review* 73 (May–June 1995): 40–50.

7. The examples and quotations in this section draw on various sources, including: P. M. Senge, "The Leader's New Work: Building Learning Organizations," *Sloan Management Review* (Fall 1990): 7–23; S. E. Prokesch, "Unleashing the Power of Learning: An Interview With British Petroleum's John Browne," *Harvard Business Review* 75 (September–October 1997): 146–168; M. Hammer and S. A. Stanton, "The Power of Reflection," *Fortune*, November 24, 1997, pp. 291–296; C. Argyris, "Double Loop

Learning in Organizations," *Harvard Business Review* 55 (September–October 1977): 11–125; S. R. Covey, *The Seven Habits of Highly Effective People: Powerful Lessons in Personal Change* (London: Simon & Schuster, 1989); A. Miller, *Strategic Management*, 3d ed. (New York: McGraw-Hill, 1998); J. S. Weston, "Soft Stuff Matters," *Financial Executive* (July–August 1992): 52–53; and M. F. R. Kets de Vries, "Charisma in Action: The Transformational Abilities of Virgin's Richard Branson and ABB's Percy Barnevik," *Organizational Dynamics* (Winter 1998): 13–14.

8. Quinn and Spreitzer, "Road to Empowerment."

9. S. Helgesen, "Leading from the Grass Roots," in Hesselbein, Goldsmith, and Beckhard (eds.), *Leader of the Future*, pp. 19–24. The Xerox example is based on A. M. Webber, "XBS Learns to Grow," *Fast Company* (October–November 1996): 115.

10. D. E. Bowen and E. E. Lawler III, "Empowering Service Employees," *Sloan Management Review* 37 (Summer 1995): 73–84.

11. The examples in this section are drawn from multiple sources, including: J. Stack, *The Great Game of Business* (New York: Doubleday/Currency, 1992); J. Pfeffer, "Seven Practices of Successful Organizations," *California Management Review*, 40(2) (Winter 1998): 96–124; A. Muoio, "The Truth Is, the Truth Hurts," *Fast Company* (April–May 1998): 100; "Open-Book Management: Sharing the Bottom Line," *Vision* (November 1996): 1–2 (a UPS internal company publication); S. Schafer, "Battling a Labor Shortage? It's All in Your Imagination," *Inc.* (August 1997): 24; C. Fishman, "Whole Food Teams," *Fast Company* (April–May 1996): 102–109; and S. Lubove, "New Age Capitalist," *Forbes*, April 6, 1998, pp. 42–43; Jack Welch, speech presented at the General Electric Company 1997 Annual Meeting, Charlotte, North Carolina, April 23, 1997; P. Meyer, "So You Want the President's Job," *Business Horizons* (January–February 1998): 2–8; N. Augustine, "Reshaping an Industry: Lockheed Martin's Survival Story," *Harvard Business Review* 75(3) (May–June 1997): 83–96; J. B. Hoppe, "Is MBWA Still Alive?" *Measure* (July–August 1997): 4–7, 27–28 (a Hewlett-Packard internal company publication); M. Goldberg, "Cisco's Most Important Meal of the Day," *Fast Company* (February–March 1998): 56; P. Roberts, "The Agenda," *Fast Company* (April–May 1988): 125.

12. C. Novicki, "The Best Brains in Business," *Fast Company* (October–November 1996): 27.

13. Peter F. Drucker used the term "theory of the business" in his article of the same title in the September–October 1994 *Harvard Business Review*, pp. 95–104. G. Hamel and C. K. Prahalad, *Competing for the Future* (Boston: Harvard Business School Press, 1994), p. 50, used the term "managerial frames." One of us has used the terms "strategic frame" and "managerial frame of reference" in prior work. All refer to the same basic sets of assumptions, premises, beliefs, and values. Portions of this chapter rely on insights attributable to each of these sources. Other examples are drawn from P. Sellers, "Sears: The Turnaround Is Ending: The Revolution Has Begun," *Fortune*, April 28, 1997, pp. 106–118; and C. Pickering, "Sorry . . . Try Again Next Year," *Forbes ASAP*, February 23, 1998, pp. 82–83.

14. The introductory discussion of benchmarking draws on Miller, *Strategic Management*, pp. 142–143. Examples are drawn from various sources, including: O. Port and G. Smith, "Beg, Borrow—and Benchmark," *Business Week*, November 30, 1992, pp. 74–75; J. Main, "How to Steal the Best Ideas Around," *Fortune*, October 19, 1992, pp. 102–106; Frank P. Doyle, executive vice president, Corporate Executive Office, General Electric Company, speech presented at the 63d Edison Electric Institute Convention,

Orlando, Florida, June 5, 1995; and W. C. Taylor, "What Happens After What Comes Next," *Fast Company* (December–January 1997): 84–85.

15. For insightful perspectives on escalation, refer to J. Brockner, "The Escalation of Commitment to a Failing Course of Action," *Academy of Management Review* 17(1) (January 1992): 39–61; and B. M. Staw, "Knee-Deep in the Big Muddy: A Study of Escalating Commitment to a Chosen Course of Action," *Organizational Behavior and Human Decision Processes* 16 (1976): 27–44. The discussion of systemic, behavioral, and political barriers draws on P. Lorange and D. Murphy, "Considerations in Implementing Strategic Control," *Journal of Business Strategy* 5 (1984): 27–35. In a similar vein, Noel M. Tichy has addressed three types of resistance to change in the context of General Electric: technical resistance, political resistance, and cultural resistance. Refer to N. M. Tichy, "Revolutionize Your Company," *Fortune*, December 13, 1993, pp. 114–118. Other examples in this section are drawn from: B. O'Reilly, "The Secrets of America's Most Admired Corporations: New Ideas and New Products," *Fortune*, March 3, 1997, pp. 60–64; D. Sheff, "Levi's Changes Everything," *Fast Company* (June–July 1996): 65–74; W. Isaacson, "In Search of the Real Bill Gates," *Time*, January 13, 1997, pp. 44–57; E. B. Baatz, "Motorola's Secret Weapon," *Electronic Business* (April 1993): 51–53; J.W. Holt, *Celebrate Your Mistakes,* New York: McGraw Hill, 1996; T. J. Tetenbaum, "Shifting Paradigms: From Newton to Chaos," *Organizational Dynamics* 26(4) (1998): 21–32. R. Mitchell, "Masters of Innovation," *Business Week*, April 10, 1989, pp. 58–63; O. Harari, "Flood Your Organization With Knowledge," *Management Review* (November 1997): 33–37; R. J. Sternberg, L. A. O'Hara, and T. I. Lubert, "Creativity as Investment," *California Management Review* 40(1) (Fall 1997): 8–21; and R. Teitelbaum, "How to Harness Gray Matter," *Fortune,* June 9, 1997, p. 168.

16. This example draws on numerous sources, including: Chaparral Steel, 1996 Annual Report; P. Ninneman, "A Company of Colleagues at Chapparal," *Iron Age New Steel* 13(4) (April 1997): 52–58; D. Johnson, "Catching the Third Wave: How to Succeed in Business When It's Changing at the Speed of Light," *The Futurist* 2 (March 1998): 32–38; C. Petry, "Chaparral Poised on the Break of Breakthrough; Chaparral Steel Developing Integrated Automobile Shredder—Residue Separation Facility," *American Metal Market*, September 10, 1997, p. 18; and D. Leonard-Barton, "The Factory as a Learning Laboratory," *Sloan Management Review*, 34 (Fall 1992): 23–38.

7

STRATEGIES FOR
IMPLEMENTATION

Significant trends and forces are reshaping the competitive environment. Commerce is becoming more complex and more global. Computer and communications technologies are shrinking the dimensions of time and distance. National and organizational boundaries are becoming increasingly fuzzy, and a new economy is emerging in which the fundamental sources of wealth are knowledge and innovation rather than natural resources and physical labor. In this rapidly changing environment, the organizations that learn how to manage their human and knowledge resources more effectively will realize significant competitive advantages.

Our research suggests that the recipes for success in this new environment include the following:

- Recruiting, developing, and retaining the best talent available
- Optimizing the efficiency and effectiveness of core value-creating activities
- Creating a flexible and responsive organizational infrastructure
- Facilitating individual and organizational learning
- Encouraging the sharing of knowledge and know-how throughout the organization
- Fostering an environment that values collective effort and cooperation, but also encourages risk taking, innovation, and initiative
- Building strong and mutually reinforcing relationships between an organization and its employees, customers, and suppliers.

Not any one factor by itself is likely to lead to competitive advantage. Rather, sustainable advantage will depend on complex interactions and interdependencies among multiple initiatives. Management's challenge is to blend human and other organizational resources into unique capabilities that create real advantages in the marketplace yet resist imitation. The focal point of these efforts must necessarily be the ongoing development and leveraging of the knowledge, skills, and know-how of the organization's people.

A Framework for Understanding

Chapter 1 outlined a conceptual framework (see Exhibit 1-2) for understanding how organizations can most effectively leverage their human capital resources. This framework focused on the linkages and relationships among the organization's:

- Human capital
- Knowledge and information resources
- Physical and financial resources
- Structural capital

Our principal emphasis has been on human capital, structural capital, and the relationships and interactions between them. We have also been concerned with the organization's knowledge and information resources because of the important connections and interactions between the tacit knowledge possessed by the individual and the explicit knowledge controlled by the organization.

Knowledge and human capital have a number of unique characteristics that differentiate them from other kinds of resources. Knowledge does not depreciate in the conventional sense, but rather becomes more valuable and more powerful through its use. Similarly, the value of the organization's investment in human capital can be increased over time through development and individual and organizational learning. And, although legal ownership of intellectual property and proprietary information is possible, the knowledge, skills, and capabilities embodied in an organization's workforce cannot be "owned" by the organization in the same sense as other assets.

Throughout, we have maintained that the design and configuration of the organization's structural capital offers the greatest potential for leveraging both its human capital and its knowledge and information resources. Before proceeding further, it will be helpful to briefly review the key concepts involved in leveraging human capital resources:

■ *Human capital.* We have defined human capital in terms of the capabilities of an organization's employees and managers, as they are relevant to the task at hand, as well as the capacity to continually add to this reservoir of knowledge, skills, and experience through individual learning. Each individual brings to the workplace a rich and varied collection of skills and capabilities, ranging from knowledge gained through formal education to everyday street smarts. In describing the individual as a bundle of resources and capabilities, we have identified eight key attributes, each embodied in and inseparable from the individual (see Exhibit 1-3):

- Motor skills
- Information-gathering (perceptual) skills
- Information-processing (cognitive) skills
- Communication skills
- Experience
- Knowledge
- Social skills
- Values, beliefs, and attitudes

Although it is sometimes useful to consider these attributes separately, in fact these elements are tightly woven and highly interdependent. Not all of these individual skills and capabilities are of equal importance in the work environment, and the relative importance of each depends, to a considerable extent, on the nature and requirements of the task to be accomplished. Nor can they all be managed or developed in the same manner. The first four: motor skills, and information-gathering, information-processing, and communications skills, are more often task-specific. These can usually be enhanced or redirected through education, training, and practice. The remaining attributes tend to reflect more general characteristics, developed over long periods of time both in the workplace and in other settings. These elements broadly influence the employee's judgment, decision-making skills, attitudes and social behavior, regardless of the specific requirements of the job. It must be kept in mind that the opportunities for leveraging human capital, and the approaches that will be most effective, depend on which sets of individual skills and capabilities the organization seeks to address.

■ *Knowledge and information resources.* Organizational knowledge and information resources include: (1) intellectual property—the explicit and legally-protected knowledge "owned" by the company—such as patents, trademarks and proprietary processes; (2) other explicit and documented knowledge—such as technical and financial data, customer lists, sales and advertising materials, and historical information; and (3) tacit knowledge—the collective process and industry know-how embedded in the organization's policies, procedures, and operating practices.

■ *Structural capital.* Structural capital can be thought of as the plumbing—or the wiring—which ties the organizational system together and helps it to function as a coordinated whole. The role of structural capital is to purposefully link the resources of the organization together into processes that create value for customers and competitive advantage for the company. Structural capital is comprised of the organization's core value-creating activities and its structure, systems, and processes (see Exhibit 1-3). The value-creating activities include the organization's core business processes; its external relationships with customers, suppliers, and alliance partners; and its reputation, brand loyalty, image, and legitimacy. The organization's internal structure, systems, processes, and culture are also important elements of structural capital. For the purpose of our discussion, structural capital plays four important roles:

1. Linking human capital more effectively to the organization's core value-creating activities by focusing and concentrating resources, using appropriate technologies, and designing processes and tasks to more effectively utilize individual skills and capabilities

2. Linking human capital more effectively to the knowledge and information resources of the organization and other individuals by using structures, processes, technologies, and practices designed to facilitate access to and use of knowledge resources and to encourage the sharing of the individual's tacit knowledge with the rest of the organization

3. Linking human capital more effectively to the organization's physical and financial resources through structures, processes, and technologies designed to enhance, extend, and multiply individual capabilities

4. Linking the organization's core value-creating activities, its human capital resources, its physical and financial resources, and its knowledge and information resources together in various ways that encourage and enhance the processes of organizational learning.

Leveraging Human Capital

Hamel and Prahalad have argued that resource leverage, an essential component of any successful strategy, can be achieved by (1) more effectively concentrating resources on key strategic goals, (2) more efficiently accumulating resources, (3) complementing resources of one type with those of another to create higher-order value, (4) conserving resources whenever possible, and (5) rapidly recovering resources, thus minimizing the time between expenditure and payback.[1] We have extended the framework that Hamel and Prahalad proposed to include the notions of *enhancing* and *extending* individual capabilities.

Human capabilities can be *extended*, primarily by the application of technology, to permit human skills and knowledge to be used and shared remotely—at a distance, or in places where the unassisted individual could not function. Individual capabilities can also be *enhanced*—made more powerful through the use of technology or the sharing of knowledge and expertise with others. Human capital can also be *enhanced*—continually improved—by training, development and practice throughout an individual's life.

Because synergies are created when individuals work together in organizations (in teams or other structures), we must also consider opportunities for leverage at the organizational level. Exhibit 1-4 summarized the ways we have discovered that leading companies are leveraging their human capital resources at both the individual and organizational levels.

Turning to issues of implementation, we have identified two ways that organizations can leverage their investment and make their human capital resources more productive. First, they can improve the quality and capabilities of the resource itself through more effective recruiting, hiring, and selection processes; development and training efforts; and retention programs. Second, they can design and configure the various elements of the organization's structural capital to improve the performance of (leverage) these human capital resources.

Most of the opportunities for leveraging human capital are related to the structural linkages among human capital, the other resources of the organization, and its core value-creating processes. We have provided numerous examples of innovative approaches used by leading companies to leverage the skills and capabilities of their human resources by building or strengthening these key linkages. For the most part, these examples have demonstrated a specific approach or technique within the context of the subject matter of the chapter. In developing strategies for leverage, it is critically important to pursue an integrated approach, using multiple approaches in concert.

Exhibit 7-1 provides a summary cross-reference between the key leverage activities (opportunities) and the approaches and techniques for leverage suggested by the examples from each chapter.

There is no one best way to leverage an organization's human capital resources. Every organization will likely require a unique combination of initiatives. Multiple tools, techniques, and approaches are available, however, and should be used in concert to develop a comprehensive plan. In devising a strategy for recruiting and retaining top-notch human capital, for example, the overall plan might incorporate technology-based recruitment processes, new organizational structures, focused incentives, and a clear statement of vision, in addition to a well-designed set of human resources practices.

In searching for opportunities to leverage your organization's human capital, Exhibit 7-1 is an appropriate starting point, helping to focus on the broad areas that should be addressed. The next step should be to probe more deeply using the kinds of questions posed in the strategic inventories provided at the end of each chapter. By effectively using both tools, it should be easier to choose an appropriate set of options and ask the right questions to narrow your focus to the best solution for your organization. We also advocate a disciplined search for opportunities, following the approach outlined in the following section.

Finding the Opportunities

The most straightforward approach to identifying opportunities for leveraging human capital is based on a process view of organizations. The basic philosophy reflects the attitude of Bob Buckman, who asked the question, "How do we take this individual and make him bigger, give him more power?"[2] We recommend the following seven-step process.

Step 1: Understand How Value Is Created

Every organization creates value in its own unique way. By adopting a process view, we assume that the organization functions by operating on inputs (resources from the environment) and producing outputs (products or services) that its customers value. Manufacturing

EXHIBIT 7-1.
Opportunities for leverage.

KEY LEVERAGE ACTIVITIES	CHAPTER 2 Recruiting, Developing & Retaining Human Capital	CHAPTER 3 Applying Technology to Leverage Human Capital	CHAPTER 4 Designing Effective Organizational Structures	CHAPTER 5 Implementing Appropriate Incentives & Controls	CHAPTER 6 Leadership & Creating a Learning Organization
Recruiting and retaining top-notch human capital	• Hire for attitude, train for skill • Employee involvement • Challenge • Culture • Flexibility	• Recruiting software • Web-based recruiting tools	• More desirable environment • Flexibility • Responsiveness	• Culture • Incentives • Recognition	• Vision • Clear direction • Culture • Empowerment
Training, developing, and shaping attitudes; encouraging individual learning	• Orientation • Involvement • Evaluation • Monitoring • Sabbaticals	• Distance learning • Self-paced training • Skill development	• Coordination • Information sharing	• Culture • Incentives • Recognition	• Vision • Clear direction • Culture • Empowerment • Challenge the status quo
Concentrating resources on top-priority activities	• Orientation • Evaluation • Monitoring progress	• Focusing resources • Automating routine tasks • Personal news services	• Modular structure • Virtual structure • Cellular structure	• Boundaries • Incentives • Culture • Recognition	• Vision • Clear direction • Culture
Designing core processes to use the capabilities of human capital		• Efficiency • Leverage employee strengths • Link value chain • Reduce cycle times	• Teams • Information sharing	• Boundaries • Incentives • Culture	• Empowerment • Information sharing
Accumulating and sharing organizational knowledge	• Hire for attitude, train for skill • Orientation	• Empower employees with information • Data warehouses	• Teams • Information-sharing techniques	• Cultural support • Incentives	
Encouraging and facilitating the sharing of individual knowledge	• Hire for attitude, train for skill • Orientation	• Collaborative technology • Communications networks • Knowledge-sharing systems	• Teams • Boundaryless structures	• Cultural support • Incentives • Recognition	• Culture • Information sharing
Enhancing, extending, and multiplying individual capabilities		• Leverage relationships • Complementary relationships	• Teams • Information-sharing techniques		
Facilitating individual and organizational learning	• Hire for attitude, train for skill • Orientation	• Information systems • Data warehouses	• Teams • Modular, virtual, and cellular structures	• Cultural support • Incentives	• Challenge the status quo • Empowerment

companies begin with materials, components, and labor as inputs; add value through the manufacturing process; and deliver products as outputs to their customers. Transportation companies add value by using their human resources and capital assets (inputs) to move people or goods from one location to another (service outputs). In each case, value is created through the complex interaction of multiple processes: the management of external interfaces, the execution of internal routines, and the application of human expertise, judgment, and creativity.

It is important to understand exactly what is valued from the perspective of the customer. In most cases, value is created by a combination of products and services, each of which may have multiple attributes. In purchasing an automobile, a customer may consider dozens of product characteristics (e.g., size, appearance, performance, reliability, price), a variety of related services (financing, service, warranty), or any one of a number of other factors (location, convenience, reputation, past experience, friendliness of the salesperson, and so on). Different customers may weigh the value of these elements differently, focus primarily on one or two, and ignore some altogether.

Understanding how value is created must begin with an enumeration and appreciation of all of the dimensions of value perceived by the customer, the relative importance of each, and the linkages and interrelationships among them. Each will necessarily be examined in the search for opportunities for leverage.

Step 2: Define Key Interfaces

Because the customer's perception of value is influenced by his or her interactions with the organization, it is important to identify and characterize the key points of contact between the organization and its customers. Similarly, relationships with suppliers and alliance partners provide opportunities for the organization to add value, and the key points of interface associated with these relationships should also be identified and defined. At each point of contact, the characteristics of the exchange should be understood: what goods or services are exchanged, what information is important to completing the transaction, and so forth.

Step 3: Examine Core Value-Creating Activities

Typically, an organization creates value for its customers by performing various functions: research and development, product design, procurement, manufacturing, distribution, sales and marketing, or customer service. Each of these functions incorporates numerous processes; some are internal, some facilitate coordination with other internal functions, and others are designed to manage interfaces with customers, suppliers, or alliance partners. Some processes are designed solely to facilitate internal coordination and control—accounting and budgeting systems, for example. The most important of these processes—in terms of creating value for an organization's customers—are called core value-creating activities. It is important to identify and focus attention on these activities, because they usually contain the opportunities for the greatest leverage.

Step 4: Assess Current Performance

An objective assessment of the organization's current performance in its core value-creating activities will help to identify the functions and processes that offer the largest potential for improvement. Various approaches have been used to assess and evaluate organizational performance in key activities, including direct observation, customer surveys, and benchmarking. Determining what the organization does well and identifying critical areas of weakness or deficiency can help it to prioritize its needs and opportunities.

Step 5: Identify Points of Exchange, Decision, Flexibility, and Delay

In most situations, identifying opportunities for leverage requires a detailed examination of selected processes. It may be helpful at this point to construct a flowchart of the process, identifying the major process steps, transactions, personal interactions, and information exchanges. At key points in the process, goods, services or information will be exchanged, decisions will be necessary, flexibility may be required, or delays may be encountered. Each of these represents an opportunity for process improvement and should be clearly identified and characterized.

Step 6: Define the Role of Human Capital

In almost every organizational process, human capital plays multiple roles. The involvement of people is frequently most critical at the points of exchange, decision, or flexibility. The role of human capital must be thoroughly understood. If information exchange is required, does the individual have ready access to what he needs? If a decision is required, does the individual have the skills, experience, information, and guidance she needs to make the proper choices quickly? If flexibility is required, does the individual understand the options available and the consequences of each, and have appropriate guidance with regard to organizational policy and preferred practice? If delays are frequent, why do they occur? What steps can be taken to minimize them and make the process (and the people involved) more efficient?

The requirements of each situation should be evaluated in terms of the skills and capabilities of the workforce. What individual skills and capabilities are brought to bear in the situation? Which are most important? Do employees have the right mix of skills and capabilities to function most effectively in the situation? Are they properly motivated? Can individual skills be developed or strengthened through education or training? Does the organization need to look for a different mix of skills in its recruiting and selection processes?

Step 7: Identify Opportunities for Leverage

In most organizations, the sequence of steps outlined will have identified and prioritized a list of potential opportunities for improving performance by more effectively employing the organization's human capital. Each opportunity will require trade-offs. Some will offer great potential for improvement, but will require a significant investment in time, effort, and dollars. In other cases, "low-hanging fruit" will appear, and relatively small gains can be achieved with limited investment or effort. Some opportunities will require changes that may be beyond the technical capabilities, outside the comfort zone, or inconsistent with the culture of the organization. Each potential opportunity must be prioritized in the light of a set of criteria unique to the organization, but which takes into account the potential benefits and costs of each.

It is important to remember our observation about the recipes for success. No one initiative by itself is likely to have a significant impact. Rather, creating sustainable advantage will require the development of a package of initiatives that creates synergy from the integration of multiple, internally consistent, and mutually reinforcing initiatives.

An Illustrative Example

We will now illustrate the application of this seven-step process with a brief example. Exhibit 7-2 illustrates an order fulfillment cycle for a typical distribution company.

EXHIBIT 7-2.
Order fulfillment cycle for a typical distribution company.

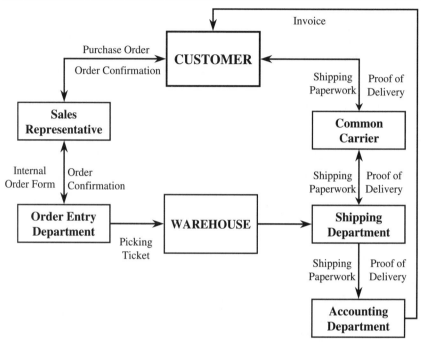

Step 1: Understand How Value Is Created

Distribution operations create value for their customers by purchasing (in large quantities) and warehousing a broad range of products, and selling and delivering smaller quantities on relatively frequent delivery cycles. Value is created through bulk purchasing (lower prices) of a broad product line (selection), prompt and frequent deliveries to the customer (reduced customer inventory requirements), and knowledgeable and responsive customer service. The customer typically perceives value in price, selection, reliable delivery, and attentive customer service.

Step 2: Define Key Interfaces

The most important interfaces are the following:

Sales representative ⟷ Customer
Sales representative ⟷ Order entry department
Shipping department ⟷ Common carrier

Common carrier $\longleftrightarrow$ Customer
Accounting department $\longleftrightarrow$ Customer

Step 3: Examine Core Value-Creating Activities

In this example, we have identified the entire order fulfillment cycle as the key value-creating activity.

Step 4: Assess Current Performance

For the purposes of this example, we will assume that the existing processes are largely manual—that the customer gives the sales representative an order, which is then mailed or faxed to the order entry department. After the order is entered and stock status is determined, the order entry department prepares a picking ticket and an order confirmation (with shipping date or backorder status) and faxes the confirmation to the sales representative. The sales representative then advises the customer.

A similar manual process takes place in the preparation of shipping documents, pickup and delivery by the common carrier, and return of the proof of delivery from the carrier to the accounting department, which prepares and forwards an invoice to the customer. The entire process, from the customer's initial order through delivery and invoicing, takes two to three weeks. A considerable amount of the sales representative's time, estimated at 30 percent, is spent in following up—with order entry, shipping, and the customer—to track the status of orders. The process is considered cumbersome and inefficient, and the organization is losing market share to a competitor who is able to confirm orders within 24 hours and deliver within seven to ten days.

Step 5: Identify Points of Exchange, Decision, Flexibility, and Delay

From this point forward, we will focus primarily on the sales representative–customer interface. The key points of exchange between the customer and the sales representative include the following:

- Customer delivery of the order to the sales representative
- Sales representative communication of the order confirmation to the customer
- Customer inquiry/sales representative response regarding the order status and delivery

With the existing manual process, numerous delays are built into the process. The sales representative is unable, at the time he takes an order, to provide the customer with current stock status and estimated delivery date. Several days may pass before the order is confirmed and the customer becomes aware of a backorder situation. Had the sales representative been aware of the stock status at the time the order was taken, he might have been able to respond flexibly by recommending a substitute product to the customer. In the absence of the necessary information, he was relatively powerless. With a more effective system, most of the status and inquiry transactions would become unnecessary.

Step 6: Define the Role of Human Capital

The role of the sales representative in this situation is as an intermediary between the organization and its customer. Because the sales representative does not have ready access to the information he needs to support the customer, his primary role is one of relaying messages. In order to perform this function effectively, he must rely heavily on his social and communications skills, but he has little opportunity to use any of the other capabilities he possesses.

Step 7: Identify Opportunities for Leverage

Numerous opportunities are available in this example to leverage the skills and capabilities of the sales representative. The most obvious (assuming technical feasibility) is to provide a laptop computer and direct access, from the customer's site, to the organization's order entry, inventory, purchasing, shipping, and billing records. The representative could then check stock status. If the item was available, he could enter and confirm the order immediately. If the item was not on hand, he could check the purchasing status and determine future availability or recommend a substitute item on the spot. If contacted by the customer with regard to order status, he could access the relevant information directly and respond immediately, saving at least two telephone calls (one to the plant to check the status and a return call to the customer), and providing significantly better customer service.

If the sales representative had the information required to support the customer more effectively, both productivity and customer service would be improved. Although it is not possible in this example to assess the technical feasibility or cost-benefit trade-offs involved, many organizations have successfully implemented similar changes with positive results. (See, for example, the case of Physician Sales and Service, Inc. detailed in Chapter 3.)

Developing Implementation Strategies

Once a set of opportunities has been identified, strategies for implementation must be crafted. Implementing change in organizations is a complex process involving multiple considerations and, not infrequently, unintended consequences. While we do not intend to define a step-by-step process, an appropriate implementation strategy will consider many, if not all, of the following activities:

- Definition of goals and objectives
- Clarification of expectations and definition of progress measurements
- Clear and frequent communication of intentions, progress, and results
- Identification of required skills and capabilities
- Initiation of efforts to retain qualified employees
- Recruitment and/or development of top-notch human capital resources
- Simultaneous implementation of multiple, mutually reinforcing changes
- Ongoing progress monitoring, with midcourse corrections as required
- Consistent support of initiatives with culture, rewards, and boundaries
- Measurement, recognition, and reward of performance.

Conclusion

As we suggested in the Preface, we believe that it is too early to define the "one best way." No one has yet written the definitive book on how to leverage human capital resources, nor do we expect that such a magic bullet will be found. We do believe that considerable progress has been made, and that leading organizations have learned a great deal through their early experiments.

We encourage you to learn from and be encouraged by the successes of others—as captured in the examples presented throughout this book—and to move forward, utilizing the guidelines provided, to explore, experiment, and learn what works in your organization.

Notes

1. Gary Hamel and C. K. Prahalad, *Competing for the Future* (Boston: Harvard Business School Press, 1994), p. 175.

2. Glenn Rifkin, "Nothing But Net," *Fast Company* (June–July 1996): 122–127.

Index